# you've got a book in you

## a stress-free guide to writing the book of your dreams

ELIZABETH SIMS

 Published by Writer's Digest Books, an imprint of F+W Media, Inc., 10151 Carver Road, Suite #200, Blue Ash, OH 45242. (800) 289-0963. First edition.

For more resources for writers, visit www.writersdigest.com/books.

To receive a free weekly e-mail newsletter delivering tips and updates about writing and about Writer's Digest products, register directly at http://newsletters.fwpublications.com.

20 19 18 10 9

Distributed in the U.K. and Europe by F+W Media International
Brunel House, Newton Abbot, Devon, TQ12 4PU, England
Tel: (+44) 1626-323200, Fax: (+44) 1626-323319
E-mail: postmaster@davidandcharles.co.uk

Edited by James Duncan
Designed by Claudean Wheeler
Cover images by mirabella/Fotolia.com
& Andriy Dykun/Fotolia.com
Production coordinated by Debbie Thomas

## Dedication

This book is dedicated to anyone who has ever looked at a shelf full of books and thought, "I wonder if I could do that."

## Acknowledgments

I'm grateful to my family and friends for their love, support, and confidence in me. Thanks also to everyone who has trusted me to help them with the writing process, whether by reading my articles and books, by participating in a workshop or webinar, or through correspondence with me. You are the reason I wrote this book.

Special thanks for wisdom-sharing, either recently or in the distant past, to Angela Brown, Gay Knutson, Philip Lenkowsky, Jennifer Slimko, and the Sarasota chapter of the Florida Writers Association.

I'm indebted to my agent, Cameron McClure at the Donald Maass Literary Agency; my editors, James Duncan, Roseann Biederman, and Kimberly Catanzarite; as well as publisher Phil Sexton and all the staff at Writer's Digest Books. To my editors at *Writer's Digest* magazine, Jessica Strawser and Zachary Petit: Thank you for being so great to work with! Thanks also to the entire staff at the magazine and F+W Media: You guys rock.

Above all, thank you to Marcia, for everything.

PHOTO © THOMAS BENDER

**ELIZABETH SIMS** is the prize-winning author of short stories and novels, including the Lillian Byrd crime series and the Rita Farmer mysteries. *Booklist* calls her work "crime fiction as smart as it is compelling," and *Crimespree* magazine praises her "strong voice and wonderful characters." Elizabeth writes frequently for *Writer's Digest* magazine, where she is a contributing editor. She has worked as a reporter, photographer, technical writer, bookseller, street busker, ranch hand, corporate executive, and symphonic percussionist. Elizabeth belongs to several literary societies as well as American Mensa. www.elizabethsims.com

## *Also by Elizabeth Sims*

*On Location*
*The Extra*
*The Actress*
*Easy Street*
*Lucky Stiff*
*Damn Straight*
*Holy Hell*

# Contents

## PART 3
# Pour it Out

# Why This Book? Read This First!

*To write a book is to open and give yourself to a world thirsty for authenticity. Writing a book is a heroic act, and it is an accomplishment no one can take away from you. When you come to THE END, you will know a wealth of things about your subject, about writing, and about yourself. You will be a deeper, richer, more complete person.*

*--from Chapter Three*

This book is for you if you've got a dream to write a book and you want simple, no-nonsense help in achieving that dream. Store shelves and the Web are crammed with books on how to write, so why this one? Because every time I meet somebody who wants to write a book—fact or fiction—but thinks it's too hard, I want to take their hand and say, "You have been sadly misinformed." And every time I meet somebody who wants to write a book but doesn't really know how, I want to take their hand and say, "I'll help you." And every time I meet somebody who's written part of a book already but feels stuck, I want to take their hand and say, "Boy, have you come to the right person!" This book is my contribution to your incredibly exciting ambition.

(If you're thinking I should have written 'his or her' instead of 'their' just above, you're right. But sometimes it feels good to break a cumbersome grammatical rule!)

In an ideal world, when you found yourself doubting your dream, a guide would appear in the form of, oh, say, a big sister who has written books herself and who will show you how to write your book with zest and honesty. Somebody who has been there, done that, loves you, and will be there for you every step of the way.

It is an ideal world.

I am that big sister.

Let's write your book together.

### *This book is not a one-size-fits-all formula for writing a book.*

The whole point of writing a book is to give something *unique* to the world, not something that sounds like it came out of a robot. This book is a guide that will help you write your book *your* way—and have fun while you're doing it.

(See Chapter Three, **Writing Blast: A Story Everybody Can Tell.**)

### *This book is not a bunch of dire warnings about how hard it is to write.*

I've written a bevy of books and talked to a lot of other authors, and one thing I've learned is that writing a book—yes, a whole book—is much easier than most people think. Trouble is, most *authors* think writing is hard! My experience and thus my message is totally the opposite: Writing a book is easy. Easy, that is, once you banish doubt and worry, and let your natural creativity take over.

(See Chapter One, **The Great Open Secret**.)

### *This book will not teach you to write well.*

It's actually impossible to teach somebody how to write well. This book will show you how to *teach yourself* to write well. That is, to write clear, unique prose, which is what readers, agents, editors, and publishers want. Moreover, you'll get started on the path of successful writing immediately, and you'll have the tools to see your book through to thrilling completion.

(See Chapter Thirteen, **Writing With the Masters**.)

### *This book is not for English majors only!*

A good many people who want to write think they're doomed to write poorly if they didn't do well in English class. Nothing could be further from the truth. I've read thousands of pages of work by aspiring authors, and I'm continually disappointed at the stilted writing coming out of people with heavy academic backgrounds. I have two degrees in English, and sometimes I feel I've done well as an author in spite of all my book learning! By contrast, I've been startled to read beautiful, coherent, inspiring prose written by people with very little experience in English literature: nonnative English speakers, math geeks, dropouts, people who work with their hands, you name it. These writers are in touch with what they want to say and explore; they're not hung up on rules and worry.

(See Chapter Eleven, **Unleashing Your True Voice**.)

### *This book is not complicated.*

Overcomplication is the scourge of writing instruction.

(See Chapter Nineteen, **A Simple Scene Blueprint**.)

### *This book is not a collection of slick tips that look good.*

The trouble with tips: They work, all right, but they don't see you all the way through your book. This book will give you an honest-to-gosh method that you can customize to your own purposes.

(See Part II **Three Touchstones for Writing Your Book: Your Truth, Your People, and Your Map**.)

### *This book is not totally new.*

The wisdom I've gained is based on my own experience—and that of other authors dating back to prehistory. I've simply combined the enduring tools of storytelling and writing with a full-speed-ahead attitude and fresh ways to develop your own natural talent and creativity.

If you're a fan of my articles in *Writer's Digest* magazine, you'll be glad to see that I've developed some of my best stuff to build the tools and techniques at the heart of *You've Got a Book in You*. These tools and techniques work. How do I know? Because with them, I've helped thousands of fledgling writers find their wings.

CHAPTER 1

# Writing a Book is Easy and Fun

Writing a book is easy and fun.

Since that sentence probably has never been put into print, I'll repeat it:

Writing a book is easy and fun.

You want to write one? Write it. This book will help you. If you've written part of a book already, stick with me and we'll get it done—and we'll have a good time doing it. By the end, you will be a different person.

How so? Because writing a book brings you to completion as a thinking, feeling person. It's sort of a paradox: Only by writing a book will you know you can write a book. Moreover, writing a book, from the first scratches of an idea on the back of a bus ticket or a grocery list, to writing THE END on page 100 or 200 or 400 is a flat-out transformative process. Just ask anybody who's done it. It takes commitment, sure. And to do a good job, it will take all the brains and heart you've got.

**THE MAGIC IS THIS:** You will end up with more brains and heart than you started with. Writing a book develops you as a whole person, it makes you realize you're stronger than you ever thought you were. You dig deep for honesty, you open your creative spirit to ideas and inspiration, and you refine your sense of direction and problem solving.

That's just for starters.

Beyond that, your book will be a part of you that reaches out to other people. It will carry your voice and your message into the vast, beautiful world. Whenever someone reads your book, a part of you becomes part of them. They might be greatly entertained by your book, they might be amused, turned on, educated, terrified, helped. And they might just say thank you. Getting thanks from a reader is a deep, smooth thrill that can't be compared with anything.

If you publish your book and people like it, money and fame might come to you.

Terrific as money and fame are, they will pale in comparison to what you've already earned: the knowledge and confidence that you're an author, by God. A real writer.

I will reveal how the professionals do it. I've been there, having written a number of successful books, some of them published in hardcover by a big New York publishing house (St. Martin's Minotaur, in the Macmillan Publishing Group), some published by a smaller publisher, and some I've self-published. Currently my two series are the Rita Farmer Mysteries and the Lillian Byrd Crime Novels. One of the latter won a Lambda Literary Award, that novel being *Damn Straight*. I'm also a contributing editor at the world's leading writing magazine, *Writer's Digest*, specializing in the art and craft of fiction. If that's not enough, I have two degrees in English, one in literature, and one in composition. For ten years I worked in the bookselling business, where I learned which books sell and why. I have experience as a newspaper reporter, photographer, and editor, and I won the Tompkins Award for Graduate Fiction at Wayne State University, back in 19-cough-cough. I'm a member of several literary societies as well as American Mensa.

As I say to everybody who asks me about writing, I wasn't born knowing how to write well enough for publication; I learned it. And I'm going to help you learn how to do it too.

I've never been able to relate to how-to formulas for writing a book. Rigid structures just don't work, especially for fiction: Rule books that say you need to have three acts, and so many story points, and you need to have dramatic moments every so many pages, and you need to put in so many twists and reversals, and then you need your ending to be big. Well, you know, duh, yeah. A book needs to be interesting.

Writing rules short-circuit my brain. I just can't seem to make the jump between a formula and lively writing. That's why I'm sharing with you what works for me: tools and ideas you can mess around with and use on your own, just like my author friends and I do. When you close this book, you won't need a teacher to help you through the writing process; you'll be your own teacher. You'll have the capacity to use any number of writing techniques your own way, and what's more, you'll adapt them and discover new ones.

The beauty of writing is that no governing body will check to see if you've done things 'right' or 'wrong.' No penalty for inventing something new!

I invite you to skip around in this book. Reading it all the way through is fine, but if you get antsy to write and you want to blast forward, do it. Read, browse, skim over the stuff that's not for you right now, slow down and savor the stuff that grabs you, close the book and do some writing. Let serendipity happen.

## Saying Nay to the Naysayers

Too many people think it's hard to write a book. Why? Mainly because writing was hard when we were kids. Rules, penmanship, rules, spelling, rules, grammar, rules. If you were a typical kid like me, you heaved that loglike pencil to your shoulder, squeezed your fingers around it tightly, and anxiously scraped out your letters and numbers trying to break as few rules as possible.

Another reason writing seemed hard to so many of us back then is that we expected ourselves to get it right the first time, ignoring the plain obvious fact that there are a thousand ways to write anything, be it a story or a factual account or an essay. The thinking was: Better bear down real hard mentally, better question every word before I write it, because I don't want to screw up.

### A SIMPLE LITTLE IDEA...

Beginners often feel that to write is to present something—to have a finished product, something completed in their mind's eye before they begin. This is false. Such a thought leads only to anxiety. The truth is that a simple little idea, if set free to run around on the page, will lead to more and better and more.

Then you got older, and in high school or even college, you had to write papers. Oh, gosh! At this point, there were so many rules that by the time you got them figured out, you forgot what you wanted to say.

Or maybe you took a creative writing class because you had a spark inside you that drove you to write. I took one in high school. The only thing I remember was the teacher telling us that Ray Bradbury wrote a thousand words a day for ten years before he got somewhat good at writing. This was supposed to be inspiring.

I left school with an uneasy relationship with writing. (Big surprise.) I could do it, but it was hard. It made me worried. Yet I wrote, and I wanted to write well. I stayed away from creative writing classes and tried listening to authors directly. They all seemed to feel that writing is hard.

Red Smith, the most famous sportswriter of the twentieth century, said, "There's nothing to writing. All you do is sit down at a typewriter and open a vein."

He was just the beginning. Tons of really famous, successful writers say things like that all the time. I won't repeat them here because you (and I) don't need the stress. If you listen to practically any professional writer talk about what they do, you'll hear it, over and over. Lots of how-to-write books say stuff like that as well. These people are believable because they're accomplished.

How could they not know what they're talking about?

So we believe them, and we try to write, and we struggle and bleed, believing that's the process. When we have a breakthrough and the writing comes as easy as breathing, we consider it a temporary gift from the gods, soon to be snatched away again.

After all, that's what they tell us will happen.

They're sincere.

But they're wrong.

Why? Because they're stuck on all those rules, which are really details that have nothing to do with the core act of writing. And because of their belief in rules, and because of some baseline insecurity that I cannot explain, they're stuck with the conviction that what they do is almost impossible.

The other thing is, and we must be honest, we must be unflinchingly honest here: It's an ego trip for lots of authors to tell how hard it was to write their books, how they almost committed suicide nineteen times during those long, long months of lonely struggle. Lonely, lonely. Struggle, struggle.

Ordeals lend writers legitimacy and charisma. Moreover, ordeals make people feel special. Ordeals give excuses for taking five years to write a book ... while drinking too much. The truth is, ordeals in writing are totally self-inflicted. Nobody's standing over us making us struggle, forcing us to suffer. Struggle and suffering in writing are matters of personal choice. We don't like to admit it, but we know it's true.

I realized that most successful writers are successful in spite of their belief that writing is hard. If they could relax and get the hell out of their own way, imagine what they could accomplish!

If you want to write a book, you can struggle and suffer too—or you can choose to write with patience, receptiveness, and a heart filled with zest. You can have fun. By the way, isn't zest a wonderful word? In our careful world, 'feeling just OK' seems to be the new normal. I want zest, dammit. Zest, joy, and ferocious awareness.

> *You know, I don't feel particularly scared of writing. I don't feel that writing is hard; I love it.*

You are an exemplar. I encourage you to share your attitude and experiences with others. Keep hold of that positive 'tude.

*But writing being fun? I'm not sure about that.*

If it's not fun, it's not worth doing. Boy, chisel that one on any spare piece of granite you've got lying around the house:

> CHISEL IT IN STONE:
> IF IT'S NOT FUN, DON'T DO IT.

Which raises the thrilling corollary, also chisel-worthy:

> CHISEL IT IN STONE:
> IF IT'S NOT FUN, MAKE IT FUN.

What's fun got to do with it? After all, this is serious business, writing a book.

The thing is, readers can always tell whether an author had fun while writing. They might not know what's wrong with a book they find boring; they simply don't like it. The book doesn't resonate with them, it doesn't sing. And that's because the author labored over it. The author didn't have fun.

It's true: No matter how serious the subject, you can only do justice to it—full-hearted justice—if you have fun with it.

I don't mean you have to make jokes or write comedy, unless that's your aim. You can have fun with the most serious—even tragic or horrifying—of subjects. By fun I mean a sense of play, an attitude of willingness to try anything, to make a fool of yourself by making mistakes, to slam down something outrageous.

If you're having fun, you can't be afraid. So don't think you need to vanquish fear; just focus on having fun.

Let's take my claim to the extreme and see if it holds up.

A man who's been thrown to the lions knows he's likely to get his neck snapped and his belly devoured before he's dead. But he also knows that he's got a chance to survive. A slim chance, but a chance! If he can figure out how to outsmart the lions and escape, somehow he'll live.

What if he goes into this fight with fear as his chiefest emotion? He'll be tight and rigid, both mentally and physically. He might survive, but he has a better chance of decisively winning if he can relinquish fear and rigidity, and bring a flexible plan to the fight.

He'll benefit by not seeing the fight as a fight at all, but as a situation that is not threatening. The greatest warriors, in fact, tell us that they approach war as an art—they're flexible, receptive, smart. The ultimate warrior brings a sense of liveliness and joy to the battle, and a fearless immediacy.

You could call it fun.

By contrast, suffering is rooted in worry.

Worry is rooted in ingrained, life-force-sapping rules and expectations. Therefore, the only thing standing between you and your book right now is worry—and those damned rules. That's it. I'm here to help you find your way past all that nonsense.

Which brings us to:

CHISEL IT IN STONE:
PERFECT IS THE ENEMY OF GOOD.

Wise people from the dawn of time have said this. Shakespeare put it in his play *King Lear*: "Striving to better, oft we mar what's well." Your grandma said, "Let well enough alone."

It's true: Perfectionism stops us in our tracks far too often in writing and in life, and it holds us back from accomplishing important stuff we want to do, especially long-held dreams.

I learned this for myself, gradually, while writing my novels, nonfiction (including this book), and countless articles, essays, stories, and poems. It came to me while counseling aspiring writers, teaching workshops, and talking with other authors. Writing, I realized, is not the problem. The problem is worry itself. Anxiety is the evil conjoined twin of rigidity. Plus, throw in fear of failure, which is maybe the incestuous offspring of anxiety and perfectionism, and you get a family tree from hell.

Once I learned to relinquish worry, my writing flowed freely. I stopped being my own stumbling block. With what I've learned I've helped lots of writers. When I sit down to write, I feel like an otter slipping into the water. I love it so much. That's how I want you to feel.

Instinctively, you know it takes guts to write a book. You need courage to keep going through the process, and fortitude to shrug off negativity. That's OK. You've got guts. And the fact is, your guts are going to work a whole lot better when you're rid of worry.

## The Great Open Secret

The real challenge is that writing requires patience—patience for yourself, patience for your work, and patience for other people's response to your work. The way to cultivate patience is to persist. And the way to succeed as a writer, by whatever standards you set for yourself, is to persist. That is the great open secret, right there in plain sight. Inborn talent is lovely to have. Good fortune is a fine thing. But over those things you have no control. You do have control over your persistence. Every day you choose what you will do. You choose what is important to be done, and you do it.

Writing also requires humility. It takes deep modesty to surrender yourself to the world as you are, to offer your work, to accept what comes to you. And humility begins with courage. You're courageous to do what you're doing right now, reading this book. You have control over whether you behave bravely or cowardly.

You have control over being persistent, and you have control over being patient. Raise your hand if this makes you think of Siddhartha ("I can think, wait, and fast.")

You have control over acceptance, because you have the power of choice. You can choose to accept all the wonderful and terrible things in the world that you cannot control.

> *If perfect is the enemy of good, then are you saying I should write without caring whether my work is any good?*

Yes! Only by giving yourself permission to write poorly will you write anything at all. Once you have something down on the page, you'll find it easier to keep going, to find the groove, the flow.

When you give yourself permission to write poorly, you are implicitly saying, "I've got the skills to make this better later if I decide it's no good." You're reinforcing your own inner strength.

To write the book of your dreams, all you really need are a few tools, starting with the calm knowledge that you can do it. Not the belief that you can do it. The knowledge that you can. That's where real gumption comes in. You're going to use your courage not in a big fight against yourself and your language and the world, but in acceptance and receptivity. You're going to allow yourself to write your book. It does take deep courage to do that, but the expending of courage breeds courage.

You're going to write your book the way you want to write it. And it'll be pretty decent, maybe even great, if you stay out of your own way. Developing flow in your writing is the thread that runs through this book.

### A GOOD PLAN...

Gen. George S. Patton said: "A good plan, violently executed now, is better than a perfect plan next week."

I love that "violently executed." Give it your all! Don't hesitate! Accept the outcome and go forward!

If your idea for a book is still so vague that you don't have a title, think of one now. What few words describe your book? They can be as simple as *My Story* or as descriptive as *Sewer Worker from the Bronx Sets Out to Solve Daughter's Murder in Peace Corps in Peru*. You can change it later if you want to, but right now you need a working title.

That's a great term right there: working title. Because when it comes out in conversation that you're writing a book, somebody will ask, "What's the title?" or "What's it about?" Instead of shuffling your feet and answering, "Um, it's too early to have a real title," you'll simply say, "The working title is __________" and give them a calm smile.

*But I don't always feel calm.*

You don't have to. You can write scared. But know that confidence calms the nerves. Confidence banishes worry, and how do you gain confidence? By trusting the skills you have. You know you can write.

*I get what you're saying, but I think you're overrating confidence. For instance, I could have all the confidence in the world, but unless I've studied and trained to do brain surgery, I can't simply walk into an operating room and cut a tumor out of somebody's head.*

Well, you could, but the results would be really poor. No, to do brain surgery you'd have to study, and you'd have to practice, and you'd have to believe when you tie on that gown and put on your gloves that you've got what it takes to do the job. Because all the knowledge in the world doesn't help a surgeon who's hyperventilating at the door to the operating room because she's afraid of making a mistake.

It's also true that no beginning tennis player will ever win the final at Wimbledon, no matter how much confidence he brings to the court. No, he must learn his sport and practice it.

*Is writing that much different?*

Yes! Because while you weren't born with a scalpel or tennis racquet in your hand, you were born into the world with the ability to use words. Your whole life long, you've been thinking thoughts and telling stories, describing things, telling jokes, making puns, making up rhymes and little songs, repeating stories you heard and remembered, making up stories of your own, telling fibs, white lies, outright lies, writing thank-you notes, forging school excuses and permission slips, getting into arguments, defending your opinions, apologizing, writing papers, writing e-mails, writing memos for work, writing blogs, texting, and writing letters of complaint, recommendations, sympathy cards, and, gosh, what else?

And you've been reading your whole life long, from ads on the sides of buses to online news, from comics to thick books, maybe even Shakespeare—maybe just a little Shakespeare?

A tennis player who's made it to Wimbledon has worked diligently to develop his skills, and he knows he can win only if he trusts those skills. He has also learned through experience that matches are not necessarily won by the bigger player, the stronger player, or the player whose parents have spent the most money on elite tennis camps.

They are won by the player who best puts aside doubt and fear, and who plays with relaxed focus, the player who lets his body and mind flow the freest.

Speaking of tennis, author Tim Gallwey explored and developed techniques for superior tennis performance in *The Inner Game of Tennis*. He also wrote *The Inner Game of Golf*, which as a golfer I've read and found wonderfully useful. I feel that my ideas about writing resonate with his ideas about sport.

You can build your talent, but the fact is, talent is the thing you have least control over. By contrast, you have total control over the amount of patience, guts, and persistence you bring to your writing. And that's beautiful.

> *But isn't writing lonely and sad? Isn't the suicide rate for writers really high?*

The suicide rate for people who are easily discouraged is high. If you are a writer, there is no need for you to ever be discouraged—at least not for long. A disappointment can sting, a sluggish day can put you in a funk, but you'll shrug it off quickly if you keep this in mind: If you can talk, you can write, and if you can write, you can tell the stories you were born to share.

Maybe it's fiction you want to write, or maybe you're feeling moved to write about your life. What's the one thing you wish you'd known earlier in life? Think about it. There's a book there! You can tell the world. If you could change one thing about your job or your workplace, what would it be and why? There's a book there, too. You can tell the world.

### JUMP OFF CLIFFS!

"You've got to jump off cliffs and build your wings on the way down." - Ray Bradbury.

I'm grateful to Bradbury for this. He wrote a lot, and he lived a lot!

The best writers are the ones who have learned to believe in and trust their natural skills. That's why sometimes a first-time author wins a major prize or gets on the best-seller list.

It does happen.

## ACTIONS

- What's the name of your book? Write down your title now. Go ahead. Print it carefully on an index card or something. How does it look? Beautiful! Put it in your pocket. That's your book in embryo.
- Find books like the one you're going to write. Of course there is no book exactly like the one you're going to write; I want you to go to the library or bookstore and find books in your category: fiction, memoir, how-to, history. Even reading only two—a new one and an old one that's been through at least a few decades' worth of printings—will give you tremendous perspective.
- If you were to start writing your book right now, what would the first word be? The first sentence? If you can't think of the first sentence, write the second sentence. Just for the hell of it, go ahead.

CHAPTER 2

# A Pen Is a Wrench Is a Magic Saber

Real writers take their tools and materials seriously. To write your book, you will need:

- **PAPER.** Even if you like to write on your computer, you'll need paper to brainstorm on. (Did you notice that that sentence ended with a preposition? If so, forget it. The rule that you're not supposed to end a sentence with a preposition is a needless one. If you thought, *Uh, I'm not sure what a preposition is,* congratulations! One less thing for you to have to forget!) Plus you'll want paper for random notes and bolts from the blue. You can use any kind of paper, from sheets of plain printer paper to yellow pads to spiral notebooks. After years of using yellow pads and sometimes losing pages from them, I switched to spiral notebooks packaged in bulk from the discount stores. After years of that, I'm now considering unlined sketchbooks for that unfettered feel of totally blank pages.

THE BOLT FROM THE BLUE

You have surely experienced the phenomenon known as a bolt from the blue: an unexpected lightning strike from a clear sky. And you surely know that bolts from the blue tend to happen when your mind is engaged in nonintellectual pursuits, rather than when you're doing original work. You'll be sliding the hot cookies off the sheet or hefting a smooth rock or touching the pool wall in your eleventh turn, and suddenly a truth will burst upon you, unbidden, unexpected. *Ah, that's how I should do it!*

Bolts from the blue are little gifts the universe doles out. They don't come often, but it's worth giving them the chance to.

They also tend to be fleeting! Write down your bolt as soon as you can, or at least stop whatever you're doing and focus on the idea until you're sure you'll remember it.

- **WRITING TOOLS.** Pencils or pens. A writing tool is as close to a sorcerer's wand or magic saber as we have on this earth. Those who master these tools have, quite literally, extraordinary power at their fingertips: the power to thrill, inform, comfort, jolt, question, build, defend, destroy. Experiment with different kinds and see what suits you, especially once you find yourself writing a great many more words at a time than ever before. I've written with just about everything, from the cheapest pencils to luxury fountain pens. I love the feel of a gold fountain pen nib gliding across paper; I like the little scratchy feel and sound that steel nibs make. These days, after having an expensive fountain pen almost stolen from my table in a coffee shop, I use a cheap fountain pen when out and about. I love gel pens for travel. Pens and pencils are your literal physical connection to your work. Do not treat them as commodities, but as friends. Keep track of them.

- **A LAPTOP OR DESKTOP COMPUTER** Anything with standard word processing software. Many fancy programs exist. Do not be apprehensive. You can't go wrong with something basic. Most agents, editors, and publishers these days prefer documents in Microsoft Word, in 12-point Times New Roman font. This font comes standard on practically all computers. (*Font* basically means typeface. In the olden times of hot metal typesetting, its definition was a bit more complicated; each point size was essentially a different font.)

- **A FLAT SURFACE.** Dining-room table, cellblock floor, desk, level rock.
- **A LIBRARY CARD.** Maybe you're already a patron of your local public library. Even though you can find out just about anything on the Web, there will come a time when you simply want to browse around, with the option of going deeper than Google or Wikipedia can take you. And if your local library is a nice quiet one, you might want to write there, or brainstorm, or just sit and think.

## THE SERENDIPITY OF BROWSING

The phenomenon known as the Serendipity of Browsing is when you find something you weren't looking for, but that you realize you want or need. It's a sublime moment.

When you're shopping for notebooks, for instance, and you pass by the pens, but suddenly a particular pen just sort of jumps into your hand and you realize you cannot live without it—that's serendipity. There's something about that pen! Maybe it's the finish or the heft of it; maybe it reminds you of something good though you can't explain why. Don't dismiss these little gut-level events. Pay attention. And buy the pen.

Serendipity can occur when you're on line, but there's no comparison to the sensation of walking around a real library or bookstore looking at books, your eyes scanning titles and covers, when suddenly something pops out at you—your hand seems to reach out on its own because something is striking a chord in you.

Maybe you pick up a book because, for some reason, it has triggered a memory of when you were seven and in ballet class and a creepy guy looked in the window at you. Or you see a book about something you were always curious about: carving canes or drag racing. Or you feel your adrenaline stir as you look at a novel about a police detective gone bad or a woman who might find true love after all—except it's with a priest and what the heck are they gonna do about *that*?

Your eyes can take in a lot, and you can feel the vibes different books give off. Your peripheral vision and senses come into play. You get such a feeling for the reality of wisdom and the worthiness of its pursuit when you're under a roof with thousands of books.

- **A DICTIONARY.** Yes, there are online versions, but there will be times when your computer isn't on and you want to check a word. There also should be times when you are using your word processor but not connected to the Internet. The time-sump properties of the Internet are well known.
- **A THESAURUS.** Also available on line but also necessary in bound form for just that reason. A thesaurus is a terrific tool that helps you banish clichés, is fun to browse, and most helpful when you're feeling a little stale.
- **POCKET SUPPLIES.** If I'm wearing a garment with pockets, I carry a Fisher Space Pen (it's reliable) and something to write on, like an index card or a piece of manila folder. (I save worn file folders and cut them up for this purpose.) Sometimes I also make mini notebooks out of waste 8.5″ × 11″ paper. These items are invaluable for getting down thoughts exactly when they occur to you, or for writing down great sentences you overhear. Being a girl, I carry this equipment in my purse as well.

*What about a grammar guide?*

Grammar guides are useful and it's great to have one like Strunk & White's *The Elements of Style* on your shelf. However, if you're stuck on a grammar issue, just Google it. Like, if you don't know whether to write:

The wolverine rushed from it's burrow.

or

The wolverine rushed from its burrow.

do not plunge into reading all the scripture ever written about apostrophes. Just Google "it's vs. its." You'll get a fast answer from any number of trustworthy scholars.

(The second sentence is correct.)

Typewriters, sad to say, are the coelacanths of the writing world: not yet extinct, but damn rare. Some writers like to use typewriters for first drafts, then retype the draft into their computer, editing as they go. I keep meaning to try this.

*Typewriter or keyboard bedammed, I don't / can't / won't type!*

You can still write a book. Ways around typing:

- Write longhand and pay somebody to type it into the computer for you. Young nieces and nephews are great for this. Another option is to Google 'typing services' or check Craigslist in your area.
- Write longhand and trade work with somebody who'll type it in for you.
- Write longhand and read it into your computer's microphone using a voice-to-text program. These programs started out horrible but are getting better and better. One called Dragon is very good. You might already have one on your computer, like 'Speech Recognition' in Windows. Sport around.
- Dictate your words directly into a voice-to-text program.

I might add that the best course I took in high school was a one-semester typing class with an autocratic teacher who forced us to learn the keyboard with our eyes closed. Touch-typing is a hugely useful skill. It helps you go faster, and it saves your eyesight because you're not looking back and forth between your words and the keyboard, and having to refocus a zillion times at short range. Touch-typing also saves your hands and wrists from unnecessary movement and strain.

Free online tutorials abound, or you can pick up a book and teach yourself.

Whatever writing tools and materials you choose, start loving them immediately. They're your essential friends. The paper *wants* you to write on it.

## Keeping a Notebook: It's a Wonderful Thing

You might have seen these little black notebooks in stores called Moleskines. Other companies make similar versions. Moleskines are trim black sturdy little notebooks with sewn bindings that were fanatically used by the likes of Matisse, Céline, and Bruce Chatwin. A tiny company in France made them, then stopped making them for a few decades. But they're available again, and thank goodness for that: The small ones fit so nicely into a purse or pocket. They're expensive compared to spiral-bound notebooks, but worth it, if you ask me. Keep one at your bedside, too. If you find yourself reaching for it frequently in the dead of night, you might get yourself one of those pens that has a light built right in.

Jot down anything that strikes you, anything you'd like to remember, even just fragments—especially just fragments. "Hooker in purple dress MacArthur Ave. looking desperate." "Story idea: A boss has to fire an employee but too scared to do it. Wishes she could murder him instead." "Paper says methamphetamine now cheaper than crack." Make sketches of stuff, even if you draw like a four-year-old.

While I'm on the subject of stationery, I urge you to treat yourself to new writing instruments now and then. Somehow I find a change of pen or pencil as refreshing as a change of scenery. They don't have to be expensive; between eBay and your local pawnshops you can find cool used pens and pencils dirt-cheap. Write with a thick line, a thin line, a blue line, a brown line. I happen to be a pencil fan—regular and mechanical—and greatly enjoyed Henry Petroski's book *The Pencil.*

When you're between writing projects, or just feeling in need of a little refreshment, visit your notebooks.

For easy ways to organize all of your stuff see Chapter Fourteen, **Keeping Your Workshop**.

## ACTIONS

- Round up two or three writing instruments. If any are pens, check that their cartridges or reservoirs are full. Re: pencils, only select those with good (not hard, old, or nonexistent) erasers and get a sharpener on hand as well. (Trivial? Someday you will be writing with a nub, cursing and turning it until you are forced to break your train of thought to find a goddamn sharpener.) Try 'em out.
- Make a list of anything else you need. Go get it.

CHAPTER 3

# Tell a Story Like a Hero, and Make Common Sense Your Writing Buddy

You picked up this book because you feel the title is true: You've got a book in you.

Congratulations: You are embarking on a fantastic journey.

You should celebrate.

I mean it.

How do you like to celebrate a life-changing event? A bottle of champagne? A long walk in the sunshine? A phone call to your favorite sibling? Let that be your next step.

Then come back to this book and write joyfully.

Writing is life.

Cherish the feeling of ink flowing onto paper or the feeling of your fingers touching keys and forming words. As a working writer I've got to pour it out every day, hell or high water. Whatever my end goals, I put them aside; they're a distraction to the process. Write what is at hand now.

> CHISEL IT IN STONE:
> WRITE WHAT IS AT HAND NOW.

## You Are the Hero of Your Own Life

What do you think of when you hear the word hero?

In ancient mythology, a hero was someone whose deeds were so extraordinary that he (yes, always he, but that was then and this is now) was elevated by the gods to a place above human level.

We earthlings like to reward people who achieve the extraordinary with praise, admiration, and trophies. Hero is the highest praise we can give.

Humans crave inspiration; this is why Charles Lindbergh got a ticker tape parade for being first to fly across the Atlantic and the second guy didn't even get a free shoeshine. What was the difference? The second guy knew it could be done; the territory was no longer unknown. No longer fearsome.

Heroes do three things:

1. **HEROES TAKE DRASTIC RISKS**, venture into unknown territory, and come back with a reward—sometimes it's an object, but most times it's knowledge: "We now know an airplane can be flown safely across the Atlantic Ocean."
2. **HEROES SACRIFICE THEMSELVES** for the sake of others. Every fallen soldier has made the ultimate sacrifice in the name of his or her cause. Parents everywhere give up their own comfort so their children can survive or have a better life. Sacrifice can be big or small, but it is always significant.
3. **HEROES PUSH THEMSELVES** beyond what they thought were their limits.

Honest writers do those three things every day. You set out across the ocean in a light plane, for the first time, over and over again.

To write a book is to open and give yourself to a world thirsty for authenticity. Writing a book is a heroic act, and it is an accomplishment no one can take away from you. When you come to THE END, you will know a wealth of things about your subject, about writing, and about yourself. You will be a deeper, richer, more complete person.

*I want to write a book, but what if I fail?*

I once climbed a mountain with a group of friends. The going was so tough that afterward one of the men confessed, "I was hoping a snake would bite me so I could quit." He had too much integrity to quit, but he'd have liked an external force to make the choice for him.

That's the kind of out a writer knows he'll never get. No matter what, writing a book is entirely self-directed. That fact can frighten some people—and exhilarate others. It's our choice.

*How do I know if I have enough talent?*

When it comes to writing a book, talent is not the most important thing.

*What?*

Oh, talent's great! You need some, and if you're seriously considering writing a book, you probably already have some. My desk dictionary (*American Heritage Second College Edition*) says talent is "natural or acquired ability." Talent can help you produce a better book, but most successful artists admit that they started with a bit of an aptitude and discovered their talent as they practiced. Their craft became their art became their way of life. You can develop your talent for writing by writing.

Writing Blasts, like the one below, are for enjoyment and exploration. They loosen you up and tune you into the flow within. I call these things Writing Blasts instead of 'exercises' because the word *exercise* has a wearisome connotation to me; also, exercise implies that it's only practice and not real. The writing you're doing with me is real, all right. Do these Writing Blasts, and they'll guide you straight through the writing of your book.

## WRITING BLAST: A STORY EVERYBODY CAN TELL

- Gather your writing materials.
- Find a comfortable place. Sit at a table or desk or sprawl on your stomach on the rug or go to your fave coffee shop and set yourself up with a nice beverage.
- OK. Where were you and what was it like when:

- JFK was assassinated
- The Challenger space shuttle went down
- Princess Diana died
- September 11, 2001

- Pick one and remember. Remember your surroundings, and what you were doing before you heard. Remember how you received the news, who you were with, what you felt, what you thought, what you did. Feelings, sensations, tastes, smells, sounds, sights. Everything we experience has an effect on us, big or small. What effect did this event have on you?
- If you are too young to remember one of those things, think of your first date or your first kiss. Remember everything about it. What happened, who said what, how did it go, what did you feel?
- Write about it. Tell the story. Write for as long as you like.
- When you feel like you've reached a good place to stop, stop.

Congratulations. You have just written a first-person narrative using a chronological structure.

*Wow.*

Yes. If I'd started this book telling you that you were going to write a first-person narrative using a chronological structure before the day is out, you might have tightened up and muttered, "Oh, hell, a writing lesson. I smell rules coming."

You see, the act of describing writing is more complicated than the act of writing itself. (By the way, a narrative is simply a story: an account of events, whether fact or fiction.)

Here's the terrible secret about most writing instruction: It is reverse engineered.

*What's that?*

A dear friend of mine is an origami master. Whenever she comes across a piece of origami new to her, she unfolds it, thereby reversing the process by which it was created. She makes notes along the way, or, if the object is extremely complex, she takes pictures. Thus, by the process of reverse engineering, she learns how to fold it herself. This works with origami, which requires exactitude and repeatability.

When it comes to writing, a theorist (usually a professor or teacher) reads something good, analyzes it, and then makes up techniques and principles that the writer supposedly used and that somebody else should be able to use to achieve the same thing.

However, because writing is such an individual practice, reverse engineering doesn't work. Why? Because good writing comes from the heart, not a science book. Analysis, rules, and theorizing are invariably disastrous for creativity.

## Your Best Friend Is Common Sense

Granted, we need a few standard agreements, like spelling and punctuation, so others can read and comprehend our work. Basic grammar helps too, though is not always necessary.

In fact, grammar rules can be particularly constricting. Here's an example to show what I mean.

You've heard this life-or-death grammar rule: **Write complete sentences, never fragments.**

If there was ever a rule that authors ought to chop into little bits and stomp into the ground, it's this one. Consider these two examples:

> 1) "The volcano!" Rupert shouted. "It's erupting!"
>
> 2) Rupert shouted, "The volcano is erupting!"

There's not a lot of difference; we easily understand both passages. In the second, Rupert yells a complete sentence. There's nothing inherently wrong with it. But isn't the first one a bit more lively? In the first, Rupert yells a fragment, then an extremely short sentence, but used together as they are, they sound like real speech. They have rhythm, and they serve well to convey Rupert's excitement. You or I might shout about a volcano in much the same way. Common sense says these sentence fragments are OK.

Here's an example of a sentence fragment that doesn't work:

When you threw.

We don't have to go into a complicated explanation as to why this is no good; it just doesn't make sense.

As you can see, the thing you need most to write decent English is common sense. Common sense is your friend in life already; now it can be your writing buddy, too.

So you write something. You let it sit.

*For how long?*

Excellent question. The answer is, for a while. It can be an hour or a day or a week, even more, depending on what feels right. Just listen to your gut.

Fresh eyes are what you're after—a refreshed perspective. In general, the shorter the piece, the shorter the time you'll need to gain perspective. For a few pages of draft an hour might be fine. For a completed book, you might need a month.

All I know is that the mental and emotional space created by 'time away' is a subtly valuable asset for a writer.

OK, after you let it sit, you pick it up. You now see worth you hadn't seen before, you see little weaknesses and how to eliminate or fix them. I guarantee this will happen.

You read it again. Does it make sense? Is it what you wanted to write? If yes and yes, go on to your next hunk of writing. If not, change it, or start over and write it again. Or let it sit longer while you go on to your next hunk of writing.

That's it.

Common sense.

## Arc: A Natural Element of Storytelling

I'd like to point out that not only have you just written a first-person narrative in the Writing Blast, but you've also written a scene with an arc.

*Arc. I've heard that word used this way, but what does it mean?*

If you've read interviews of filmmakers, you might have seen the phrase 'story arc' or 'character arc.' The word arc is a verbal tag for 'change that happens to one or more characters as the result of an event.' It's a natural element of every good story. Usually the term 'arc' is used to describe a vast sweep of action, like what happens during an epic story or a whole season on a TV show: The main character or characters go through many adventures, they confront troubles, and they come through the troubles bigger and better—or at least wiser—than at the start.

But every scene, small or large, if it's worth its salt, should have a mini arc as well. Something happens; change occurs, even if it's just a shift of mood.

By the way, whenever I use the word character, you can take it to mean fictitious person or real person.

## Who, We?

Speaking of persons: first person, second person, third person: what exactly are they? The short answer: First is 'I,' second is 'you,' third is 'he, she, they.'

Examples:

> **FIRST PERSON:** With a shriek, I leaped into the canoe and pushed off just as the panther reached the shore.
>
> **SECOND PERSON:** With a shriek, you leaped into the canoe and pushed off just as the panther reached the shore.
>
> **THIRD PERSON:** With a shriek, Joe leaped into the canoe and pushed off just as the panther reached the shore.

Generally, the second person comes off as bizarre in a long piece, with all those yous. We tend to use the second person more in conversation, thus it works in dialogue like this:

> The reporter stuck his microphone into Chris's face and asked, "How did you feel when you ran into that burning building after those children?"

> Slowly, Chris said, "Well, you always think you'd do that for somebody. Kids, especially. I guess I didn't really think about it. I'm just glad it worked out."

Writers almost always use either the first person (telling the story from the point of view of one character) or some version of the third person.

A story in the third person may use an omniscient narrator (one who sees into the brains and hearts of all the characters) or a limited narrator (one who sees into the brains and hearts of one or a few characters, but not all).

## Stories Move Forward on Change

In newsrooms around the world, a news article is called a story for one excellent reason: People live on stories. And a story isn't a story unless it has change somewhere in it. Newspapers and magazines are a world of stories. Books are a world of stories, be they fact or fiction. Movies and television are a world of stories. The most effective TV commercials are the ones that tell entertaining little stories.

> CHISEL IT IN STONE:
> STORIES MOVE FORWARD ON CHANGE.

By the way, if you're intent on selling your stories someday, rejoice, because not only book buyers but movie and TV companies are insatiable maws in search of stories.

### ACTIONS

- Pick up a newspaper or news magazine. Read one of the stories. What is that story's arc? It's got one, or an editor wouldn't have considered it newsworthy. What makes this particular story a story? What happened, what changed in whose world? From now on, you'll be aware of arc.
- The next time you're listening to somebody talk, look for arcs. What change is being described? If none, no wonder you're bored. The next time you're talking to someone, have arc in mind.

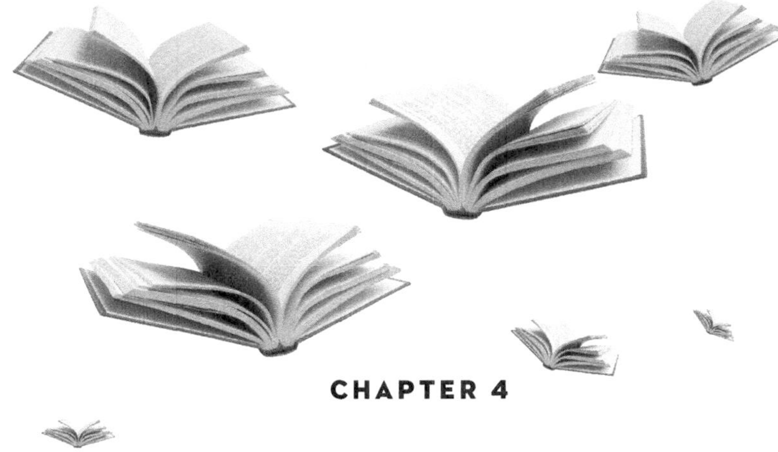

CHAPTER 4

# Find Your Garret:

## Your Space and Time

Right now I'm roughing out this chapter in longhand while sitting in a straight chair next to my eighty-eight-year-old mother's bed in the ICU at Blake Medical Center in Bradenton, Florida. An ultrasound technician is making pictures of her kidneys with a portable machine. Having done all I could for my mother this morning, I realized I could work right here as she dozes and gains strength.

And I'm writing and thinking about a writer's time and space. Literature abounds with examples of writers locking themselves away in garrets—

*Wait. What the hell is a garret, exactly?*

An attic. Attics are places where you can be alone—hidden, even—and no one will bother you. That's usually because nobody wants to climb that ladder or tricky narrow staircase just to tell you about the iguana they just saw recite the Pledge of Allegiance on YouTube.

For our purposes, garrets are real places, but they are also infinitely movable, changeable, and adaptable to our needs. Every writer needs a garret. This is beyond a room of one's own, so lovingly described and honored by Virginia Woolf in her book by the same title.

A room of one's own is fine: a place that's yours, where you can go to do your own thing. However, an intruder who presumes that his need to talk to you is more important than your need to write, can knock on the door of your room. Even if unanswered, the knock itself is an intrusion.

Therefore, such a room is beside the point. What a writer needs is psychic isolation, a mental place where you can focus on what you want to do without much chance of interruption.

The idea of a garret is perfect for our purposes. The garret, there beneath the peak of the roof where the rain pounds loud, the place equal in height to the streaming eaves, is the place where nobody with important business goes. It's the place that's hard to get to, the place that says, "If somebody's writing up there, they must *really* want to do it."

*I don't have a garret. Will the basement do?*

I will say basements can be depressing. The summer after getting my first university degree, I wrote in the unfinished basement of my ancestral home, and it was just plain awful. No windows, no natural light, cold, musty. I came to realize how great garrets, real garrets are. You're warm, you might have a little window, and even though it's probably musty, you're literally above it all.

If you have access to an attic garret, grab it. Try it out. Not everybody, however, has such a place. Plus, we writers sometimes travel, and a physical-world garret is not portable.

Therefore we must *create our garrets.*

In order to do this, we must realize that the garret is 1) a frame of mind, coupled with 2) a workable physical space. The world abounds with such spaces. Therefore, you can make and take your garret with you.

This is tremendously freeing.

Your personal garret might be:

- a study carrel at your local library
- a corner of the garage that you've barricaded off and lighted
- a table at the local coffee corral
- a stand-up counter spot at your favorite deli

- a park bench
- your car

Stephen King wrote his first novel, *Carrie*, in the laundry room of his single-wide trailer. If you've ever been in a single-wide, you'll know that its laundry room is a spot tighter than an ant farm. But it was his garret. He made it work!

> CHISEL IT IN STONE:
> WHEN TO WRITE? NOW.
> WHERE TO WRITE? HERE.

As I said above, a writer's garret is first a frame of mind. The physical space matters as well.

*Quiet*, however, is not always necessary. Some writers find a little white noise to be helpful, but a lack of disturbances is prime. The definition of 'disturbances' for our purpose is anything from your ordinary life or routine that can grab your attention. Sometimes these things lurk.

The phone is one, but just about anything at home can do it. The computer, needless to say. The quickly growing lawn. The list of stuff to do that you got partway through and then put down. The curling wallpaper seam. The preparation of lunch. Beware the crossword puzzle in the bathroom. Then there's your kids, or your little siblings, spouse, parent, the cat, the dog, the parakeet.

> *I live alone, so I don't really need a garret. I can just sit at my table and—*

Listen.
Every.
Writer.
Needs.
A.
Garret.

I lived alone for years, sometimes in a simple studio apartment with few possessions. But I used a coffee shop as a garret. Why? Because of writing enemies in my apartment: The stack of unopened mail; the friend I owed a call to; the jeans that needed a patch before I could wear them again; the last of those tasty potato chips. And on and on.

No wonder 'anywhere out of the house' equals a garret for so many of us writers. Now I have a home office and work there a lot, but often I have to get the hell out. The landline rings. The voicemail gets it but I sit there hearing it ring and wonder who's calling and when I can call them back …

My garret, as I began this chapter, was that chair in that hospital room. (By the way, my mother recovered from that illness.)

A regular garret is a good thing to have. You might find yourself gravitating to one or two regular garrets. If you're lucky enough to live near a beach or a terrific park, you can write there. Bring a folding chair or spread a blanket.

Coffee shops are just great for writers, for so many reasons, but resist all temptations to connect to the Internet. I rarely bring my laptop to a coffee shop, preferring to write longhand. In a coffee bar it's so much easier to block out distractions like some song you don't admire or the conversation next to you, because these things are not personal to you, unlike your ringing phone or seductive significant other.

I might add that you can feed off of lots of the stimulation of a coffee bar. Besides the lovely hit of caffeine (or theobromine, if you do hot chocolate instead of coffee) and the heavenly aromas, you can eavesdrop and learn a lot about writing realistic dialogue. (See Chapter Seventeen, **Eavesdrop!**) You can use the creative energy of the music coming over the sound system, no matter what kind it is. You can feed off the personalities of the staff.

Anywhere you go to write, feed off the ambient energy: the cars and people going by on the street, the vibes of the books in the stacks, the vitality of the very air currents on your face. Grab the vibes at your local burger biggie. The snacky cache.

And in any eatery, always be sure to buy at least a beverage. Be nice to the crew; make it so they smile when they see you coming. If you come in frequently, consume some comestibles and tip decently, you'll make friends with the staff. When you're friends with the staff or owner, sometimes they give you free stuff. Besides, even if the business is a chain, like Starbucks, and even if you're against chains or Starbucks in particular, it's not right to take advantage. Anything you do to take away sales (like hogging a table for hours without buying anything) will not harm headquarters and shareholders. The brunt will be borne by the local employees.

To me, caffeine is a wonder drug, boosting brainpower and energy. If you use it, use it wisely. I try to save it for when I'm really settling down to work on important, original writing. When I need to be at my peak.

Otherwise, I dial it down by drinking pale tea.

## Space Can Change

Here's another angle. Your garret can be the busiest room of the house—if you're there when nobody else is. Getting up before dawn, sitting at the kitchen table with a mug of something hot, you've found your garret. Or your garret might be a hot bath. Bring your materials and write for thirty minutes until the water cools.

Make your environment comfortable however you can. My friend Jamie Morris, a stellar editor and writing teacher, has learned that having food nearby helps her students relax and focus better. Even having something as simple as a bottle of water and a packet of nuts or crackers gives you a sense of adequacy and comfort. No anxiety. You're OK.

So you see, your garret is the space you're claiming right now for your writing. Long term or just for this hour! It's good. It's safe for writing. It's yours and it's glorious.

Claim it. Write in it.

### YOUR PERMISSION SLIP

Write yourself a permission slip to do whatever the hell you want. To go anywhere and write. For fun. For serious. Sign your own permission slip.

## The Mental Angle: Garret Mode

Garret mode is the frame of mind when you're in a good physical place and you're ready to write. To enter garret mode, simply choose to free your mind from worry and inner babble. Say to yourself, "I'm ready to write." Bam, you're in garret mode.

You can bring your own portable music device, but I think it's distracting to listen to anything that competes with the ambient music and sounds of your surroundings. It's good for your concentration to write in a public place and deal with the sounds, sights, smells, feels. Your concentration improves under such stimuli. This carries tremendous advantages, along the lines of Buddha's admonition to meditate on Main Street, for if you can meditate while sitting next to the busiest road in town, you'll be able to carry your peaceful core everywhere. Ultimate liberation!

## Dancing With the Clock

Most important is making time for your writing.

Just as you claim space by creating your garret wherever you choose, claim your time to write.

I know what you're thinking. Go ahead, say it.

> *OK. I don't have enough time to write.*

Listen to this.

I used to go to an inventor's group where people discussed their ideas and shared strategies. (Everybody signed a confidentiality agreement.) At those meetings I learned a central truth of inventing:

Ideas are a dime a dozen.

It's development and execution that separates the moguls from the chumps. And I realized that this is a profound truth in life. And of course there is a direct parallel to writing. Having an idea for a book is a terrific thing. The thing that gets your idea from dream to bound volume is simple execution, word by word, sentence by sentence, chapter by chapter.

Some writing coaches feel you need to set an inviolate time, to write routinely, and to adhere to a specific schedule, or you'll get annihilated. The trouble with that is, the first time you skip a session—whether due of necessity or a passing attack of laziness—you tend to feel like a failure. "Ah hell, I've blown it. I've just proved I'm not a professional: I don't have the discipline I need."

And then you feel like you have to promise yourself even harder that you'll write in your regular time slot from now on without fail ... which sets you up for more unhappiness and more ridiculous, unproductive self-talk.

That is all bullshit.

Do you see how perfectionism is your enemy? Remember "Perfect is the enemy of good"? You are perfectly good the way you are.

Here's the well-guarded secret held by every professional writer: None of us are as productive as we feel we should be. None of us writes as much or as regularly as we know we ought.

But we write where we can and when we can. We strive to be reasonable with our inner selves. We don't wait until conditions are 'right'. We bring our garrets with us—very light bundles, actually!—just about everywhere we go. We enter garret mode easily.

> CHISEL IT IN STONE:
> TIME IS NOT THE POINT. PRODUCTIVITY IS.

Good time slots for writing:

- Lunch breaks at work. A friend of mine wrote the first draft of his noir novel over six months of lunch hours!
- After your regular work shift. Stop at one of your away-from-home garrets and throw down your words before going home.
- Early morning. Here's a trick to quit hitting the snooze button: Transfer your heartbrain from "Oh, this bed feels so good and I deserve comfort," to "My book awaits me."
- A weekend day. You can throw down a ton of words in one focused period in a weekend day. Using the whole day is great, but a morning is very good, too. I will note that it requires iron discipline to write on a weekend afternoon, given the many opportunities for goofing off. If you do it, brag to me. You're entitled.

*Wait, go back. What's a heartbrain?*

## Heartbrain

The mysterious, writerly core of you is your heartbrain. More than brain, more than heart. It's where your magic lives.

Make this mental shift: Write constantly, and squeeze in life around the edges. It's a simple but powerful shift. As you can see, getting a book written is a matter of priorities. Give writing a high priority, and you'll find yourself making excuses to drop other stuff like sitting in front of the television or dicking around on the computer.

> WRITE LIKE YOUR LIFE DEPENDS ON IT.
> BECAUSE IT DOES.

When you start writing regularly, your life opens like a great vista: It becomes richer, bigger, more beautiful, more compelling.

Now, what about this concept of 'time,' anyway?

## Hours Spent Writing Are Irrelevant. Word Count Is Gold.

For all writers, word count is gold. Getting the words down is gold. Sitting there staring at your paper for an hour because you can't think of something good to write is demoralizing.

Commit yourself to a minimum word count per session and start writing. Or you could do a minimum page count.

Aim low.

*What? I thought I was here to reach high goals!*

You are. I'm your champion and I want you to reach the heights. But this is one case where aiming low is essential.

In the early stages of writing, set yourself a goal of 200 words per writing session. That's not a lot. The beauty of aiming for low output is when you arrive at your minimum, if you're fascinated by what you're doing, you'll keep going. This will happen naturally. You'll see.

If you're anxious about your word count as you go along, count the words on every page of writing after you finish it. You'll soon get a feel for how many words you typically write per page. Then you can just count pages to get to your goal.

Today, the word-count issue is nonexistent thanks to the word processing software that comes with your computer. You'll see a running total at the bottom of your screen. I love that feature.

When you've reached your minimum or beyond and you sense that you're at a good stopping point, stop. You've achieved your writing goal for the day and you're entitled to feel good.

No matter how tempting it is, do not get more rigid or self-demanding than that about your writing routine. If you miss a day or two—or a week or two—be at ease in your heartbrain.

Simply persist. Gather your writing materials at the next opportunity, enter garret mode, and pick up where you left off—or try another direction. Write your minimum, and write it where you can, when you can. Without stress, without self-drama. Small pieces of writing will add up quickly over time. Never mourn lost time.

As you get used to it, you can set your daily word-count goal higher. Most professionals write between 1,000 and 2,000 words per day. You can boost your output to 5,000 or even 10,000 words in one marathon day. Select your day and plan for high output. Before you begin, eliminate distractions, take care of pending business, and get your food and supplies lined up. On Marathon Day, start early. Don't go on line or screw around with anything but original writing, going forward, always forward. Take short breaks every hour, and pour it out.

That's not a pace you can sustain every day (at least if you want to turn out quality work), but you can do it now and then, when you really want to kick it into high gear.

## The Best Strategy for Reliable Output

As you see, a writer's best strategy isn't rigidity. It's flexibility combined with persistence.

*What if my writing seems fragmented, with all these little bits and pieces?*

That's OK. Trust the process. When we write freely, stuff goes on deep within us that's wiser than we know. Eventually, fragments will either be thrown off or absorbed into the whole during rereading and making-it-better.

## The Dreaded Day Job Question

*I'm serious about writing, and my job gets in the way. If I quit my job, I'd have the large blocks of time I feel I need to get my book done. Should I take the leap?*

I remember being a corporate executive, riding in an elevator to some meeting, thinking about the insane hours I was working and about the novel I'd started four years earlier. I thought, *I know of ten ways I can make that manuscript better, but I don't have ten minutes to do it.*

Since I was in position for a big promotion, that moment led me to ask the Great Question in life: **What do you want carved on your tombstone?**

As it happens, I intend to be cremated, but somebody might put up a marker. At that moment, I felt my choices were two:

SHE WAS AN EXECUTIVE VICE PRESIDENT.
*or*
SHE WENT FOR IT.

I went for it.

I quit my job and wrote fiction full-time. However, it took four years for me to find a leading house (there were no digital publishing programs yet) that wanted to publish my book. It was a tough, poverty-strewn road. I went from an income of $90,000 per year to nothing, for years. I had some savings, but they got used up, and I was fortunate to have a life partner who willingly supplemented my meager income.

I had to do it, I felt a strong compulsion to do it.

You have to listen to your heartbrain.

It's a challenging situation either way. It's challenging to write on a tight timeline without a regular income, and it's challenging to try to fit in writing around your regular employment.

There is a third way.

## The Garret Vacation

Do you get paid vacation or unpaid leave?

Take a week of it and set yourself up in a cheap getaway—an off-season vacation rental, like Florida in summer or Ohio in winter, or a motel right in your town. The point is to get out of your normal home and take a Garret Vacation.

Bring your writing materials, comfortable clothes, and healthful snackies. Make yourself a little garret. Write intensely there. See how much you can get done. You can do a 10,000-word day, or you can set yourself a 10,000-word week.

You'll get a lot done.

The Garret Vacation can be taken repeatedly, using hunks of time as you get them—a weekend, a four-day holiday, two weeks, you decide.

If your garret is boring, fine. Just as a too-noisy writing environment will teach you how to block out distractions, a dull, unstimulating one will prompt you to dive more deeply into the world you're writing about.

Focus and execute.

You can also take a few months off your regular work. If you have some savings and don't mind a little risk, ask your boss for unpaid leave. If that won't work, you can quit, write for a while, and then get another job if you need to.

Would-be writers are consistently told to keep their day jobs. I say, listen to your heartbrain. As long as you have a good survival plan and can keep up whatever financial responsibilities you have, do what you feel driven to do. If you make plenty of money with your writing, great! If not, you'll find employment to pay the bills. If another job doesn't come right away, maybe you'll go through some hardship. That's the risk. But you won't die. And you'll probably keep writing.

*I'm retired with an adequate income. But I still have trouble finding time to write.*

Chores, recreation, and sleeve-tugging spouses expand to fill your time. Get tough with all of it.

Make a list of stuff that takes up your time. Look at each item and ask, "Is this necessary? How necessary?"

Eliminate the bullshit stuff and cut back your commitment to semi-bullshit stuff. Make your significant-other time count. (Watching television together doesn't count and can be cut back.) Claim your writing time. No one cares about your writing as much as you do.

*I have small kids. What do I do?*

Successful writing moms I've talked with advise four strategies:

- Hug the chaos.
- Teach yourself to write in short bursts.
- Be at peace with the fact that your output might not be as high as you'd like. This is actually the condition of every writer, not just moms.
- Save up and splurge on a sitter now and then. Go find your garret, and write like hell!

## Don't Eat Crap

It's more fun being a healthy, fit writer than a sluggardly one. Slugs tend to get depressed from eating crap, drinking too much alcohol, using drugs, or downloading too much porn.

A strong mind doesn't make your body stronger, but a strong body strengthens your mind. You become more confident. You are all one thing.

Your writing life will be more fun if you:

- Get a little exercise. There's no better physical activity for a writer than walking. Pay attention when you walk. Let the world come in, and don't obsess about what you're writing.

- Don't eat crap regularly. Indulge once in a while. To paraphrase St. Thomas Aquinas, eating crap is its own punishment.
- Eat a good breakfast every day. High protein is good. I like to start my day with a hard-boiled egg or two and some hot tea.

## ACTIONS

- Take a few hours to look for garret spaces. At home, elsewhere. Try them out.
- Keep a time diary for a week. Write down everything you do and when you do it, then review for opportunities to cut useless activity. I know you will not do this, and I know why. Because we all waste time doing brainless, unproductive things. Whenever you think, "I don't have time to write," threaten yourself with a time diary. You'll choose to do fewer brainless, unproductive things and use the time you save to write.

CHAPTER 5

# Fact or Fiction?

Do you know whether your book should be fiction, memoir, regular nonfiction, or even how-to? Once you write some basics about your book, you'll be ready to make that decision.

Even if you are sure, read this chapter. I won't try to change your mind but I do want to save you from barking up the wrong tree.

Why try to figure out your form in the first place? Why not just jump right in?

Simple answer: An initial focus will help your ideas flow.

A story can be fact or fiction. A newspaper story is a factual narrative: *Yesterday a pedestrian was killed by a drunk driver.* or *Last night the city council met and voted to give a raise to the librarians.*

Here are the basic forms of books you could write. Even if you're just focused on writing one book right now, you might write other books later, so it's good to have an idea of these things.

**FICTION:** Stories you make up. Fiction can be based on fact. Most novelists use material from their own lives.

For instance, we know that Harper Lee based her famous novel *To Kill a Mockingbird* on her childhood in small-town Alabama. She used bits and pieces of it, inventing the plot about a black man fighting a trumped-up rape charge, his word against that of his white accusers. The book rings with authority because Lee knew what she was talking about.

It can't hurt to set a novel in a milieu familiar to you.

Here are rough word counts for different forms of fiction, although there are no hard-and-fast rules about it:

Microshort story: 5 – 100 words

Short-short story: 100 – 1,000

Short story: 1,000 – 5,000

Novelette: 5,000 – 10,000

Novella: 10,000 – 40,000

Novel: 40,000 – infinity

Most novels and short story collections run between 50,000 and 100,000 words.

## Genres (a.k.a. Categories) of Fiction

**MAINSTREAM.** This encompasses everything that doesn't quite fit a subcategory. Tell an interesting story that is not a mystery or romance or science fiction, and you might be writing a mainstream novel. Authors mainly known for their mainstream fiction: Charles Dickens, Pat Conroy, Anne Tyler.

**LITERARY.** Books that get kind of philosophical. You'll find these assigned in college literature courses. These books explore deep human themes, like love, death, alienation, religion, and ultimate purpose. Literary authors include William Faulkner, Isabel Allende, Kazuo Ishiguro.

I'm going to go into some greater detail in these next couple of categories, mystery and thriller/suspense, because they're the widest-read categories in fiction, and if you're thinking of writing a novel, ten bucks to five says you've got a mystery or thriller in mind.

**A MYSTERY** is a puzzle, the classic example being: Here's a dead body, now whodunit? Most mysteries try also to answer the questions howdunit and whydunit. It's a venerable form. Most writers start out being great mystery readers.

Examples of mystery writers: Agatha Christie, Arthur Conan Doyle, Umberto Eco.

**A THRILLER** is a pursuit. This category often overlaps with mystery, but the key feature that distinguishes a thriller from a mystery is *time pressure.*

Like so: The bad guys are planning something dreadful for innocent parties. In order to avert catastrophe, the evil must be stopped. Usually the bad guys and the good guys take turns pursuing each other.

The element these two forms—mystery and thriller—have in common is suspense, and I'll get back to that.

### *Mystery Subgenres*

A few major subgenres of mysteries: The **NOIR** novel, which features a morally ambiguous hero; Jim Thompson's underground classics *Pop. 1280* and *The Killer Inside Me* are examples.

Then there's the **COZY**, in which the violence takes place offstage—no explicit violence. Alexander McCall Smith's *The No. 1 Ladies' Detective Agency* novels are cozies.

The **DETECTIVE** novel usually means a private investigator, and you can start with Arthur Conan Doyle's Sherlock Holmes and keep going through Dashiell Hammett, Raymond Chandler, and beyond.

**POLICE PROCEDURALS** usually involve police detectives and the technical details of how they solve a crime; Elizabeth George writes these.

The **AMATEUR SLEUTH** is not a law-enforcement professional, but something different, like maybe a reporter or an actress. Most of my books feature amateur sleuths.

More categories exist because people like to categorize things. I don't think much of categorization, because like rules, categories can make for rigidity. But it's wise to have a passing familiarity with this kind of thing, because then you'll know what the hell authors, critics, and booksellers are talking and arguing about.

### *Thriller Subgenres*

A few major thriller subcategories: The **GEOPOLITICAL** thriller, which includes espionage, global politics, and intrigue. Richard Condon's *The Manchurian Candidate* is one, and some call Dan Brown's *The DaVinci Code* another.

The **TECHNO** thriller verges on science fiction, with hot technology figuring large in the action. Tom Clancy's *The Hunt for Red Octo-*

*ber* would be a well-known example, with most of Michael Crichton's books thrown in.

**PSYCHOLOGICAL** thrillers usually involve a psychopath of some variety, a murderous nut on the loose. A prime example being Thomas Harris's *The Silence of the Lambs.*

You might notice that many of the novels I'm mentioning have been made into movies. This is not by accident! Hollywood goes after the most powerful material it can find in these popular, categorized genres.

There's the **HISTORICAL** thriller, which these days usually means low-tech; Ken Follett's books could be placed in this category.

**DISASTER** thrillers feature humans who must cope with forces beyond their control. Paul Gallico's *The Poseidon Adventure* was an early and a famous example.

For all this, the categories of mystery and thriller eventually break down into similar elements. In order for a mystery to hold the attention of your readers, you need to inject some suspense, like the sleuth who's unraveling the mystery becomes endangered himself or herself. That's an element of the thriller. And in a thriller, you can't have a prolonged, pointless pursuit—with the possible exception of the 1974 made-for-TV film *Killdozer*—without injecting some intrigue into it.

To reduce the terms mystery and thriller yet more, you could say that the mystery is cerebral while the thriller is gut-level. And you can see that writing a purely cerebral story without some element of danger can feel flat, and a story with nothing but chases and explosions can feel juvenile, not to mention monotonous, without an element of human intrigue.

### *Plenty Good Recipe for a Mystery:*

- **A PUZZLE TO BE SOLVED,** one that usually involves a death.
- **SUSPENSE:** Will it be solved, and how?
- **HERO OR HEROES:** Who will solve it?
- **HIGH STAKES FOR THE HERO OR POTENTIAL VICTIMS.**
- **THE SOLUTION GETS REVEALED:** Who did it and why?
- **TRIUMPH OF THE GOOD OVER THE BAD.**

High stakes might involve the hero's reputation, or his very life, or the lives of other people at risk. A story needs villains, of course—and when I use the words hero or bad guy, of course I mean either male or female, and I will use both interchangeably.

### *Plenty Good Recipe for a Thriller:*

- **PURSUIT:** The bad guys are planning something awful!
- **SETUP:** What's the danger?
- **STAKES:** *Very* high, involving large numbers of people.
- **SUSPENSE:** Will the good guys be able to prevent the danger from happening?
- **URGENCY:** Will the good guys prevail *in time*?
- **TRIUMPH OF THE GOOD OVER THE BAD.**

You see that some elements are shared between the two forms, but you probably knew that intuitively already. The boundaries between the two forms are pretty liquid. I will note that in a mystery, a crime has already been committed, but in a thriller, the crime, or at least much more crime, is *impending.* And as one of my correspondents suggested, a mystery can be a thriller, but a thriller is not necessarily a mystery. In fact, I routinely posit that every novel is a mystery, because wanting to know what happens keeps you turning pages!

Contemporary mysteries tend to focus on a small world: maybe a family, or a few people, maybe a town. Contemporary thrillers tend to involve great swaths of society: secret organizations, armies, governments.

### *Back to the Other Genres of Fiction*

**SCIENCE FICTION.** Stories set in other worlds, or the future or distant past, involving scientific discoveries and made-up technologies that seem plausible, given the fictional conditions you set up as an author, fall under this category.

For instance, if you have a story set on a huge, solid planet, you know you're going to have to account for gravity. You can't have near-weightlessness occurring there without some good explanation, or your story won't seem plausible.

Our friend Ray Bradbury wrote lots of sci-fi, as did Ursula K. Le Guin and Arthur C. Clarke.

**FANTASY** is often set in mythical/magical times, for example when unicorns roamed the uncut forests of what we now know as Europe.

Top fantasy authors include J.R.R. Tolkien, George R.R. Martin, and J.K. Rowling. I don't know what it is with the initials.

**ROMANCE.** This huge category features love stories of all stripes, but the one absolute requirement is a happy ending.

Top authors in the genre include Nora Roberts, LaVryle Spencer, and Jude Deveraux.

**HISTORICAL.** These novels are set in actual historical times, like Edwardian England or Renaissance Italy.

James Clavell, Robert Graves, and Pearl S. Buck all wrote historical fiction.

**CHRISTIAN.** A story of any kind—family saga, romance—with a Christian theme.

Examples of Christian writers: C.S. Lewis, G.K. Chesterton, and more recently Tim LaHaye.

**PARANORMAL/SUPERNATURAL.** This one can bleed into just about any other category. Usually the action starts in a real-life situation, then the supernatural creeps in. Some of Stephen King's work could be called paranormal, as well as that of William Peter Blatty and even Edgar Allan Poe. Vampire stories fall into this category as well as the next.

**HORROR.** This category can be supernatural or not. Horror is the land of the eerie, the haunting, and the flat-out terrifying. Here we also find the work of Stephen King and Poe, plus authors such as Mary Shelley (*Frankenstein*) and Bram Stoker (*Dracula*).

**YOUNG ADULT**, or **YA**. Another huge category, written for readers aged fourteen to twenty. YA literature is often about—what else?—growing up.

Successful YA writers include Judy Blume, Philip Pullman, and Stephenie Meyer. (The paranormal often finds its way into many young adult books.)

**CHILDREN'S.** This massive category includes picture books and books for very young readers. The information and advice in *You've Got a Book in You* might seem aimed specifically at writers of books for grownups, but in fact it all holds true for writers of children's books as well. The young need great stories, freely told!

Well-known picture book and children's authors are Eric Carle, Dr. Seuss, and Laura Ingalls Wilder.

**OUTSIDER FICTION.** Also known as minority fiction, this subgenre offers stories geared toward gay/lesbian/bisexual/transgender, Black, Hispanic, Native American, and Asian audiences. It centers on themes thought to be of interest to these groups. Increasingly, outsider fiction addresses the immigrant experience, no matter what country of origin.

Also in the outsider fiction category is fiction by or about inmates. If you're in one of these groups, sometimes it's just a relief to pick up a book that's about your subculture.

**FAN FICTION.** These are novels that are written based on fiction that already exists—be it books or TV shows or even video games—by fans of the original material.

If you wrote a book using the characters from your favorite TV show, putting them in different situations but having them behave consistently with their already established personas, you're writing fan fiction.

This is a controversial category, as fan fiction is both a tribute and, in some ways, a rip-off.

**BLENDED FICTION** is any combination of genres: Historical YA, literary mystery, Christian sci-fi, gay paranormal romance ...

## The Weird and Exciting Arena of Creative Nonfiction

We next segue into the oddly stimulating gray area of creative nonfiction. That seems like a contradiction in terms, like 'cheap Rolex' or 'liquid ice.' But this is a contemporary category that means a factually accurate account of something that happened, told in a narrative form that might include dialogue and inner thoughts of the characters involved.

For instance, if you wrote a piece of creative nonfiction about the Battle of Gettysburg, you might write it from the point of view of one fictitious soldier or many, or even soldiers and officers with real names who were known to be in the battle. You might make up dialogue and their inner thoughts for them. You might make up incidents that happened on or around the battlefield.

However, creative nonfiction must stay true to known facts. If you wrote the story so that the Confederacy won the Battle of Gettysburg, you could not call it creative nonfiction.

Truman Capote blazed an exciting path when he wrote *In Cold Blood*, which told the true story of a home invasion, mass murder, and its subsequent investigation, trial, condemnations, and executions. It wasn't strict reportage. It was Capote putting himself at the scenes and imagining what it was like based on known facts: What were the people thinking and feeling when those events occurred?

Of course, gory murders make compelling material no matter what genre you're writing in.

## Nonfiction

In the simplest of terms, nonfiction is something that really happened.

### *Categories*

**AUTOBIOGRAPHY.** This is the story of your life, written by you. A category usually reserved for people of historical significance and celebrities, like Nelson Mandela, Lee Iacocca, and Katharine Hepburn.

**MEMOIR.** Essentially the same as autobiography in that you're writing about true incidents that occurred, but you're not necessarily writing the story of your whole life. This is a great form if you want to write about a specific period in your life, like when you were in a post-grunge band or when you fought in Vietnam.

Today lots of people are writing memoirs, which is good because lots of people lead interesting lives. A guy who took a job as a Christmas elf at Macy's wrote about it and he made it big: David Sedaris, *Holidays on Ice*. His work is memoir.

Your memoir might be of a particular episode in your life and its aftermath, like when you got fired for turning in your company for malfeasance, or how you escaped an abusive parent by running away and living on the streets for three years. If you think your personal story is compelling and might help others, consider writing a memoir.

**FAMILY HISTORY.** Every family needs one!

**BIOGRAPHY/MONOGRAPH.** This is the life story of somebody who is not you. (A monograph is simply a book that features or is about the work of one person.)

**ORAL HISTORY.** A collection of transcriptions of recorded interviews that usually focuses on a particular subject or time period. These are great fun to do. Consider writing a family history as an oral history, with all of your relatives participating.

**HOW-TO.** Do you know how to do something exceptionally well? Have you succeeded in business or developed a new way to do something that other people would want to know about? You can tell them about it. A how-to book can be on any subject under the sun. All you have to do is know what you're talking about.

**TOPICAL NONFICTION.** Things like true crime (an account of a murder and its solution, for instance), history, politics, psychology, sports, science, the story of an organization or place, and other such things all qualify as topical nonfiction. This genre usually requires research, meaning you will have to go out and dig up information.

Fun stuff about doing research:

- You get to surf the Web.
- You get surprised.
- You get to talk to new people.
- You get to be bold!

**ESSAY.** Do you like to offer your opinions? More important, do you find writing a way to explore issues and figure out where you stand on things? If so, the essay form might be for you. Book-length collections of essays usually consist of individual essays first published elsewhere, usually in magazines or as part of a blog.

**BLOG.** This is shorthand for 'web log,' which is basically a place on line where a person posts her thoughts, ideas, opinions, and experiences. Blogs can be terrific writing practice. If you start a blog, you might theme it according to your chief interest.

## More Help in Deciding Fact vs. Fiction

So, is it going to be fact or fiction for you? Ask yourself the following vital questions. It might help to write down your thoughts as you go so you don't forget. Spend some time on this, let your thoughts develop.

- Do you love to tell stories?
- Are you good at making them up?
- Or are you mostly focused on true stuff?
- When considering your story do you find yourself thinking 'What if?'
- Like this: What if this person had fallen in love with someone different? What if an earthquake hits and ruins everything? What if the adopted kid turned out bad instead of good? What if Bernie and Skip went in together on a lottery ticket and won?
- Is there a moral to the story? (Crime does not pay, crime pays great, love conquers all, love is for fools ...)

### *If Your Book is Centered on a True Story*

- Is it your direct experience?
- Is it a family yarn, valuable as much for the embellishments it's gained over the years?
- Is it something you observed?
- Is it an event, perhaps historically significant, that you participated in, or affected the outcome of?
- Does your story center on a memorable person?
- Are interesting, fun embellishments occurring to you?

### DRAMATIZE YOUR LIFE

A good friend of mine is an editor for Amazon's self-publishing subsidiary, CreateSpace, so she sees a great many newbie manuscripts. Recently she told me, "The quality of these manuscripts is all over the place. Some are wonderful! But the absolute worst thing somebody can do is fictionalize their life story. They change the names and tell their story, but there's no dramatic structure to it. It's just this sequence of events, and some of them are cool, but the whole thing really doesn't work as a novel."

So if you're considering fictionalizing your life story, you *must* treat your experiences as a starting point—as inspiration. Then get some drama in there! See Chapter Ten, **Your Map**, for how to do it.

## *If Your Topic is Concrete*

Are you an expert at something? Does your book center on a skill or set of skills? Perhaps your thing is business savvy or how to make/do/survive something? For the purpose of writing a book, you're an expert if you've taught it—if you've lectured at the college level or at companies.

Want to become an expert? Teach a seminar or course at your local college, free or for pay if you can. Agents and editors talk about a writer's need for a 'platform' in order to sell nonfiction books. That simply means that you have basic credentials, and a following of some sort, or the potential for one.

Credentials = Credibility.

Do you enjoy asking questions and searching for the answers? If you're passionate about a subject or if a subject keeps pushing itself into your heartbrain—whether it's the quest to cook the ideal meatloaf or wanting to know what's going on in the meth lab next door or coming up with an idea for the perfect embezzlement—explore it. Look into it and see how you feel about it. If you find yourself thirsting to know more about a subject, a nonfiction book might be the ticket.

Do you suspect that your true story, while compelling at least in parts, lacks pizzazz or the kind of ending you'd expect in a gripping novel? If your story is true, what about the other real people involved? While it's acceptable to change names and identifying details and still call it nonfiction, if your subjects will recognize themselves in an unflattering light, you might want to change things still more and call it fiction.

What if you decide to fictionalize a real individual who you want to take revenge on, and/or be acidic about? Go to drastic lengths in the portrayal of this character. Otherwise I guarantee you the person will recognize him or herself. Give the person a totally new name—do not get cute—and change every one of their physical characteristics: hair, eyes, body type and height, skin tone, nationality, mannerisms of speech and movement, and so on. Even race or sex. You can't go wrong changing the sex, because it will throw off every reader out there. I also suggest making the fictional character much more physically attractive than the real one. Save your vitriol for the personality.

So: Fact or fiction? Pick a way to start, get going on it, and see how the project feels.

## ACTIONS

- Tinker with titles. If you were to write a fictional piece, what title would you give it? If it were factual, what title would you give it? Which sounds like the better book?
- If you're still unsure which—fiction or nonfiction—is the right choice, try on both decisions. Spend a short time—say an hour—having made the decision to write your book as fact. How does it sit with you? Now decide the opposite, and live with that for an hour. Which seems most right now? If you're still unclear, try living with each decision for a whole day and see what happens.

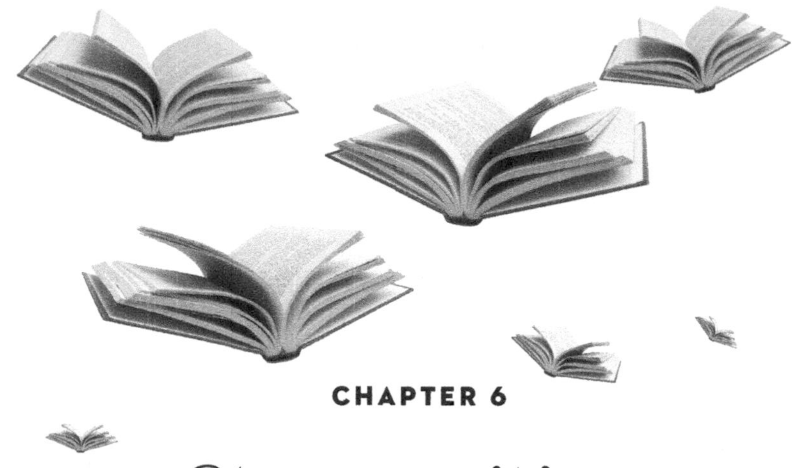

CHAPTER 6

# Stormwriting:

## The Tool of Tools

Now you're to the point where you're ready to start crafting your book.

You've done a bit of brainstorming, and perhaps you've done some writing. But there's something about brainstorming that's only partly right. After years of writing, teaching writing, and talking with writers, I've come to realize that brainstorming is a critically misunderstood process. Bad practices have become common.

Most people have been told that brainstorming is where you sit with a blank piece of paper and you're supposed to just, like force out new ideas. Well that's fine, but how?

Too often we get stuck in a rigid idea of what a brainstorm is supposed to be. We figure we're supposed to go fast, so we're supposed to write only ideas. Single words, little phrases, just get the gist of the idea down and move on to the next. We're supposed to 'think laterally', but lateral all too often winds up being shallow, a few interesting thoughts but no depth.

There is a better way.

The answer, I found, lies in the very word 'brainstorming.' I don't like that word. It puts too much emphasis on thinking.

You need to use something deeper and more productive to write a good book: You need to engage your heartbrain, that is to say your whole, deepest self. When you tap into your heartbrain, you'll be writing up a storm, which is why I call this next technique stormwriting. This is a results-driven tool that you'll use time and again. I use it constantly.

Stormwriting is essentially a heartbrainstorm, a process by which you open your heartbrain and provoke it to not merely dump stuff out, but generate new questions and ideas that lead you to more good stuff: The stuff that becomes building blocks for your book. How do you provoke it?

In one of my mystery series, my main character is an actress. In gathering background on acting, I often talk with a friend of mine who's a professional actor. One day we were talking about improv. You know, improvisation, a theatrical situation in which actors play off of each other unscripted. They create little dramas and comedies just by speaking dialogue and acting out scenes they think up as they go.

I said I thought improv must be awfully hard.

And my friend Phil said that what makes improv hard is having the wrong attitude.

"What attitude is that?" I asked.

"No," he said.

"You mean as in *No, I don't like that idea*?"

"Right." Phil then revealed the most important attitude to have when doing improv.

It is, simply, "Yes, and—"

Meaning that no matter what somebody comes up with, no matter how much it's not what you're expecting, no matter how off the wall or even *dumb*, you don't resist it or ignore it. You run with it. You say, "Yes, and—" ... and the room begins to fill with the mutant ions from the forgotten medical waste facility next door! "Yes, and—" ... and suddenly your ingénue character is on a ten-million-dollar yacht with the dictator's son, who just opened champagne and proposed marriage.

You never say "*No, but—*." You never even say "*Yes, but—*." You say, "*Yes, and—*." You accept it and you go with it, and you build on it and you play off of it. The whole act might stumble and change direction anytime, but you'll be in harmony with it.

And I realized that writing is improv.

I thought about that some more and the idea of stormwriting came to me. I realized that in practically any stage of writing, when you're brainstorming, trying to create new material, it's like doing improv. And just like improv, it requires more than your head. It requires your heartbrain.

So now we have:

## The First Stress-Free Guideline to Stormwriting

### *Yes, and—*

Use this when you're forming ideas for your book. Don't just write down the beginning of a thought and then sit and stare at it. Move with it. Let it move with you.

**Yes, and—** goes perfectly with:

## The Second Stress-Free Guideline to Stormwriting

### *What if?*

The golden guideline all excellent storytellers keep in their back pocket is **What if?** They're never without it.

**Yes, and—** and **What if?** together, are the most fruitful, lively activators you can use in mining your heartbrain and crafting creative material. These two tiny phrases will take you as far as you can dream of going.

Let me demonstrate how they can conduct you from an initial idea to a whole book.

One day I got an idea for a novel I wanted to write, using my actress hero, Rita Farmer. I thought, wouldn't it be cool to have her dressed in police costume on a movie shoot, and she wanders away from the set for some reason, and gets drawn into a real crime scene?

That was the nugget I started with. I thought, that's a terrific opening. That's *all* it was, an opening, but I immediately saw that mistaken identity, costume, impersonation, could all become themes going forward, subjects for me to explore and have fun with in the book.

I stormwrote. It stood to reason to use Los Angeles as the setting for this story, since that's where Rita lives. Questions that I asked myself were: OK, what's the main plot, and what are my subplots going to be?

OK, we're in a big city. What's a typical street crime in a big city? Well, there's drug dealing, there's assault and battery, there's rape. I'll make my initial crime a combo: I could have a young guy being beaten up by two gang-bang types. **Yes, and** Rita will walk into this assault and stop it. **What if** she gets shot while she does it? **Yes, and** she'll ride to the medical center with the beaten-up kid, and they will find out that they have something in common. But what? I'm not sure right now, but I know the young kid will be the messenger in this heroic adventure that Rita will take.

*Wait, what do you mean by 'the messenger'?*

I think you already have a sense of what I mean, but for the full deal see the **Hero's Adventure Foolproof Story Map**, Chapter Ten.

Suddenly I was writing lots more than just little isolated words or phrases on the page. I was stormwriting, going off on major tangents, writing half a page, two pages, or more per idea, then returning to my main idea page. My head was engaged. I paid attention to my emotions, too, letting them come and go with the flow from my pen.

I wrote a couple of pages on what the assault might look and sound like; I started a list of stuff I needed to look into. Started a list of characters I needed: the movie crew and the other actors, the young kid, the thugs who were beating him. I wrote half a page about what kind of movie might be shot in a gritty area of L.A., then a page about the kid. On and on.

## The Power of Tangents

As you can see, stormwriting is all about tangents. Because when you start with a single idea or concept, everything that comes off of it is a tangent.

Yet we're conditioned to reject tangents. "Now, don't go off on a tangent; stick to the point." Too often we stop a new thought in its tracks because, well, maybe it's irrelevant.

The thing is, in the early stages of creative work, *we don't know what's relevant*. Something that's totally off-the-wall today could be tomorrow's central driving force. Sometimes an idea just grabs you, or some scrappy little thing pops up and your first instinct is to just make a quick note and keep going, trying to generate more ideas. This—temporarily quashing an idea so you can go on to the next one—is the novice's critical mistake that you will now avoid forever. Because the thing is, that tangent never comes back as fresh as when it first bursts upon you.

**Tangents are the key to fresh, great material.**

You must follow them.

This is a tremendously liberating thing to realize. You're free! No more hobbles. No more rigid process. Each tangent, when you write on it, becomes a building block for your book. Just as a builder doesn't use every scrap of material he hauls to a building site, so will you sort through and keep or toss these chunks of writing.

Run, my dear writing hound, run! Follow your nose, your heart, your mind. Chase down those tangents, revel in them, chew on them, and write deep.

One chunk at a time, all this will add up to your book.

> CHISEL IT IN STONE:
> WHEN IN DOUBT, DON'T OVERTHINK IT. MOVE FORWARD.

Now back to my stormwrite on the Rita book. I went deeper. I thought about the urban experience in general, and I thought about my own experience living in big cities, and I decided to make use of my fascination with street people. Just out of my own interest, I had observed street people, talked with them, talked to police who dealt with them, talked with service organizations who provided help to them, and I had kept up with my cities' efforts to solve an intractable social problem.

And I thought, *OK, where can I go with this*? What are the elements of street-person-hood? Well, there are shelters and missions that offer help to the homeless and the needy.

The farther I let my thoughts roam, the more ideas came to me, and a plot began to take shape. It felt good.

**What if** I had a mission run by a sort of charismatic figure? **Yes, and** she seems to be hiding some kind of trouble. **What if** this angel of mercy has a dark secret? **What if** this dark secret involves a long-ago crime? **Yes, and** maybe the dark secret that involves crime wasn't what it seemed? Well, how could that be? Well, **what if** there were two dark secrets? (My heart started to beat fast. I paid attention and kept going.) **Yes, and** one exists to cover up the other one, the worse one! Yeah! **What if** the root secret had nothing to do with homelessness or drugs or violence, but something else altogether? And **what if** the angel of mercy was the grandmother of the kid that got beat up in the first scene? Yes, they're related!

You see, it doesn't have to hold together at first. Just allow yourself to reach out and gather stuff, and keep asking your heartbrain questions, prompting yourself with questions about the world you want to write about.

So, all that got me going on a plot and a subplot. You can see layers of complexity forming as we go.

This novel became *The Extra*, the second in the Rita Farmer mystery series. The story ranged all over Los Angeles, and up to a ramshackle farmhouse in Bakersfield with an old widow living in it, back down to a mansion in Hancock Park where a prize-winning beagle stud has gone missing, over to streetcorners in South Central Los Angeles and the secret rooms in a rescue mission with a very bad vibe.

This is the same approach you should take. Unleash your curiosity; fling open possibilities. If you do, ideas will come up faster than you can address them. The key to developing ideas in writing is to *plow up questions and chase down tangents.*

That's what stormwriting does.

In a minute I'll show you an example of a nonfiction stormwriting session.

Every now and then check in with your gut, with your heart, and consult your feelings. If you go dry while stormwriting but you don't want to stop, try starting a list. Just write down a list of things related to your stormwrite, such as, 'What locations might be useful in telling this story?' or 'What do I need to learn about to write my book?' or 'What are all the things that might happen at the beginning? Who are the people the reader should meet? What am I sure of? What am I unsure of? What stuff should happen near the end?' Lists themselves will become idea generators.

## STORMWRITING STEP BY STEP

1. Gather your writing materials.
2. Find a comfortable place.
3. Enter garret mode.
4. Write down your subject or idea to explore at the top of a blank page. Or write it in the middle of a page, if the idea of spinning off ideas in a cluster sort of way appeals to you.
5. Throw down everything you can think of relating to your subject or idea. Use more paper if needed. Write line by line if you want, or go off and group words together and connect them with slants and circles, or leave them orbiting alone, whatever feels right.
6. Using **Yes, and—** and **What if?**, let each item suggest a new one. Welcome tangents. Write on them as long as you want (even for pages and pages!), then come back to your original stormwrite.
7. While you work, if your gut suddenly jumps or your heart starts to beat faster, notice and follow.
8. Keep going, don't stop to criticize or censor. Open your heart-brain's throttle wide. Plunge into your subject.
9. When you feel you're ready to stop, stop.
10. Take a break.
11. Come back and look over what you've done. Look for patterns and anything that strikes you as important or thrilling. Explore those things some more or set them aside for their own stormwriting sessions.

Do you see how stormwriting is a totally individual way to develop your book?

You start with an initial idea for your book, just a general idea like the one I demonstrated above. This leads you to sub-stormwrites, all of which will help you write your book.

If something off the wall occurs to you, go ahead and write it. It might be:

- an odd way to say something

- a different way to organize a cluster of information
- a sideways, subversive twist to a situation

Never go, *Well, I've never seen anything like this before, so maybe I should trash it.* Always go: *New? Yes!* And open it up, write deeper, write long, write relaxed, write loose.

And never ever worry about your finished product in the midst of all this messy glory.

## STORMWRITING FOR NONFICTION

Stormwriting is the best way in the world to get a nonfiction project going. Start with your initiating idea, and proceed with a massive brain dump, using **Yes, and—** and **What if?** the whole way. Which will lead you to sub-brain dumps. Write lists as they come to you. Here's an example.

> Main subject: How I coached a high school track team to 3 state titles.
>
> My background—Dad—how I grew up loving the sport—My first coach, Mr. Cole—Yes, and that kid from 32nd Street—My record as a miler. What if my knee had popped when I hit that hole at regionals?
>
> How I came to coaching. Yes, and how Shirley helped me.
>
> Our marriage as a coaching tool? Coaching helped me to be a better husband. Explore. Is that true?
>
> The Wildcats—their history before I came to that school…
>
> What do I need? Get at school archives—local library—yearbooks—talk to veterans of earlier teams.
>
> What made me go for the job?
>
> Drills, workouts, nutrition, and hydration plans.
>
> What if I'd done that vertical-jump drill differently?
>
> Opposition to my ideas. Fears, doubts.
>
> The kids were open, but the parents and principal had issues with me. Yes, and that one little jerk that tried to get me fired.

The incidents with parents.
What if we'd lost that first championship?
What if we'd won the 4th one?
Regrets?

In this case, an example of a tangent might be this: You're making a list of the outstanding kids you worked with, then you remember a coach from a rival school whose son was on his squad, and you find yourself writing about that man and that boy and the things you learned from watching their relationship twice per season. Keep writing! You might use all that material in your book. Write down as many incidents as possible, knowing that you'll winnow out, save, and use the most illustrative ones later.

## FOCUS

If you try to keep your whole project in your head at one time, you'll keep trying to write it all at once, and that's a recipe for a self-inflicted gunshot wound. Just focus on one small part at a time, and really write the hell out of that part.

After you've done a bunch of this kind of work, read it over and look for patterns and gaps. Is there a thing, a person, an idea that keeps cropping up? How's your comfort level with it? Do you feel curious, weary, resistant, inflamed? Pay attention. Write more. Patterns can lead to interesting places.

Same with gaps. As you look over your stormwrite(s) do you get the feeling that something waits under the surface and is straining to come up? Tune in, get calm, listen. Let it come. Write it down. Patterns and gaps will point you forward to more writing, more learning, maybe some soul-searching.

I want to make clear that when I say don't censor yourself (under No. 8 of Stormwriting Step by Step), I mean that literally. If you find yourself using a swear word or some extreme vulgarism, don't stop to decide whether you ought to use it or not—just throw it down and keep going.

And certainly don't stop yourself from writing on a taboo subject. If for instance you find yourself thinking, "Oh, I shouldn't write about sexual abuse," do a mini stormwrite. Ask your heartbrain, "What if I did?"

The best artists know that if they dedicate themselves to *the process*, a beautiful result will follow. It might not be the result they first envisioned, but it will be honest and true.

Launch a stormwrite anytime you need ideas and anytime you need original material. The beauty of stormwriting is that you can use it anytime, anywhere, for any purpose of development. Be liberal with paper and ink, be happy, be sloppy, follow tangents, and let tangents develop as far as you want.

**Remember you are more than your head.** Be sure to pay attention to your feelings as you go. Maybe some fear is coming up, maybe some anger about what you're writing. Whatever emotions come, never resist them. Allow them to be. Notice them, and neither suppress them nor go drama queen about them.

As you write, ask yourself: How am I feeling now? Is my belly nice and loose, is my breath coming freely? Are my neck and shoulders loose? Am I having fun? Have I smiled in the last few minutes? Have I smiled at all since I started doing this? Am I taking myself too seriously?

## Challenge an Idea With Stormwriting

Alternatively, you can *challenge* an idea using a stormwrite. If you have an idea that you're a little unsure of, do a stormwrite on it.

What ideas, what characters, what events excite you as you write? What catches at you in an uncomfortable way? What begs for more attention? What do you feel like shying away from? How come? As you stormwrite, this emotion will resolve one way or the other. Maybe it's a subject you should plunge into with more depth and honesty, maybe even with more courage than you thought you needed at first.

You can use the stormwriting technique to address large issues such as, "Should I write a book about my grandmother's past as a marijuana smuggler?" or small ones like, "Should my fictional tank commander be religious?"

List pros and cons; write it one way then the other.

Let's go back to improv for a minute. Imagine the pressure and the excitement of it: You're in a studio or on a stage with other people, and everybody's watching one another, everybody's thinking, feeling, talking when they're moved to do so. All of your senses are alive, you're attuned to the others, you're attuned to yourself, you're striving to let the moment be whatever it wants to be, you're striving to be in harmony, you know that trying to force something could ruin the moment.

Yet you can't be passive because, if you are, the moment will either die or pass you by. You can't stop to evaluate the idea or emotion that has just come to you; that takes time and moves your focus away from creativity. You've got to pour it out and keep going.

What exquisite aliveness actors and actresses must feel!

This kind of aliveness is what we hope to achieve when we engage in the writing process. This is the aliveness we can achieve when stormwriting, and of course it is the flow of unfettered life.

As you can see, stormwriting is all about taking your initial ideas logically further and turning them into building blocks for your book. Doing this makes your unwritten book unfold before you like a flower or a road or a landscape you've never before seen.

Some teachers say, "Be in the now, and your creativity will flourish."

They're right, but the hell of it is that now you have to figure out how to meditate your way into the now (whatever that means). You have to do this homework assignment of getting into the now before you can be a good writer. Sure, just attain Buddha-hood and then maybe you'll be able to write well.

No!

Here's the great fun of it: If you get into your creativity via the guidelines in this chapter, you will *already* find yourself in the now. You don't need perfect consciousness to start. Perfect consciousness is your reward when you tune into your creative core, when you unleash your heartbrain.

Don't seek the Buddha. *Be* a Buddha.

Perhaps **Yes, and—** and **What if?** are stress-free guidelines for not merely writing, but for living.

## ACTIONS

- If you haven't done so yet, stormwrite on your initiating idea for your book. What's the big idea? Write down everything you can think of for your book: How does it start? Improvise! How does it end? Improvise! What might happen between the beginning and the end? Improvise!
- Write deep on one of the tangents you've generated. Your beginning, perhaps? Write Chapter One. What's the story? Who is it about? What are you going to tell about? Tell it! If fiction, what's going to happen in it? Tell it! If fact, what will you tell about? Start telling. Write your tangents. When you stop, how do you feel? You've begun your book. Your first stormwrite has readied you for more writing and more progress.

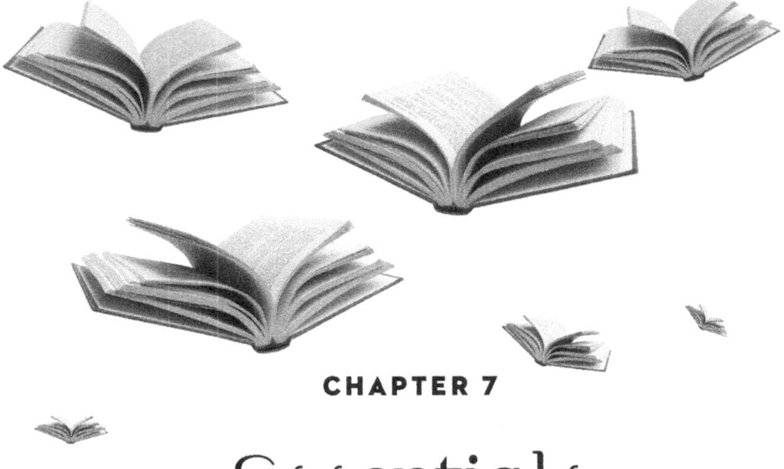

CHAPTER 7

# Essentials

When you strip any book down to its chassis, you find three things and three things only:

1. **TRUTH.** The book is about something.
2. **PEOPLE.** Or characters; the two terms are interchangeable within the pages of this book.
3. **A MAP.** The plan the author used to put the people and the truth together to create a story.

These are your essentials. An essential is something that can't be taken away without destroying the whole.

Sometimes when you're in the thick of working on your book, you'll come up for air and realize you're totally confused; you don't know *what* you're doing or what you should be working on.

In every case, this is because you've inadvertently loaded your mind with too many things at once.

The next three sections—Your Truth, Your People, and Your Map—are all you need to stay on track. They are your touchstones. From beginning to end, they'll see you through.

If you ever feel lost, come back to them.

*What exactly is a touchstone?*

The term comes from geology. Touchstones are fine-grained stones or tiles of neutral properties used to test rocks and minerals. You rub a rock or mineral on the touchstone to make a streak, then check the color of the streak. Knowing what minerals make what color streaks helps you tell, for instance, fool's gold (gray streak) from real gold (gold streak).

So a touchstone is a test of authenticity. For writers, a touchstone is a gut check, something to come back to in moments of uncertainty. What's real? Am I writing in harmony with my original, genuine ideas? A touchstone is a list of notes on the most essential elements of your book, something that brings you back to a focused, effective, productive state of creativity.

I like the thought of having something in my pocket that I can reach for and feel reassured.

Real stones have a kind of power. They have, well, gravity. Hefting a smooth stone in your hand makes you feel more grounded than you were a minute ago, perhaps a bit calmer, a bit quieter.

No companion is as silent as a stone. When you touch on one, it helps restore your appetite for taking your journey, it reminds you of where you're headed. It helps settle the compass needle of your heartbrain.

In these next sections, you'll further flesh out your book using these touchstones. Then, if you ever find yourself at a loss for direction, return to them. Write on them. Never make it more complicated than that.

CHAPTER 8

# Your Truth:

## Finding the Heart of Your Book

**Q:** How is writing like politics?

**A:** Both deal with a slippery thing called truth.

The difference is that while politicians can make a living obscuring truth, writers must relentlessly find, explore, and present truth. And whether any particular truth be pretty or ugly, it must be presented—that is, written about—beautifully.

Not a tall order, right?

This is where the fun and the mystery of writing surfaces.

Your **truth** is the honest essence of your book. It is the core, or motivating idea behind your book and behind your desire to write it.

Your truth might be a big one like:

> Here's who really assassinated JFK.
>
> or
>
> Divorce sucks.

Or it might reside on a smaller scale:

> A man and a woman meet in a fender-bender and now the man realizes there is such a thing as love at first sight.
>
> or

One troubled person can bring down a whole family.

What is your book *about*?

This section will help you figure out your truth, there beneath 'the stuff I want to write about.' Then, when you write, you'll be able to home in on it, frequently asking:

What's the truth I'm writing right now, right here?

What's the point?

What do I want to accomplish?

What do I suspect is true, but must 'write into it' in order to find out?

*Gosh, I don't really know what my truth is.*

If you feel a little uncomfortable now, that's fine. No writer has her whole book in her head to start with, much less can any of us conduct a philosophical discussion on a book's core parts before we've written the thing.

I don't want you to force anything at this point, but I do want you to bring up ideas from the depths and get friendly with them. This will help you go forward with clarity and confidence.

And just like anything mysterious and worthwhile, it's futile to try to head-butt our way into it. Best to get at it from a gentler angle.

*But my book is going to be simple and factual. Do I really need to deal with this?*

No and yes. Skip forward if you feel like it, or just close this book and do some writing. As I said at the beginning, not all parts of this book are for all people. Your truth might indeed be straightforward:

I want the world to know what a son of a bitch my dad was.

or

I'm writing about how to succeed as an electrical contractor.

Still, I ask you to bear with me. Your truth might be deeper than you think.

This is about your relationship to your truth, it's about getting comfortable with what you'll be writing about.

## What Is the Book of Your Dreams?

By dreams I don't mean the stuff that happens in your subconscious when you sleep. I mean the aspirations you hold in your waking mind and heart. What is your highest dream as a writer?

To add to the historical record or to set straight an event you were part of?

To share your personal story of struggle, triumph, loss, or redemption?

To produce a work of fiction that will entertain, inform, provoke?

To convey your knowledge of how you do something—run a welding shop, make terrific pies (I'll be over later), design a website?

To document the family history for next year's reunion?

To blow the whistle on an injustice?

To make people laugh?

To become famous?

To unburden yourself about something?

To earn money?

To get revenge?

Think about it. See your book. Feel it in your hands. Spend some time doing this. I might add that just sitting and thinking is a fine habit for a writer to get into.

Do you wish to write a book that will make you richnfamous? Most writers do. It's good and fine to wish to be richnfamous, to see your name on big posters in stores, to win a literary prize. And it most certainly is good and fine to actually *be* richnfamous, to see your name on big posters in stores or to win a literary prize.

But it is not OK to tie those desires to your dream of writing the best book you can.

*Why not?*

Because if you do, you will become a miserable wretch.

Look at it this way. A long time ago a man told me, "You can do whatever you want."

I thought that was the silliest thing I'd ever heard. It was so obviously untrue, so clearly wrong. Why would this man, who I respected, say such a stupid thing?

I thought about how wrong he was. Sure, there were some things I could do. But whatever I want? Come on! As somebody who's never run the high hurdles before, I thought defiantly, I can safely say I can't win an Olympic medal in the high hurdles. So there! That's one of many things I *can't* do!

But I thought some more. The simple phrase "You can do whatever you want" kept ringing in my head. On some level I knew it must be true. But I couldn't prove it.

I kept thinking of my high hurdles, and I finally realized that *nothing was stopping me from running the hurdles.* If I wanted to, I could go out to the track at the local high school, set up some hurdles, run up to one, and try to jump over it.

It dawned on me that I literally could do anything I wanted. If I wanted to run the hurdles, by God I *could.* And if I wanted to spend the time and effort to train really hard and compete and devote myself to the goal of winning an Olympic medal, I could.

Yet qualifying for the U.S. Olympic track team and winning a medal was not something I could *do.* It was only *one possible* result of my running the hurdles incredibly fast.

Do you see?

Writing a book is something you can do now, today. Getting on the *New York Times* best-seller list is not something you can *do*; it is a possible result of your writing the best damned book in your power. It's also the possible result of your marketing your book well. But first things first.

It's OK to fantasize about getting on the NYTBS list. But if you think about that while you're writing, you will paralyze your writing muscles and become a miserable wretch. Because you can only do one or the other: either write or think about possible results. You can't do both at the same time.

*What if my writing is awful?*

You'll get better as you go. Trust me. You'll learn by doing, and if you're honest with yourself and everybody else, you'll write something of value.

If you want to become richnfamous, go ahead and daydream about what it'll be like: autographing books for a block-long line of adoring fans, buying a new car, searching for a sophisticated house, socializing with richnfamous friends who think you're the cutest, smartest thing in the world.

*Yeah, that sounds pretty great!*

And it all might come your way—*if* you write truthfully and fearlessly, starting today.

Now about your truth: We need to make it clear. As clear as we can right now!

## The Power of Theme

Theme is a way of getting at truth. Theme is also a word learned in school and if it still makes you go *Unhh*, it won't in a minute. The way to instantly understand theme is to look at some examples.

### Novels and Their Themes

Mark Twain, *The Adventures of Huckleberry Finn*: social issues like racism and the meaning of friendship.

Dorothy Allison, *Bastard Out of Carolina*: child abuse, growth.

F. Scott Fitzgerald, *The Great Gatsby*: moral corruption, thwarted love.

Dashiell Hammett, *The Maltese Falcon*: deception, greed, individual justice.

Margaret Atwood, *The Handmaid's Tale*: sexism, the complicity victims can develop in a totalitarian state.

Chuck Palahniuk, *Fight Club*: the meaning of masculinity, materialism.

### Nonfiction Books and Their Themes

Dale Carnegie, *How to Win Friends and Influence People*: human nature, the desire to love and be loved.

Tom Wolfe, *The Right Stuff*: idealism, risk vs. reward, the complicated relationship between politics and science.

Isaak Dinesen, *Out of Africa*: love, brutality, endurance.

Richard Wright, *Black Boy*: racism, poverty, intellectual potential, the initiative of one person to escape.

Annie Dillard, *Pilgrim at Tinker Creek*: religion, death.

## How to Focus on a Theme

Theme represents a taproot through which authors delve into countless aspects of being human. Consider what is important to you. What would you like to explore?

If you've chosen to write a book of fiction and you deliberately choose a theme for your story, you can let your theme suggest characters to you. Let your theme help you pour out your story. Consult your theme when you have to decide what to write next. Just think, "Hmm, what might this character do next? Well, my theme is X. My character must try to find X, overcome X, or something related to it. How might that motivate the character?"

Let's say your theme is the cruelty of humans toward other humans. Let's say you've chosen an avenue for that theme, and that avenue is 'vicious gossip.' Let 'vicious gossip' suggest characters to you. You might first think of stereotypical gossips, like bored homemakers and talk show hosts. You might then challenge yourself to think up characters who are nontraditional gossips.

What if we chose to write a story about a camp counselor who is a pathological gossiper and liar? What fun! A trusted confidante who routinely betrays her vulnerable charges! How might her compulsions come out in her behavior?

How about a captain of industry, someone who is supposedly above passing gossip and lies (he's got minions to do that sort of work), who decides to destroy a competitor by word of mouth? How might he go about doing it? And why would he put himself at risk engaging in such a stunt?

What if we chose to write about a very young child who tells a vicious lie about an adult? We might first think of an allegation of abuse, and we could make that fly, but what about another kind of allegation? What motive might a young child have for hurting someone else by telling a vicious story about that person?

And what of the opposite? An old character: Gramps is on his deathbed, and his last words are vicious gossip. Why? Is there an ancient score so important to him that he would compromise his own last moments on earth?

Let's say you choose as a theme the resilience of the human spirit, and you decide to get at it by writing about 'hopeless optimism.' What sorts of people might spring to mind? A cancer patient. A battered spouse. An unpopular politician. A Third World village riddled with disease. A drug addict.

All of these examples demonstrate theme and also show you how easy it is to come up with a story to tell. You see, the magical thing isn't so much the story you choose to tell. It's *your telling of it* that makes magic.

Another note on theme. Theme is subjective. Two people may read the same story—or write similar stories—and have two very different opinions as to what the theme is. Take for example a story in which a man and a woman have sex. One person may see that story's theme as male sexual aggression, while another might see the theme as female sexual manipulation. Both views can be valid!

Sit and think about this stuff.

## Theme Is Your Servant

If you've chosen to write a nonfiction book, you probably have a pretty good idea of your material, that is, your content. Theme can help you organize it and present it. It can give you a thread that you can use to unify the book.

If you're writing a book about 'what a son of a bitch my dad was,' you might wish to use an aspect of your dad's life as a theme. What aspects might there be? Poverty might be one, or the fact that he moved the family around constantly. You could use his addictive relationship to street drugs/alcohol/pornography/food/his career/his hobby as a thread through your story. You could use the progression of his work life or his mental illness or his relationships with women (mother, sisters, wife, daughters).

If you're writing a book on how to be a successful electrical contractor, you might use efficiency as a theme. What's the most efficient way to do something, and why is it so? How did you learn that? What's the most efficient way to invest in your business, to organize your tools, to outfit your truck, to advertise, to set pricing and keep your books?

A theme can be a guiding light for a writer. You needn't limit yourself to one. A couple of themes can work well together, but too many will dilute your results.

## WRITING BLAST: YOUR FIRST TOUCHSTONE

Your Truth: The Heart of Your Story

- Gather your writing materials.
- Find a comfortable place.
- Enter garret mode.
- Consider your desire to write a book. Think about the book you'll write. Check in with your gut as you go along. Let your heartbrain loose. Use **Yes and—** and **What if?** liberally. Do a full-on stormwrite using the following questions:
- What is your story? What will your book be *about*?
- What things, ideas, events, and people do you want to explore?
- Is a theme starting to coalesce—or simply a central idea? What is it?
- Write answers to one or all of these questions, in no particular order. Write for as long as you like.
- When you're ready to stop writing, stop.

Congratulations. You've now focused your heartbrain on your book. What's more, you've written the basis for your Statement of Truth, a living document.

*What's a living document?*

A living document is one that comes out of your heartbrain, one that can grow and change with you.

## Your Statement of Truth

Take a crack at distilling what you've written into one or two simple sentences. Write them on an index card or small piece of paper. Post this document in a place where you'll see it frequently, like next to your computer or inside your medicine cabinet.

*I don't want to bother with this, I just want to get started writing.*

You are writing. The reason to write a Statement of Truth is this: A month from now, when you're in the thick of writing your book, and you realize how much you've put into it, but how much there still is to do, you will start to question what the hell you're doing, fun bedammed. This happens to every writer. You will then look up to the wall behind your desk, or flip open your mirror to get your toothpaste, and you will see your Statement of Truth, and you will know. You'll find focus and you will remember your strength. You will remember your joy.

You might alter your Statement of Truth as you get into your writing experience. You'll constantly develop a better understanding of what your truth is as you write and explore. You can even rip it up and write a new one. Make your Statement of Truth anything and everything about what you want to do with your writing.

Sample Statements of Truth:

- I'm going to write a novel about a family that survives a sadistic home invasion because I'm fascinated by the courage and ingenuity it would take to do that. I've always had a knack for writing, and I want to see if I can do it. I want people to see me as a great writer.

- I want to help people stretch their grocery money by following tips I use myself. My theme is thrift! When my book is finished, I'll feel great.
- My book is about a guy who drank too much and lost everything. I'm writing it because I want others to learn from my mistakes. I'd like to write for television someday.
- I intend to write a memoir of my grandfather because he inspired the whole family during WWII. I'll feel happy at the end of writing it, because it will be an achievement. I want his story to inspire other people.
- I'm writing about my experiences being a nurse in Alaska where we flew into the little towns to care for people. That way of life is disappearing, and I think people will enjoy reading about it.
- I'm going to write a whole book of short stories, because that's the kind of writing I do best. My stories are funny, and I think the world needs more humor. My theme is the absurdity of modern life.

Your truth is simply the focal point of your book. When uncertainty hits, go back to it. Are you and it in harmony? If not, it's probably because you're overcomplicating whatever you're doing. Ask "What's the truth am I trying to write about in this moment?" Simplify. Write one thing at a time.

## ACTIONS

- Visit a place that evokes your truth. It might be an urban alley, a wooded trail, your workshop, a highway, a stadium, a shopping mall, you pick. Hang out there. Make notes on stuff that occurs to you. Do some writing if you feel like it.
- Just for kicks, think about a book you've read that you really liked, or think about a song you've found meaningful, or maybe a poem. If the writer of that piece had written a Statement of Truth, what might it have looked like?

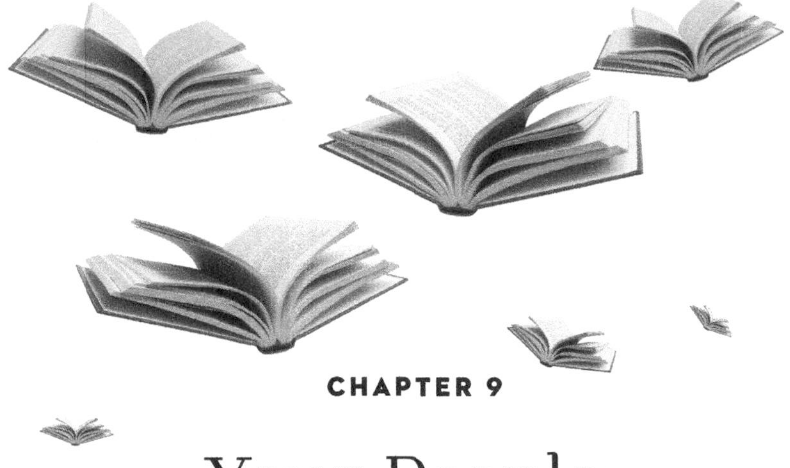

CHAPTER 9

# Your People:

## Breathing Life Into Your Book

Every book starts with people.

Some writers strictly use human characters, some create animal characters, some create inanimate characters, such as HAL the computer in Arthur C. Clarke's *2001: A Space Odyssey*. For the purposes of this book, *people* means any kind of characters, real or fictitious.

Your people can and will drive your book, whether fact or fiction.

Somebody does something. Somebody wants something he doesn't or can't have. Somebody loves somebody.

And every compelling book has a hero. You know them:

> Odysseus, Don Quixote, Gulliver, and Nathan Hale.
> David Copperfield, T.E. Lawrence, and Scarlett O'Hara.
> Ma Joad, Dorothy Gale, James Bond, and Atticus Finch.
> Rosa Parks, Nancy Drew, Yuri Zhivago, and Harry Potter.

Forgettable books have weak heroes or no heroes.

Your book needs a strong hero. Who is your hero? Explore this. Your hero might be your main character. If your book is a memoir, you might be the hero. If your book is nonfiction, there is probably one figure who stands above the rest.

In fact, if you're writing a nonfiction book, I encourage you to read the whole of this chapter, even though much of it seems aimed at fiction writers, because this chapter is about making the people in your book vibrant and fully realized. The best nonfiction reads like great fiction, and much of its appeal comes from the personalities that populate it. I'm just in love with the biographer Robert Caro, whose books on the life of President Lyndon B. Johnson read like the most gripping fiction.

Heroes are the ones we all remember and look up to. People read books because they want to be inspired. We all want to be brave in the face of danger. We like to *believe* we'll be brave in the face of danger. We want instruction on *how to be* brave in the face of danger. We want to be smart, and we want instruction on how to be smart. We want to be independent. Sassy. Irreverent. Original. Loved. Loving. Sexy. We want to learn how to *do* and how to *be*.

We read books because, in a way, every book is a guide to life. The people in books, specifically the heroes, give us examples of how to act—and how not to act. The hero speaks to our deepest self, the thing-that-aspires-to-greatness that we all carry deep within: the Heroic Kernel.

Take a few minutes to visit your Heroic Kernel. Get in touch with it. Like this:

- Lift up your eyes.
- Square your shoulders.
- Rise from your chair and be the ideal you: a competent adult, a calm, strong person with a clear, generous gaze.
- Feel the receptivity and readiness that marks your Heroic Kernel.
- Go take care of something: a phone call, some tidying of your space, repair something, write a to-do list. Carry yourself well: unhurried, purposeful, noble.

Now how do you feel?

> *Especially good! In fact, I feel the way that, as a child, I thought I would feel when I grew up. But I hardly ever feel that way.*

You've got it. Why not feel this way all the time? Just choose it. Instead of betraying insecurity by being slumped or unhappy or too quick or loud or proud, become your Heroic Kernel.

Be inspired by the greatness you see in this world, whether manifested by a sports star or a spiritual teacher or a beautiful machine or the little kid down the block who, no matter what he's doing, gives it everything he's got. Be inspired by the romance of the world, whether a night-blooming jasmine or a mountain peak or two people dancing slow near the jukebox.

All right, now that you have heroes and their mind-set in place, it's time to put them into motion.

Heroes have adventures; they go on journeys.

Let's do some writing.

## WRITING BLAST: YOUR SECOND TOUCHSTONE

Your People: Breathing Life Into Your Book

Do a general stormwrite on the people who will be/are in your book.

- Gather your writing materials.
- Find a comfortable place.
- Enter garret mode.
- Who are the people in your book?
- What are their names? If you're writing fiction and you don't have a name yet, that's OK; later we'll talk about how to name characters. If you're writing nonfiction, use this writing blast to focus your heartbrain on your important people.
- Who else is going to be in your book? List as many people as you can who might be an influence in your book.
- Do they have names yet? If so, write them.
- What are their relationships? Boss, cousin, neighbor, lover …
- Do any minor characters come especially vividly to mind? The taxi driver who delivers the baby, the masseuse who overhears the plot to ruin the movie star's reputation, the college student who finds the ancient coin …

- Who are the people you'd like to get to know better? That is, who among the bunch is your attention most drawn to and could this person be your hero? Why?

This general stormwrite will prime you for upcoming stormwrites about your people.

## A Hero's Traits

You've probably heard the word *protagonist*. It's from the Greek word *protagonistes*, which means primary actor. Your hero is your protagonist. Now a hero doesn't necessarily equal 'good person'. Or 'thoroughly principled, flawless character.'

You understand. Nobody's perfect. Only in cartoons do we find perfectly heroic heroes—and perfectly villainous villains. Real heroes, male and female, are flawed. A realistic hero might be narcissistic, afraid of someone or something, might have an inferiority complex, might be a liar or a criminal.

We pull for Michael Corleone in Mario Puzo's T*he Godfather* because we identify with him. He doesn't want the criminal life of the mob, the life that promises worldly gain at the cost of souls, but after enemies try to assassinate his father, he feels he has no choice but to become a criminal and murderer.

Puzo does such a great job of making Michael real and human that even when Michael draws the revolver and kills Captain McCluskey and the crime boss Solozzo in cold blood, we're stirred with excitement and admiration—not revulsion. We feel the tension before he shoots and we wonder what we would do in that situation. And we go along for the ride, and we feel the release when he does shoot.

In being loyal to his family's code, Michael betrays the codes of his society and his religion. The story is compelling because we know life isn't simple. We all have to make tough choices: whether to fudge facts on a job application, whether to stay faithful to a suboptimal spouse, whether to leave the last piece of pizza for someone else, whether, when our brakes give out, to crash into the red car or the blue car.

*What distinguishes a hero from everybody else?*

A good hero will have doubts, will suffer for their weakness, then come to grips with it, then prevail over that weakness. Sometimes a hero will be a criminal who goes straight in the end, or vice versa, like Michael Corleone, or perhaps your hero is a criminal who conquers a problem but remains a criminal, like Dexter Morgan in Jeff Lindsay's novels (the first being *Darkly Dreaming Dexter*). Dexter's a fellow who feels compelled to murder and who solves the compulsion by adopting a code of ethics: He will only kill people who are themselves killers of innocents.

## Antiheroes

You've also possibly heard the term antihero. An antihero is *not* the villain in the story.

An antihero is a heroic character who doesn't have typically heroic attributes or one who operates as a force for good outside the common moral code.

Robin Hood was a prototypical antihero: He robbed from the rich (stealing is wrong) but he gave the booty to the poor (charity is good). Today's outlaw bikers might consider themselves antiheroes, living outside society's common codes but adhering strictly to their own codes of fair play, however unconventional.

Scarlett O'Hara, the protagonist of Margaret Mitchell's *Gone With the Wind*, could be called an antihero. She behaves abominably at times, she lies and manipulates, but instinctively she knows the painful truth that many a leader has learned: In times of strife, real gains require ruthlessness and sacrifice. In the end, Scarlett's actions save her family and their land. Meanwhile, she recognizes true love and lives to pursue it.

Tom Ripley in Patricia Highsmith's *The Talented Mr. Ripley* is an antihero. He's basically a Midwestern college boy who wants a much more privileged and romantic life than he's got. He gives in to strong temptation to turn into a murderer. Yet we pull for him because we sympathize with his desires, and we live his exciting transgressions vicariously.

As you can see, your hero might have a quite complicated code of ethics.

Keep in mind that the most compelling heroes take an inward journey as well as an outward one. Sal Paradise, the narrator of Jack Kerouac's *On the Road*, leaves home to seek adventure, freedom, and the great truths of life. That is the outer journey. Sal's inner journey develops when he becomes disillusioned with the immature, hectic life he's pursuing with his buddies and he becomes more introspective. He realizes that the 'road-as-religion' has severe limitations, and he begins to quiet his mind and listen more deeply to the wisdom that's already inside him.

I want you to think a lot about heroes. A good believable hero will drive any book, fact or fiction.

Your hero must be brave, but all of your people must be strong, in one way or another. Here strong doesn't necessarily mean physically strong, or even morally good.

Daisy Buchanan, the object of Jay Gatsby's love in *The Great Gatsby* by F. Scott Fitzgerald, is a physically slight woman who once made a dreadful mistake (she married the wrong guy); she's careless, older now, morally weak and dissipated, yet she is a strong character. She's memorable because she causes things to happen in the story, she's conflicted, and she understands true love. She is believable. She is genuine.

> CHISEL IT IN STONE:
> WHEN IT COMES TO PEOPLE, GENUINE = STRONG.

## WRITING BLAST: THE HERO STORMWRITE

Stormwrite specifically on your hero. This will get you SO GOING. Remember to use **Yes, and—** and **What if?**

- Gather your writing materials.
- Find a comfortable place.
- Enter garret mode.

- Who is your hero? (Simply who: A six-year-old boy with ADD, a middle-aged investment banker with international connections, a 35-year-old army wife who wants out …)
- Name?
- Physical description. Personality description. What does she dress like?
- Where did he grow up? Who are his parents?
- Where does she live, and what is her occupation? Hobbies?
- Marital status, kids, pets?
- Basic traits, likes, dislikes, idiosyncrasies. Smart? How smart? (The hero is usually the smartest person in the bunch.)
- Strengths, special abilities? Spend some time on this. What is her Heroic Kernel?
- Weaknesses? Spend some time here too. Strengths and weaknesses are deep things. Most people are insecure about something to some degree, so you can't go wrong with giving your character a few insecurities. (Maybe he's afraid he's not a good lover, father, spy, or he's ashamed that he didn't finish school, or he's embarrassed that he cries at sad movies …)
- What are her problems? Or, what conflict is going on in your hero's life when we first meet her? (Examples for fiction: In the middle of one murder investigation, she is called to a crime scene to open another; she gets abducted at a day spa; she gets kicked out of the house for smoking dope and decides to hitchhike out West to look up an old friend… Examples for nonfiction: She's a small-time businesswoman who can't get a loan to expand against competition; she just kicked booze but her husband leaves anyway; the town she's the mayor of just got blown away by a tornado.)
- What does he want and why does he want it?
- What does she think will happen when she gets it?
- Who are his friends? (Who might be able to help him?)
- Who are her enemies? Does she know them yet?
- Who might come into her life later?

- Make a list or two, just for kicks. How about five things he likes to eat? What cars/bicycles/knives/suits has he owned?
- Might there be a journey or adventure in the offing?
- Follow any and all tangents that come up.

You're not going to know the answers to all of these questions at first. Not all of the questions will even be relevant. One question might prompt a different, better one. Invent your own questions as you go, and that will help you write your way into the character.

*Can I write more than one hero in my story?*

You can, but having one main one is important to cement reader loyalty. Readers don't like to be confused; they want and expect one main hero. While Dr. Watson shares Sherlock Holmes's values and even behaves heroically at times, he's still a sidekick to Holmes, the boss hero dude.

The same goes for Dorothy Gale and her friends, Harry Potter and his friends, and countless other heroes and heroines and their friends. The friends are great, the friends are helpers, but the hero is the hero.

Every book needs conflict. Every good story from *Genesis* to today's psycho-thrillers puts its characters in conflict. Every gripping memoir begins with conflict. Something must be overcome!

What's a great way to create conflict for a character?

Other characters!

Stormwrite about a few of your other characters, just get to know them.

## SIMPLE STORMWRITE FOR CHARACTERS

A stormwrite for a less important character might go like this:

- Gather your writing materials.
- Find a comfortable place.
- Enter garret mode.
- Tune your heartbrain into your character or person.
- What is that person doing in the story?
- Name?
- Description?

- Background?
- Occupation?
- Smart, dumb?
- Strengths, special abilities?
- Weaknesses?
- Problems?

In fiction it's useful for every significant character to have a special ability. You can draw on that ability later. For instance, a child is little and can wriggle into tight spaces where grown-ups can't go; someone with musical ability can identify voices particularly well; a home-brewing fanatic might know some chemistry...

> CHISEL IT IN STONE:
> LET YOUR PEOPLE TELL YOU WHAT THEY WANT.

Get to know your people on paper as intimately as you can.

Conjecture! Let 'em loose to tell you what they're about! Feel free to ask them things:

What are you doing?

Tell me about your childhood.

What's your favorite drink/car/TV show/book?

If you're uncomfortable with a character, what do you not know about him that you wish you did? What do you think he would do in a life-and-death emergency? How would he react to a surprise birthday party?

If there was a government coup, what kind of role would he take in it? Profiteer, idealist, doomed loyalist?

## How to Supercharge Your People

Readers get hooked on a book when they meet a character they enjoy spending time with. Characters we love—or love to hate. Here's how:

- **LET YOUR READER INSIDE THEIR HEADS.** Sure, we see your characters in action, but show us their fears, their misgivings, their secret vanities. Most amateur authors expect the reader to assume too much along these lines. Let readers know what your characters are thinking via inner monologues or dialogue, or even through unexpected action. ("Yes, dear," he sighed, giving the cat a discreet kick.)

- **GIVE A CHARACTER A SECRET.** Think *Sophie's Choice*: You can bet William Styron built the whole novel backward from Sophie's main, huge, character-defining moment, having thought of the choice first. If you bear in mind your character's secret as you write, it will inform your whole book, lending substance and subtlety.
- **BUILD IN A LOVABLE QUIRK.** Holden Caulfield (in *The Catcher in the Rye* by J.D. Salinger) was as cynical as they come—except when something charmed him. Pure sincerity pierced his heart, whether it was two nuns in a coffee shop or his naïve yet sharp-witted little sister. Without that vulnerability, he'd be just another insufferable teen.
- **CREATE AN UNPREDICTABLE CHARACTER.** Shakespeare's witches (*Macbeth*), Boo Radley (in *To Kill a Mockingbird* by Harper Lee), Kurtz (in *Heart of Darkness* by Joseph Conrad). A character with a screw loose, or a character that's hidden in the shadows, will prevent your readers from ever feeling safe.
- **MAKE THEM SHARE.** Do your research (see Chapter Twenty-Two, **How to Write What You Don't Know**) and, through your characters, share cool stuff you've learned: about a time, place, person, or pursuit in depth. Frederick Forsyth's *The Day of the Jackal* gave specific, compelling information on covert ops; Dick Francis brings his readers into the world of horse breeding and racing. Other current authors go deep into detail on subjects ranging from domestic arts to international terrorism.

## People Dossiers for Fiction and Nonfiction

Whether your project is fiction or nonfiction, a fun and productive thing is to make dossiers as soon as you've done some stormwrites on your people. When writing a major project, I make up a file folder for each main character or person. You can do this with real manila folders and throw all your stormwrites and notes for each person into them, or you can make the files on your computer (or both, for belt-and-suspenders thoroughness).

**SKETCH HIM.** Get to writing about what he's like via your stormwrites. Where is he from, what are his strengths as a person, what are his weaknesses? What does he look like, is he big or little or medium? This is called a **character sketch** because you draw the character with words. Take down as few as a hundred, as many as a thousand, or more, if you feel like it.

Which character would you rather write about:

1. "He was just over six feet tall, with blond hair and blue eyes. He wasn't very clean."
2. "He could have been a J.Crew model, if given a shower and a shampoo. What was this pretty kid doing crouched behind a garbage can, reciting Milton to a litter of raccoons?"

My point is, don't get caught up telling the obvious. I'm not saying don't tell us what color hair your hero has. I'm just saying it might not matter. It might be more fun to describe him in a different way. Nobody knows the shape of David Copperfield's mouth or how tall he was. It didn't matter.

Write down and add to the folder anything else about that person that comes up.

**FOR FICTION**, for example, you can clip pictures from magazines or print out shots from your camera that evoke the character.

I keep books on hand that have lots of face shots and pictures of people. You can find good people shots by browsing through photography monographs.

Looking at pictures of faces helps me imagine characters for my fiction. In describing a character, I can borrow an anonymous face from a picture. Or I can borrow a famous face. If I decide that my main character has a high forehead, a direct, burning gaze, and a reddish beard, no one need know that I'm basing his appearance on Vincent van Gogh.

**FOR NONFICTION**, invest some time in remembering and writing about what your people look like. It's surprising how we can know somebody well and yet have a hard time painting them in words. Relax and take your time about it, and it'll come. (The banker that turned down the businesswoman squints habitually and wears an expensive suit, while her brother-in-law wears a trucker cap but lends her $5,000…) You can keep any information about that person in their dossier, including a list of questions you want to ask that person (if living), notes from interviews, impressions and remembrances other people told you, family information, anything. If you make a dossier, you can keep all this material nicely organized.

I highly recommend that you take up drawing. As a writer, sketching a person or an object—even crudely, with no training or innate skill—opens your heartbrain and makes you more tuned in to your subject. It makes the world seem fresh.

In a person's dossier you can put a list of idiosyncrasies of how they talk. Like this guy habitually uses the word *dashed* instead of damned; this gal talks with a Tennessee twang; and so on.

A fun way to make a person come alive is by attributing animal traits to him or her:

- He was quick as a lizard.
- She stalked over to the bar, switching her tail as she went.

Or even inanimate ones:

- He sat there with all the energy of a slag heap.
- Her expression blossomed when she heard his voice.

Just go off on any tangents that pique your interest.

## How to Deal With a Real Person You Can't Get Out of Your Head

Sometimes a real person, whether famous or not, is the keystone for a book you want to write. Maybe you don't know him or her personally, maybe you do. People you've known can be terrific templates for characters. Whatever the case, go with it. Do a stormwrite on that person. Write everything that comes to mind. Is this person admirable or despicable? Why has this person become lodged within you? What is remarkable about him or her? Why do you want to write about them? What is the story you want to tell? Or, what is the story *you wish you knew*?

If a real person compels you to write, pay attention and go deep. Explore. Sometimes the person's extraordinariness is obvious: This woman saved my life by pulling me out of a burning car. Sometimes the person's extraordinariness is obvious but complex: This woman saved my life by pulling me out of drug addiction. Sometimes the person's extraordinariness isn't obvious at all: I've seen this woman every year for five years in a row at the bluegrass festival, playing her fiddle, jamming with whoever comes by. One year, so many things had gone wrong in my life I was practically suicidal. But just being around this musician lifted me up. Somehow, everyone who jams with her walks away a better player (as far as I can tell). It makes me wonder: What does she give away so easily, invisibly, and mysteriously?

Stormwriting about somebody you know can help you get at that person's essence. If you feel there's something special about someone, do yourself a favor and make a character out of that person. It's worth exploring because people like that usually lead to intriguing, deep places in your thinking and your writing.

Maybe this person really needs a nonfiction portrayal. Maybe your book should be a memoir about your years-long experiences at the bluegrass festival, and maybe this year you should talk with that fiddle player and make a special effort to get to know her.

Imagine somebody you know, or somebody you knew a long time ago, and then put him or her into difficulty. She just got laid off. He just found a cache of stolen treasure. She just accidentally broke a valued heirloom belonging to her significant other, and the significant other doesn't know yet.

Difficulty, by the way, doesn't have to be relentlessly negative. You could bestow upon your hero a stroke of good fortune—an important award, a reprieve from illness, an unexpected inheritance—which is inherently good, yet might pose interesting problems.

## How to Steal Characters

Another way to form a character is to steal from somebody else's work. Before you shout in protest, let me just say that I am not suggesting you plagiarize. Read on.

Here's how you 'steal' from someone else's work: Pull out your Chaucer, for instance, and canter through a few tales, get reacquainted with somebody like the Canon's Yeoman or the Wife of Bath. Or pull out your Shakespeare, or your Brontë, or even your Old Testament, anything that's at least a century old. Pick out a personality. Now place that personality into your contemporary story. What if you made King Lear the president of his condominium homeowners' association, and he had to deal with dog litter enforcement? What if Samson ran a gay bar? What if Jane Eyre married somebody like Captain Ahab? How would Coach Solomon deal with a horde of Little League dads who all think their kid is the next Hank Aaron?

Your life is richer than you think, and you can 'steal' from your past as well. Mine through your memories and dig up unique people that you can spin off into new characters, such as: Your neighborhood delinquent, grown up. The first person you deeply admired or feared or loved. The last person you'd want to be stuck on a desert island with. The smartest person you know. The dumbest. The vainest. The most confident.

## Feel the World Surging Through You

Relax repeatedly. It's so important to eliminate tension. It's such a pleasure, such a relief to do it. Last night as I practiced my mandolin, I had trouble playing a fast tune I know well. What was the matter? Without noticing, I'd gotten tense. The first flubbed note led to another, then another, and another. I stopped, relaxed my hands and arms, let a big breath out, and played the tune again—fast and easily, with enjoyment. Being relaxed and ready helps you do everything better.

Allow yourself to relax. Shut off your inner editor and refuse to second-guess anything that comes out of you. Just throw it down on the paper. You can go back and make things read better later. Just plain refuse to jabber at yourself while you're writing. (I've been heard to mutter, "Shut up! Shut up!" to myself while writing first drafts.) For more, see **The Little Bitch or Bastard on Your Shoulder** in Chapter Twenty-Three.

## When It Boils Down to You

As I suggested above, if you're writing a memoir or other nonfiction, your main character might be you. Do a stormwrite on yourself. In fact, no matter what your book is about, I think doing a stormwrite on yourself as the hero of your own life is a great idea.

Give it a go.

Because you must feel comfortable with yourself, you must make peace with your weaknesses and acknowledge your strengths. You have to be OK with exposing yourself, because that's the way we best relate to real stories. Your story, any story. We feel the most deeply when we see gut-level honesty in another.

When hunting for characters, explore your own dark side. Think about something you did that was really rather horrible, and that you're not sorry for. That's some powerful stuff there. Now think about something you did that was horrible, and that you're ashamed of. There's power there, too. Think about writing a story about that shameful thing from a *sympathetic* point of view.

## A How-To Book Needs People as Much as Any

The how-to books that readers relate to best have a human element. Funny or serious, hard-assed or warm, let your personality come through.

Say you're writing a book on how to grow roses. You'd naturally put in the basic facts of what kind of soil, sun, water, and nutrients roses require, grafting techniques, and so on. But you can bet that lots of people who want to grow roses would benefit from knowing how you, personally, solved particular problems or figured out new methods or arranged your plants for best effect in your unique backyard or made a beginner's mistake and learned from it.

People love to read tips from other enthusiasts like themselves.

In the case of rose growing, they'll love to read about gophers overcome, frost damage averted, a catastrophe of flood or fire and the rebuilding afterward. You can include these things from your own experience—your readers will want to know about the best rose gardener you met when you took that trip to England!—and you can beef things up by talking to other growers and asking them about their experiences. Then add what they say to your book. Give credit where credit is due.

## All People Sense Things

Writers sometimes forget to bring the reader in via sensations, because we're so intent on showing action. As you're motoring along in a scene, take a moment to clue the reader into what that rose bed or that Italian kitchen smells like, or how the mountain air tastes or how those heels clicking along the wet pavement sound. Mention the infrared warmth from the end of a lit cigarette, the strips of light and shadow cast by a venetian blind.

Just for fun, do a Writing Blast on sensations. Explain to a space alien what an ice cream cone is, how you eat it, what it's like to eat it, and three reasons why all space aliens should eat ice cream every day.

## Getting the Good Stuff

I once heard a successful radio reporter tell the secret of how he got people to tell him such good stuff. He said, "After they finish talking, I just keep holding the microphone right where it is. When they finally say something else, it's always good."

If he had tried to cajole or force sources to talk more, they wouldn't have.

> CHISEL IT IN STONE:
> RECEPTIVE PERSISTENCE CREATES BREAKTHROUGHS.

This holds true in all things.

## ACTIONS

- Make a dossier on one of your people. What are the facts of this person? What do you know, what can you guess at? Have fun. Range far.
- In the spirit of receptive persistence, do an intense stormwrite on a character. Perhaps you will concentrate on your hero or perhaps someone else. Just pick someone you feel attracted to. When you notice yourself veering off on a tangent, follow it. Get to the end. Then keep going on that tangent. Then go further. Open up your heartbrain. Don't press hard, just stay with it. Let words and ideas bubble up, whether they seem disconnected or connected. Look at it from another angle: a worm's-eye view, perhaps, or a bird's-eye view. Look at it inside out, upside down, backwards. Like an athlete ignoring fatigue or an inventor persevering in the face of blown gaskets, you just might break through to a whole new level of creativity. Give it a go.

CHAPTER 10

# Your Map:

## Planning Your Book and Setting Off on Your Journey as an Author

Maps are funny things. When we're heading off to new places, the first decision we must make is whether to grab a chart because we know that having no map, no plan at all, can create problems. We can set off in a general direction with excitement and a light heart, but if we have any desire to travel with some purpose, we can get awfully frustrated if we find ourselves going in circles.

Fun but no accuracy.

However, a map can be daunting. If it's extremely detailed, as most modern maps are, it can be hard to read, confusing us with information we don't need or want. If we've paid good money for that map, we might be reluctant to toss it aside and take our chances by the seat of our pants.

That's not to mention the experience of driving somewhere with a GPS unit. You punch in your info and a voice tells you exactly what to do and when to do it. There are no surprises, pleasant or otherwise. Plus, if you diverge from the route the computer has selected for you, you hear a dismayed voice urging you to turn around.

Accurate but no fun.

You may be aware that a great deal of what is called "commercial fiction" is plotted out in microscopic detail before the first sentence is written. Another word for this kind of fiction is formula. Many mystery and romance novelists thoroughly plot their books before they write them. In the case of a mystery, a certain amount of plotting is essential to a coherent end product. If you begin a story with a dead body, you have to know in advance who did the murder and why. Lots of mysteries are plotted backwards.

Margaret Mitchell, author of *Gone With the Wind*, said that she did not plot the book out in sequence. She knew the ending she wanted, so she wrote the last chapter first. Then she worked her way toward it.

Ken Follett, author of *Eye of the Needle* and *Pillars of the Earth*, is a master of deliberate, precise plotting, and his books are bestsellers. He's come up with a formula that pleases a great many readers, and he has the talent, patience, and brainpower to execute it. His formula includes a certain number of story points, with a certain number of dramatic events dispersed strategically between the story points.

I want to draw a distinction between this kind of formula and rigid writing formulas.

What is the advantage of thorough plotting? Well, all your worrying about plot is done in advance. When it's over, it's over. While you're plotting, you can figure out whether your core idea is any good, before writing 200 pages of prose. If you run horribly dry trying to work out a plot, you can go back and rethink—and re-create, if need be—your characters, setting, premise, and theme. Or you can scrap the whole idea, and set to work dreaming up another book or story.

*Why would anybody want to do it any other way?*

Because there are disadvantages to working this way, too. When you plot with rigidity, you take away spontaneity. You take away the element of surprise, at least for you, if not for your reader, and a book without that can be satisfying but it won't be unforgettable.

I believe a writer must always allow for the element of surprise.

One best-selling—and critically respected—writer whose method of plotting was drastically different from Ken Follett's is E.L. Doctorow. He said he never plotted his work in advance. He tried to write something every day. One day, he was so unfocused and desperate to write something that he began writing about the wall he was sitting facing. Then he wrote about the house the wall was in, which was built at the turn of the twentieth century, and that got him to thinking about that era, and one thing led to another and the end result was *Ragtime*.

Bestseller.

He literally did no planning. Here is an excerpt from Doctorow's 1986 *Paris Review* interview with George Plimpton:

> **DOCTOROW:** "[The way I write is] like driving a car at night. You never see further than your headlights, but you can make the whole trip that way.
>
> **INTERVIEWER:** "How many times do you come to a dead end?
>
> **DOCTOROW:** "Well if it's a dead end, there's no book. That happens too. You start again. But if you're truly underway you may wander into culverts, through fences into fields, and so on. When you're off the road you don't always know it immediately. If you feel a bump on page one hundred, it may be you went off on page fifty. So you have to trace your way back, you see. It sounds like a hazardous way of working—and it is—but there is one terrific advantage to it: each book tends to have its own identity rather than the author's."

That's a beautiful way to put it, I think.

Just start writing and see what happens: What fun! This can be an especially attractive way of working when you're in a playful mood—or when you get an idea that's making you so excited that you're impatient to get writing. Well, write away. If you find yourself at the end of a cul-de-sac, big deal. Back out and go in another direction. Repeat as necessary.

This can eat up a lot of time, but beyond what Doctorow said, it's educational. We learn from our mistakes. Writers who write without lots of advance planning—and do it successfully—have stumbled and staggered around quite a bit over time, much of it early in their careers. After you stumble and stagger, you invariably develop a sharper set of instincts. Not that you stop stumbling altogether and forever, it's just that you become more sure-footed over time.

Harlan Coben is a best-selling contemporary author who says he does all his plotting in his head—sometimes taking months—then sits down to write without notes. That's pretty intriguing!

Another hugely successful author, James Lee Burke, told *Writer's Digest* magazine that he writes 750 words per day, seven days a week. And he starts out with only two scenes in mind, no more. He just goes forward with those two scenes, no outline, no idea of how it'll end. Cool!

Mapping a story is much like "sense of direction." People talk about sense of direction the way they talk about VD: You either have it or you don't. But that's not so. Improving one's sense of direction amounts to practice, and the willingness to get your head into it. Use your map and compass, and take responsibility for where you're going, and your sense of direction will improve.

So it is with writing long-range. The more you do it, the more comfortable you become with your tools and your skills. And the more successful you become at avoiding wrong turns and dead ends in the first place. How? Simple experience. It adds up!

## Between the Extremes of Plotting: The Route 66 Placemat

In the cool populuxe era of the United States—the 1950s and 1960s, that halcyon postwar period when cars were cars and the Interstate Highway System had barely begun, Route 66 became the most romantic highway in the world.

Running some 2,400 miles from Chicago to Los Angeles, it was the road that led travelers from the familiar (OK, *boring*) Midwest to the paradise of California, the destination of dreamers, seekers, misfits, and maniacs. Restaurants along the way served meals on paper placemats, which showed the route with crude accuracy: It featured the states and main towns and that was it.

More than one traveler used that placemat as their sole guidance system. Think of it! How much more would you really need?

Sure, you could make a wrong turn trying to find cheap gas in Albuquerque, but you could always ask somebody or just keep trying roads out of town until you found your way again.

And if you saw something interesting down a side road, why, you could go have a look and get back to your regular route at your convenience.

Writing a book is so similar to making a long journey that the simple equation practically writes itself:

> Desire to write a book
>
> +
>
> Desire for a basic plan that allows for spontaneity
>
> =
>
> A Route 66 placemat (Naturally, I mean the *writer's equivalent* of a Route 66 placemat.)

I used to think that writers needed more than a simple map to write their book, but having seen the damage that can be done by too much planning—anxiety, doubt, dead-sounding prose—I know otherwise.

Your map, of course, is what puts your truth and your people together and makes your story go somewhere interesting. And the perfect solution is a map that's neither too vague nor too complicated.

Let's make one.

## WRITING BLAST: YOUR THIRD TOUCHSTONE

Your Map: Planning Your Book

- Gather your writing materials.
- Find a comfortable place.
- Enter garret mode.
- Consider your truth, and consider your people. Dwell on those things for a few minutes. Open up your heartbrain.
- Now consider the stuff your people will do during your book, fact or fiction. Simply, what's going to *happen* in your book? Start writing about it. Be loose, don't push anything.
- Consider the stuff you *want them to do*, and what they will *need* to do, and what they just *might* do on their own. What they might be *forced* to do!
- Write on any of the ideas you've generated already. Use **Yes, and—** and **What if?** liberally.

- Write for as long as you like.
- When you're ready to stop writing, stop.

Now you have some basic mapping material.

## Your Map for Fiction

Today's best novels make readers so desperate to know *what happens next* that they'll stay up reading past two in the morning, thumbs blistering, until THE END. Then and only then will they be able to relax, their souls flooded with satisfaction, relief, and peace.

Only to be followed—ideally!—by a gnawing sense of unfulfillment, anxiety, and a compulsion to *read more books by you*.

It's our responsibility to feed their addiction.

Looking at successful authors and their polished products, you might conclude they must have some literary alchemy at their fingertips, or they really are slightly superhuman, or they've made a deal with the devil. (If only it were so easy!)

But no: writing a page-turner is an art and a craft, and you can learn to do it.

Remember, you have been listening to stories, reading stories, watching stories, and telling stories your whole life long. I want you to go over to a mirror and say, or write on a card and keep, "I have an instinctive understanding of good storytelling."

Because you do.

You will craft a whole tale that readers will relate to, deep in their hearts. You have skills and talent already, or you wouldn't have the ambition to write a gripping story, and right now you're going to learn how to harness the strengths you've already got.

You're going to do what storytellers from the absolute dawn of time did, and you're going to do what the books on the front-of-store spinner racks at the airport bookstores do. You're going to tap into timeless human drama.

You do that by learning what works. You already know what doesn't work: We've all unwittingly wasted time reading a book or watching a film where at the end, you go, That's it? That was so lame! Why was it lame? Because it didn't move me at all. I didn't believe it. I didn't care.

OK. Right there you know that you must engage your readers' emotions. You have to make them feel. There's your start: The most successful storytellers engage the readers' emotions first and foremost. You need to make them believe what you're telling them, and you need to make them care about what you're telling them.

These are your two test questions, as you go forward and write:

> Will they believe it?
> and
> Will they feel it?

## Two Sure Ways To Plot Your Book

There are two foolproof ways to make a Route 66 Placemat Map for your book. The first is to plot from your gut.

You've got a good idea for a story, you've got a few characters developed, and you've got some stuff-that-happens.

Now what?

At this point, most aspiring authors just start writing, hoping that their book will take shape as they go.

Such a plan can lead to interesting things, but hope isn't good enough for most new authors to go on. In fact, the streets of New York City are littered with queries from such first-book authors.

To lift your work from the gum wads and pigeon *merde*, you need a coherent plot.

Alternatively, you can get pretty complex with plotting. You can try to follow this or that guru's rules, you can try to emulate this or that best-selling author. You will feel like putting a bullet through your brain. Why? Because the whole thing gets horribly complicated way too soon.

The following method, I'll tell you right now, is as good as any and simpler than all of them. It will help you forge a compelling plot.

## The Heart-Clutching Moment Foolproof Story Map

When you were first thinking about your book, and then when you were working on your Truth and your People, you undoubtedly thought of some heart-clutching moments, or HCMs. Remember the information about arc in Chapter Three? An HCM will give you arc, boy howdy will it.

OK, what is a heart-clutching moment? Here are some classics:

- love at first sight (Marius Pontmercy meets Cosette.)
- a huge moral lapse (Judas takes the money.)
- murder (Miles Archer's sets Sam Spade in motion.)
- death by other means (Injun Joe starves to death in cave.)
- a refusal of grace (Mayella Ewell sticks to her story in spite of taking courtroom oath.)
- nature gone wild (Shark dines on first recreational swimmer.)
- someone standing up to corruption (Shane picks up his gun again.)
- a change of heart, for good or ill (Michael Corleone offers to kill Solozzo and Captain McCluskey.)
- an act of depraved violence (Bill Sykes cudgels Nancy.)
- a maturing (Dorothy realizes the problem wasn't Kansas, it was her.)
- betrayal (Sandy puts a stop to her eccentric mentor Jean Brodie.)
- forgiveness (Melanie insists Scarlett join her in the receiving line.)
- a revelation (Pip's secret benefactor is none other than …!)

HCMs can also be active, whole scenes:

- a lifesaving attempt
- a chase
- a battle
- a seduction
- a caper

Bear in mind that an HCM is not the same thing as a story point.

*I've heard the term story point, but it's not clear in my mind.*

You will instantly grasp the difference by considering this example:

**STORY POINT:** Jack Woltz shows off his prize racehorse to Tom Hagen, the Godfather's representative.

**STORY POINT:** Hagen asks Woltz to give Johnny Fontane the part he wants in Woltz's new picture.

**STORY POINT:** Woltz refuses.

**HEART-CLUTCHING MOMENT:** Woltz wakes up to find the severed horse's head in his bed.

**STORY POINT:** Woltz changes his mind and gives Johnny Fontane the part in the picture after all.

**STORY POINT:** The Godfather continues on to the next order of family business.

See, story points precede the HCM, and story points follow the HCM. You can use any number of story points to build suspense to an HCM. Scriptwriters call them 'beats.' Same thing.

**NOW:**

- Do a stormwrite focusing on the HCMs you thought of while you worked on your Truth and your People, plus whatever bubbled up during your writing blast on your map.
- Come up with some more HCMs.
- Construct your story around them.

I emphasize the difference: Don't focus on your inchoate story *line*. Focus on the *key* moments in your story.

*Wait, what was that word,* **inchoate***?*

*Inchoate* is a great little word that means 'newish and therefore as-yet unformed.'

So: stormwrite a list of HCMs and put them on index cards in rough order.

There's your Route 66 placemat right there.

Add other dramatic moments and scenes as they come to you.

Going forward writing your book, if you ever feel you're going dry, do any of the following:

- Start writing one of your HCM scenes. The scene itself will prompt ideas and suggest new courses of action or characters.
- Write deeper into an HCM scene you've written already, and think about the bridges between scenes, the story points that might lead up and follow your HCM, and you'll find yourself thinking of more good scenes and more HCMs.
- You can't go wrong adding conflict, suffering, or frustration.

For example, Shakespeare wanted to take Macbeth from conquering hero to murderous traitor whose decapitation at the hands of one of his countrymen is the only possible, imaginable end.

How does he do it? Reread the play and you'll realize that one HCM leads to the next, fast and furious: The witches' stunning prophecies, Macbeth's realization that he could be king, his wife's corrupt ambition, one murder, two more murders, and more upon that, and prophesy again, and insanity, and suicide ... All in the space of ninety-eight pages!

You can't go wrong with the heart-clutching moment plotting method. But if you're writing a novel and you have a hero in place, I advise exploring the Hero's Adventure as a way of making your map. This is the second foolproof way to plot your novel.

## The Hero's Adventure Foolproof Story Map

How do the most successful authors of our time construct their stories? If you read them, and if you also read some ancient myths, you will begin to see parallels. You will feel smacked upside the *head* with parallels. You'll realize that the top authors of today use storytelling techniques that writers used back when plans were being drawn up for the pyramids.

An excellent book to read about ancient myths is *The Hero with a Thousand Faces* by Joseph Campbell. The title says it all. Across cultures and generations, some variation of a hero figures into every beloved story. And the typical story is about an individual who goes on a quest or a journey. By the end, the individual becomes a hero. This is the Hero's Adventure.

What is a beloved story? One that people can't get enough of, one that's passed from person to person, generation to generation. One that you want to hear again and again. The prototypical hero story is that of Heracles, or Hercules, with his exciting quests and labors and brave deeds.

The hero's adventure stands out and is the most archetypal story of all, becoming the basis for more novels than any other kind of story. Novels of *all* different genres are based on the Hero's Adventure, from romances to thrillers to sci-fi.

What is the Hero's Adventure? You know it already, and you may even have elements of it in the story you're working on. But I suspect you haven't *yet* methodically and thoroughly appropriated it for yourself. You might not know how, or you might have found it too complicated, or you might not have realized just how important it is.

Some story analysts make the Hero's Adventure quite intricate by breaking down the parts into many subparts, which can easily overload the creative spirit. Others try to force the whole thing into a three-act structure, that is, try to make it like a typical stage drama, divided into chunks A, B, and C.

There's merit to all that in-depth stuff, and I invite you to study up on it when you feel like it. But simple works best, and simple will take you a long way, just like the Route 66 placemat. So, stick with me.

1. Start with the HCM Plotting Method. Do a stormwrite on all your heart-clutching moments, and throw in any other highly dramatic moments you can think of.
2. Use the following basic recipe, developed by all of our ancestors who told stories around the fire (including Joseph Campbell). This is my simplified version of all that. I call it a recipe instead

of a formula because recipes are by nature flexible, not rigid. They are inspirations, not handcuffs. When I say 'use' the recipe below, I mean adopt it as a framework to insert your HCMs, ideas, and other story points, specifically in the italicized sections, and to come up with new ones that will complement them and make them work irresistibly as a Hero's Adventure.

## Hero's Adventure Basic Recipe

*A messenger comes.*

The messenger might be human, or a message might come from an experience—like a brush with death or a dream. At any rate, something has gone wrong; the natural order of the world has been disturbed.

*A problem is presented.*

Perhaps something has been taken away from the tribe, or some misfortune or malfeasance has occurred.

*Someone is marked out as the person to solve this problem.*

She is chosen according to some past deed of her parents or by her own reputation or by happenstance.

This person, of course, emerges as the hero at the end.

*A challenge takes shape.*

The challenge may be refused, at first. "No way, I'm not gonna risk my neck for that!"

*A refusal, often.*

But eventually the hero decides to accept the challenge. She might even be forced to accept it by circumstances.

*The challenge is accepted.*

And the adventure begins.

*The hero leaves the familiar world.*

And she sets off into another world. It's dangerous. The hero could use some help, and very often, helpers show up.

*Helpers materialize.*

A helper might have special skills the hero doesn't have, or he might have special insights or wisdom, in which case he is a mentor.

*Setbacks occur.*

> The hero is tested, she makes gains, she endures setbacks, she fights for what is right, she resists evil. The going's tough!
>
> *The hero regroups and gains some ground again.*
>
> Maybe she needs another visit to a mentor, or maybe she makes a personal breakthrough and overcomes a great inner obstacle, perhaps her own fear.
>
> *The foe is vanquished or the elixir is seized.*
>
> Eventually she vanquishes the foe or comes into possession of something that will restore the natural order—an elixir. That is, a cure, or new knowledge that will bring justice, or the return of prosperity. And she returns to the familiar world with this elixir.
>
> *The hero returns to the familiar world.*
>
> And the problem is fixed, or justice is done. The natural order is restored.

The person who accepts the challenge and prevails is elevated to a special position, somewhere above human, somewhere below god. She is the hero. And it all feels so satisfying and good. You have seen endless manifestations of this story, you've read it and seen it over and over again.

Famous stories from King Arthur and Excalibur and the Round Table to *The Wizard of Oz* to *The Little Engine That Could* to Harry Potter and everything in between are based on the Hero's Adventure.

As a matter of fact, every story worth telling is a Hero's Adventure in some way. This framework will help you see the hero's story in your story. It will help you develop a terrific novel, and it will help you figure out how to write a nonfiction narrative.

> *It still seems rather abstract.*

OK, I'll get more concrete now.

## The Hero's Adventure Foolproof Plot Recipe Made Concrete

Just about everybody has read a Sherlock Holmes story, or at least understands the gist of those wonderful tales by Sir Arthur Conan Doyle, so I'll use Holmes as an example. This will help you identify the heroic journey in the novels and stories you read, and it will help you create one for your own story.

> Holmes and Watson are hanging out in the familiar world of 221B Baker Street when a young lady comes calling. (What follows is the exact same sequence of events that I just presented, only we're talking about a specific mystery story now.)
>
> *A messenger comes.*
>
> The young lady tells Holmes that her sister has died under weird circumstances, and she now fears for her own life. In other words, there has been a disturbance in the Force.
>
> *A problem is presented.*
>
> Knowing of Holmes's reputation, the young lady asks him for help.
>
> *Someone is marked out as the person to solve this problem.*
>
> Holmes asks many questions, and perceives the seriousness of the situation.
>
> *The challenge takes shape.*
>
> Holmes rarely refuses a challenge, though he has been known to be reluctant at times.
>
> *A refusal, often.*
>
> But in this case, Holmes senses great urgency, so he doesn't waffle.
>
> *The challenge is accepted.*
>
> And the adventure begins.
>
> *The hero leaves the familiar world.*
>
> Holmes sets off from 221B Baker Street and enters the busy, raucous streets of London, thence to a creepy old mansion in the country. It's dangerous. The hero could use some assistance.
>
> *Helpers materialize.*
>
> And guess what? He's got Watson at his side! Much investigation occurs, with progress, and then…
>
> *Setbacks occur.*
>
> Things go wrong, problems turn out to be more difficult than anticipated.
>
> *The hero regroups and gains again.*

> Holmes perseveres.
>
> After a nail-biting, death-defying climax, Holmes prevails, discovering a deadly plot and a bizarre method of murder. The perpetrator is killed by the very method he had used to kill another.
>
> *The foe is vanquished or the elixir is seized.*
>
> Holmes and Watson wrap up the case for the local police, and return to their flat in London.
>
> *Hero returns to the familiar world.*
>
> And we feel totally secure because we know justice has been done; the killer has been killed and cannot kill again.
>
> *The natural order is restored.*

There you have it. For this example I used the bare bones of the story "The Adventure of the Speckled Band," but you could substitute just about any other.

The Holmes stories are all more or less *alike in their structure*, differing only in content. This satisfying structure is what keeps us reading them one after another like I eat potato chips on Friday nights. Furthermore, you could take any Sherlock Holmes story and expand it, give it some subplots, make it bigger, longer, and uncut, and you'd have a novel. But each one is a polished gem of a heroic adventure.

Going further: Read practically any good, successful dramatic novel and you will find similar story bones. *This is not by accident.* Good authors have an instinct for such things. We can sharpen our instincts by studying, as you're doing right now, and by writing, which you've been doing all along.

> *Must my Hero's Adventure begin and end in exactly the same place, like the Sherlock Holmes stories?*

Great question. It can if you want, but no, it doesn't have to. Many terrific stories end with the natural order being restored, but not necessarily in the same physical or psychological location as the beginning. A Hero's Adventure can still begin in Chicago and end up in Los Angeles.

The Hero's Adventure is a fail-safe model for storytelling. However, it is not the be-all and end-all. As you can see, it's simply a way of organizing and linking your heart-clutching moments for **maximum effect**. It was good enough for the ancients, it was good enough for the most memorable authors of recent centuries, and it's good enough for us.

Best of all, it's so flexible. You can follow it quite literally, or you can use it as a general guide. The template I've presented to you is simple and stress-free. You can use it to make your novel reach deep into your readers' minds and hearts.

The more I think about it, the more I bet that the story you do have, however much of it you have, contains elements of the Hero's Adventure already. Have you been yelling that to me through the time/space continuum?

*Yes!*

Good.

Why does the Hero's Adventure affect us so? Because it taps into the deepest human dreams, desires, and fears.

To make a hero's adventure even better, let your hero have doubts about what he is doing; let him have an inner conflict that must be resolved along with the outer one. Dig it: An inner journey to go with the outer journey. You started thinking about this while you were developing your people.

A very simple example of inner conflict would be a husband who storms out after an argument with his wife. He gets in the pickup and drives, and he's angry, and he's continuing to shout at his wife even though he's alone, and he's justifying what he's done and said. Then, since there's nobody there to contradict him, he cools down. Then he has to decide what to do. He might go to a bar and tell his troubles to strangers, or he might go to a friend's or find a prostitute or go to the river and take a swim or find a dice game and lose his pocket money and his pickup.

During this adventure he might ask for advice and get some. It might not be the advice he wants. Or it might be. He might realize he'd been a jerk. He might make an effort to understand his wife better, in spite of *her* faults. Eventually, he will go home. He might overcome his pride and apologize for being a jackass and beg for forgiveness. Or he'll pack his bags and leave. Or maybe he'll arrive to find a note from her and all her clothes gone, along with his guns.

You can see how this basic story of an inner journey can be explored, embellished and suspense-ified any number of ways. Self-destruction followed by humility followed by courage followed by enlightenment is a typical, and deeply satisfying, sequence.

Here are some questions to open up your heartbrain while you're working with the Hero's Adventure. Take your time and consider each one separately. Some might especially pop out at you and you'll think, *Oh, yeah, I'm gonna write on that, right now.* Savor and enjoy!

- Who? Who is active here? What are they doing before order has been disturbed, and why?
- How has the natural order been disturbed? Is somebody dead, is somebody about to become dead, is somebody—or are a lot of somebodies—in danger? What is out of balance?
- Who or what is my messenger?
- Who is my hero?
- What is his familiar world?
- What heart-clutching moments do I have so far? Do these heart-clutching moments suggest others?
- Who are my hero's helpers?
- What is their world like?
- Where will my hero go on his adventure/journey?
- What is the unfamiliar world my hero will enter?
- What is the quest, or mission?
- What is my hero's inner conflict? (One idea to prompt you: In what way(s) is my hero flawed?)
- What is the puzzle? Do I know the answer yet?
- What is the pursuit?
- Who is after whom?
- And why?
- Who is my villain? What is my villain's story?
- What or who will my hero have to fight?

- What are the stakes? What will be gained with victory? What will be lost with failure?
- What weakness might cause my hero to screw up?
- What's the most exciting ending in the world?

Keep using **Yes, and—** and **What if?**

You'll soon have your Route 66 placemat map for your book.

## The Magic of Surprise

Coming upon something surprising while writing is the most electrifying thing that can happen to you as a fiction writer. (You can argue with me about seven-figure publishing contracts and Pulitzer Prizes all you want, but I stand by that statement.)

I'm not talking about writing something that will surprise the reader, like a corpse falling out of a cupboard. I'm talking about this: You're writing along, pursuing your characters as they carry out what you think you want them to do, but suddenly one of them does something that you hadn't anticipated at all. It's as if that character has taken on a life of his own. In a sense, he has. Rejoice when this happens. Follow that character, let him and your other characters tell you what they ought to do next. When it's time to put away your writing for the day, open a bottle of something to celebrate. (Not necessarily alcoholic!) You've tapped into your mother lode.

If you do much unfettered writing, such a thing will happen any number of times. I remember it happening to me most vividly while writing a short story. When I sat down to write a particular scene I had no inkling that a brand-new character was going to drop dead of a heart attack. But it just happened. An appropriate moment for a heart attack happened, and I saw the character clutch his chest and fall over, and I sat there thinking, *No, this character does not have a heart attack. We haven't even seen his face yet!* But he just kept clutching his chest and falling over, so that after a few minutes I had to write it. Then I had to adapt the next scenes to accommodate the death of that character, and those scenes turned out to be much more interesting than what I'd vaguely envisioned in the first place.

You can't force surprise to occur, but you *can* be receptive to surprise.

Creating a *basic* plot, a Route 66 Placemat Map, leaves you wiggle room. It leaves space for surprise.

And that's magic.

## Your Map for Nonfiction

Drawing a Route 66 placemat map for your nonfiction book is so much fun. I enjoyed making my simple map for this book before I set out on the journey of writing it, and I look forward to mapping future books.

If your nonfiction book is story-based, either a memoir or an account of an event, like how your ancestors survived the Holocaust and made it to America, or the history of your neighborhood, or the story of how you rode a skateboard from San Diego to Fairbanks, that makes it narrative nonfiction. And readers respond wonderfully to drama in narratives like that.

Start with a Heart-Clutching Moment, and stormwrite it. Luxuriate in this stormwrite. Take plenty of time with it, just letting dramatic moments and scenes tumble out of you, with plenty of **Yes, ands**—and **What ifs?**

Examples of HCMs from real life for nonfiction might be:

**A BIG DECISION:** *Instead of go to jail, I told the judge I'd enlist in the Army.*

**A BETRAYAL:** *The detective reported to me that my wife was in Las Vegas with my cousin Earl instead of visiting her old college roommate in Poughkeepsie.*

**A TRIUMPH:** *My granddad won the city tennis championship two years after being diagnosed with polio.*

**A DISASTER:** *Someone who had a grudge against the social worker torched the halfway house.*

Each chapter of your book should be based on or include a dramatic moment. That seems obvious, but I've read too many beginner manuscripts that spend whole chapters describing a place or a few people without anything really happening.

Explicate whatever you need to explicate—give background information, technical insights, whatever, just don't devote entire chapters to it solid. Use the cool, interesting stuff you're telling to lead you to the bits of hard information you want to give.

CHISEL IT IN STONE:
DRAMA = READER LOVE

Put your list of your heart-clutching and dramatic moments on index cards, or make a list by hand or electronically.

Write 'em all down, big ones (Finding Ivan's body after his suicide) and little ones (My five-year-old son took my hand and said, "I'll take care of you, Mommy.")

For any kind of narrative nonfiction you'll be using your best and strongest material, of course. As you're putting it in order, material that's weak and easily weeded out should be tossed. But if it's iffy, keep it for now. You can segregate it in a separate folder marked *iffy.*

You can add to and subtract from your map anytime.

Your map will firm up by itself as you get deeper into the writing of your book.

We'll soon get into how to structure and write individual chapters.

For memoir you can:

- choose one period of your life to write about in great detail, with chapters—the events you describe—being fairly contiguous; or you can
- write chapters that are essentially complete on their own and thus independent of sequence.

Each chapter simply has to tell its own little story.

You can jump from big to little scenes, back and forth in time. For example, if you want to write the story of how your mother went from being a vibrant, accomplished person to enduring the oblivion of advanced Alzheimer's, you might want to start with a chapter about her life today, then skip back in time to when she was the renegade PTA mom who did a belly dance to raise funds. And so on.

It's fun to start with an HCM from real life, and then to move to telling the early story of how that came to be.

If, say, you want to tell the story of your deployment in Operation Iraqi Freedom, you could begin with a description of a battle you were involved in. Then you could go back and tell the story of how you came to enlist in the Army. But from then on, a chronological narrative would serve well, because so much of a military story depends on action and time and sequence of events. Readers expect a military story to be chronological.

However, you might serve your story just as well by alternating sections about your personal story with sections that tell what was going on in the big picture. But keep it chronological.

Say you've come across the notebook/diary your great-uncle kept when he was on an archeological expedition in Turkey in the 1930s. If you want to publish that account, you could intersperse his words with your own educated conjecture, plus some historical information about the political and scientific situation in Turkey and the greater region. You might research (that is, learn about) the natural history of the area and put that in, too.

Another way to do it: You can select a theme for each chapter, like "Uncle Roscoe's Workshop" in which you relate several anecdotes, perhaps widely spaced in time, all of which took place in Uncle Roscoe's workshop. A chapter can center on a specific person, idea, animal, or thing.

## Mapping for Instructional Nonfiction

The best, most useful how-to books are stories. Or they have an underlying story. The chapters of Donald Trump's first book, *The Art of the Deal*, aren't divided into theory, explication, and quiz questions. They are story after story after story about how he did it—and how you can, too.

If you use a story as a framework for your how-to book, you'll be light-years ahead of authors who think that information is the only worthwhile thing. Your information is the main reason for your book, to be sure. But readers will relate on a deep level to the story and actual experience you tell about.

Do a stormwrite on everything you want to tell.

Break everything down into the smallest practical units or steps.

Put them on index cards, then put the cards in a good rough order.

What's the personal stuff you want to put in that's relevant to your material? In this book, for example, I include little stories about my own life experiences, all of which support the points I make about writing.

Good how-to books start with the author's personal story then move into the guts of their material, like this:

> I was the worst woodworker in the world.
>
> Embarrassing anecdote about failed project I. (An anecdote is a quick account of something that happened. An antidote is what James Bond always needs to find after someone has given him poison. An anaconda is a big snake.)
>
> Embarrassing anecdote about failed project II.
>
> After painful experience, I realized that quality results absolutely must start with the right tools, not just good materials.
>
> Anecdote of success I.
>
> Anecdote of success II.
>
> Here's how I learned about tools, and here's my guide on how to buy or make excellent tools for woodworking.
>
> Then move into your how-to information, which will be the bulk of your book. You can sprinkle in additional personal anecdotes as you go, in order to illustrate the points you want to make.

Stormwrite on all this stuff. Get your raw material on paper one way or another. Have fun thinking of all the things you want to tell, even little things, which sometimes stick the best in readers' heads. ("I found that keeping my dust brush on the left side of the workbench works best. I'm left-handed and I don't have to reach across for it.")

## A Map for All Writers

If you want to, you can even draw a literal Route 66 placemat map of your book.

Get yourself a big long piece of paper (or tape one together) and write your sequence of HCMs and dramatic scenes in a line. I like to start with index cards because they're so easily changed around, and you can lay them out on a table and try different sequences. If you do this first you'll make a map with fewer cross-outs.

Everybody's different in what works to unite our eyes, our hands, and our heartbrain. So long as we're comfortable with our materials and tools (like our woodworker!), we can be happy and easy as we work.

## ACTIONS

- Read a good book, fact or fiction. As you go, be aware of the author's map. Do you notice heart-clutching moments? What are they? Do you notice elements of the hero's adventure? What are they?
- Everybody's life, young or old, has traced a course. Just for fun, get a piece of paper and list the heart-clutching moments of your own life. Are there elements of the Hero's Adventure in your own life? What are they? Are some of them happening right now?

## *COUNT ON YOUR TOUCHSTONES TO SERVE YOU*

At any time in your writing, if you start to feel confused or stale, or if your pen stops moving and you get an uh-oh feeling inside you—which is nothing but worry—go to any of your touchstones: Your Truth, Your People, Your Map. Dive into them, feel them, write on them deeper and longer, and they will point you toward what to write next. They'll open up your process again.

CHAPTER 11

# To Be Great, Strive to Be Ordinary

As you plunge into writing your book, here's the main thing to do:

**Strive for the ordinary. Because that's what the greats do.**

*If I were a person who used vulgar talk, I would say, "You are shitting me."*

I am so not shitting you.

Do not even strive for near-greatness. Look, do you think that every time Joe DiMaggio stepped into the batter's box he strove to make the most perfect swing in all of baseball? Hell no! He strove to hit the damn ball.

Do you think that every time Picasso picked up a paintbrush he scrunched up his face and said to himself, "OK, boy, whatever you do, don't blow it. Don't ruin this canvas. What you've got to do is try really hard to produce another triumph that will make the art world sob with emotion." Right.

Picasso probably didn't say *anything* to himself, he dove into that canvas with a child's bright, open anticipation.

Do you suppose that every time Shakespeare or Jane Austen or
Virginia Woolf
Henry David Thoreau

J.D. Salinger
Martin Luther King, Jr.
F. Scott Fitzgerald
Winston Churchill
Dorothy Parker
Charles Dickens
Isaac Asimov

sharpened their quill or uncapped their Parker Duofold or clicked their Bic or sat down to their massive gorgeous loud clunky Underwood, they thought, "Ah! Now to unveil brilliance to the world!"

They sat down merely expecting themselves to relax and write.

So, then: I want you to behave just as the greatest geniuses behaved. I want you to strive to write an average book. A decent book. An OK book. In order to do this, you must first write an average sentence. And you have to start somewhere. And that is no sweat.

> "The funicular car bucked once more and then stopped."

That is the first sentence of Ernest Hemingway's short story "Cross-Country Snow." It's fashionable to bash Hemingway these days (mostly in the form of scoffing at his machismo), but whatever you think of him, you have to love that sentence. A whole writing lesson lies in it: There's the lesson of beginning a story by writing a simple, declarative sentence, and there's the lesson of where to start your story.

He could have begun the story: "Nick slept in, and while he ate breakfast at the hotel he thought about his girl. He imagined her kissing that bullfighter chap, and then he ordered some fine Riesling wine to take away the sting of the thought. By the time he decided to do some skiing, the sun had just about finished rising. He paid the funicular car man, and got on. The car bucked as it climbed the strand of cable up the mountain."

But he didn't. He began the story with some action. He knew we didn't need to begin at sunrise. We didn't need to hear all about what Nick ate for breakfast and what he did before the funicular car stopped.

What I love about the "bucked once more" is that he's telling us that the car was bucking all along, without telling us. I just love that.

Whenever I get to feeling anxious about the writing I'm doing, I remember, "The funicular car bucked once more and then stopped." In fact, if you pick up my second novel, *Damn Straight*, you'll notice that I sort of ripped off the structure of Hemingway's sentence for my first sentence:

> The power struggled back up for about ten seconds—ten brown little seconds—then failed again.

You don't have to start at any obvious beginning, no matter whether you're at sentence one or in the middle of Chapter Fifty.

Get right going.

## Unleashing Your True Voice

Another aspect of being ordinary—and being yourself as a writer—is unleashing your own voice.

> *What does that really mean?*

Voice. English teachers talk about it; writing teachers talk about it. Agents and editors talk about it.

Professional authors never talk about it.

We just write the best we know how.

Voice is simply your style of writing, your way of expressing yourself. Authors write in different styles, we know this. Ernest Hemingway wrote blunt and punchy, for example, while Virginia Woolf wrote smooth and delicate.

Readers love a unique, authentic-sounding voice. Agents and editors hunt assiduously for original voices.

Your voice as a writer is the words you choose, the rhythm you use, the colors and inflections that characterize you.

No one kind of voice is better than another.

All you want to do is be yourself. Like everything else good in writing, a free, unique voice stems from flow: from you, the writer, being in harmony with your world and your material.

### *How to Kill Your Voice and Disappoint Your Readers*

- Overthink your writing.
- Be extremely careful; that is, try to write totally grammatically, as if the world's meanest teacher were looking over your shoulder.
- Try to write as if you're smarter or dumber than you are.
- When you want to show that you're being casual, write down the first cliché that comes to mind.
- When in doubt, get tight.

### *How to Write With Your Own Original Voice*

- Stay in touch with your heartbrain.
- Write it how you'd say it.

I know I'll drive my copy editor to distraction in this book because I don't always use perfect grammar and I do use idiosyncratic constructions. So what?

> CHISEL IT IN STONE:
> TALK PLAIN. WRITE PLAIN.

## Clichés: How We Hate Them

News flash: Agents and editors hate clichés. Readers sometimes tolerate them, but acute readers don't.

Writers with dull, undeveloped voices use clichés, which are simply hackneyed, overused expressions that were once groovy and new.

Examples of clichés:

- The greatest thing since sliced bread.
- Fit as a fiddle.
- Cat got your tongue?

This list could go into the thousands.

How to know when you've written a cliché: a) when you've heard it before more than once, and b) when you suspect it's a cliché.

You have two weapons against clichés:

- Cut it and say it plainly. "Cat got your tongue?" can be transformed into, simply: "You're quiet tonight."
- Give it a twist: "The greatest thing since sliced bread," can become "The greatest thing since MTV," or "The greatest thing since beer-can hats."

However, do not trouble about clichés while you're writing. If something lame occurs to you and you realize it's probably a cliché and won't make it into your book, go ahead and write it anyway; don't stop to chaw over it. You'll get it out of the way and it won't form a clot in your brain. Take time later to think about it, perhaps with thesaurus in hand.

## ACTIONS

- Go over to your bookcase or local library. Pick out two books, by different authors. Bearing 'voice' in your heartbrain, read a few pages of one, then read a few pages by the other. You'll immediately see differences in how they write. This is voice.
- Rewrite these clichés or choose a few on your own.
    - All thumbs.
    - His bark is worse than his bite.
    - She went off half-cocked.
    - A heart of gold.
- Write on your book. By 'write on it' I mean write a hunk of it, or more than one hunk. ('Write on it' is the best combo of 'write it' and 'work on it'.) You might already have a pretty good start on it. Keep it going. Write on it using the ideas and words you've generated so far. Do more, go as far as you feel like going! Have fun while you're at it, otherwise why bother?

CHAPTER 12

# Writing Flow and Your First Draft

If you thoroughly read only one chapter of this book, make it this one.

Good writing, like the blood in your body and the currents in the ocean, is all about flow. Bad writing, like sludge, is about friction and resistance.

Do you believe in writer's block?

Watch out; that's a trick question. (And it's the only trick question in this book.)

Are you smiling? If so, it's because my question made you realize that writer's block is a matter of belief. Do you *believe* in writer's block? For writer's block to exist, you have to believe in it. Just like the monster under your bed. Therefore, you realize that you can choose to believe in it or not. I don't believe in it. Please join me for a moment of not believing in writer's block.

Ah! How does that feel?

Writer's block is a term invented by some author who needed an excuse for believing he couldn't write. That writer did not know he had the power to be prolific.

The more you chew over a piece of writing, the tighter you clench on it, the less benefit you gain by your effort. That's not to say the first thing that spills onto the page is always best, but if you find yourself obsessing, move on. Obsessing on details leads to so-called writer's block, which does not exist in any material way. It's a mythical monster, which requires belief to live. Deprive it of belief.

By contrast, if you allow yourself to write free and easy, if you don't strain, if you attempt to write like a lion dashing across the veldt rather than a dung beetle grunting up an incline, you'll do fine. Not that you don't have to put in effort. Accomplishing anything worthwhile takes effort. It's just that you want to eliminate *excess* effort, and eliminate self-impedance.

The key is to work with the language, not against it.

### YOUR ADDICTION

Give up your addiction to struggle. You know what I'm talking about. Just let it go. *The struggle itself is the effort.* What some of us find hard is getting out of our own way. That's what this book is for. I also recommend the book *Flow: The Psychology of Optimal Experience*, by Mihaly Csikszentmihalyi (Mee-hy Cheek-sent-me-high-ee.) Dr. Csikszentmihalyi is a professor who's figured out that humans are happiest when they're so absorbed in what they're doing that everything else falls away.

Ernest Hemingway famously said, "The first draft of anything is shit." For years I didn't understand. When I started writing fiction seriously, I kept trying to get it right the first time. Every night after clocking out from my shift in a bookstore, I'd hit my favorite coffee shop with my yellow pad and the gimme pens I collected from publishers' reps, and I'd carefully work on my first novel. I'd write my minimum requirement of 300 words, staying inside the lines and squeezing out every word with great thought and deliberation. Grant me, at least, that I was disciplined: I counted my words, and if I got to 299, I wouldn't go back and add "very" to a sentence, I had to at least begin the next one.

Using this word-count method I managed to produce quite a lot of pages. But guess what? My prose did not consistently swing, sizzle, or startle. It took me a long time to figure out Hemingway's hidden meaning, and longer still to apply it. Over time, paradoxically, as I got rougher with my first drafts, my finished work got better and better.

> *Why does a coherent first draft usually give birth to a stilted finished product?*

Because it means you haven't let it flow.

Perhaps you haven't given yourself permission to make mistakes because you haven't forgiven yourself for past ones!

Admit it: Unless your throttle's wide open, you're not giving it everything you've got.

One day I realized that creativity in writing isn't a linear process. Granted, we read in a linear fashion, and the words must go on the page one after the other. And, yes, we must put our thoughts and words in order, so that the reader can make sense of them.

The act of writing, in fact, is the only art that is literally one-dimensional. Remember Descartes establishing that a point in space has zero dimension, a line has one, a plane two, and intersecting planes—or a solid—has three. A solid moving through space represents time, a.k.a. the fourth dimension. (When we attempt to insult a piece of fiction by calling its characters 'one-dimensional,' we need to do better than that. I note crankily that the put-down began as 'two-dimensional,' meaning 'flat,' but just as 'a hundred and ten percent' has come to substitute for 'a hundred percent,' we've corrupted this simple geometric concept the same way.) (End of rant.)

So, yes, writing is a linear process but creativity is a sprawly, multidimensional process. That's one of our keys to freedom.

> CHISEL IT IN STONE:
> CREATIVITY NEEDS ELBOW ROOM.

For your writing to come alive—to be multidimensional—you must simply give your creativity room to breathe and expand. A great way to do this is to barter away some control. That is, give away neat-n-tidy for ferocious, disorganized creativity. The rewards are worth it. Stormwriting is not linear.

*How do I stop worrying and learn to love anarchy?*

Very simply:

Ignore sequence while writing your first draft.

From listening to writers at all levels of accomplishment—from rank beginners to published authors with fan bases—I've learned that worrying about sequence is the biggest gumption trap. You have the basic story figured out, but you don't know how to present it so it hangs together—you're not sure what should come next.

Here is the key to freedom: *Write what comes to mind next*, not necessarily *what must come next*. After you've written a bunch of pages you can go back and take another look with sequence in mind. You can move stuff around and sort it out then.

What about transitions? Writers get hung up on them. Why? Because most of us had high school teachers who kept saying we needed more of them in our papers. If I had a nickel for every English teacher who has scribbled, "You need a transition here," I'd be shopping for my *second* Lamborghini.

I might note that as an ETK (English teacher's kid), I have nothing against English teachers as a group. There are some pretty cool ones out there.

But as authors, we don't need transitions. We don't need to know the unimportant stuff that happens between the important stuff. Just leave it out, or skim over it quick.

Some examples might help here.

Say you're writing about someone named Carlos who needs to confront a guy named Sid about something. We want to see that, whether the story is fact or fiction. We don't need to read that Carlos got in his car, started it, backed out of the driveway, and drove the five miles to Sid's house. You can just write, "After dinner Carlos drove over to Sid's."

If you're struggling with some passage or other, ask yourself if it's very important. If not, try cutting it altogether and see if your narrative suffers from it. (Narrative = Story.)

Exposition, too, is always less important than you think it is. What's exposition? Exposition means to give information, to *expose* information. Say you're writing about a police detective who is investigating the disappearance of a teenaged boy. The detective might inspect the boy's bedroom, looking for clues.

You could write this:

> Guitars were strewn around the room. A teenage boy into guitars: pretty typical. There was a black one without strings, and another with a long crack going all the way up the neck. There were packs of guitar strings all over the place. There was a guitar with a starburst pattern painted around the sound hole, a guitar made of shiny metal, an all-blue guitar, and a nice-looking beige one with the name *Gibson* written on the top in pearl letters.

Or you could write this:

> The kid was big into acoustic guitars. There must have been half a dozen, in various stages of repair. The best appeared to be a lustrous honey-colored Gibson, a brand Detective Watney recognized. Expensive.

Which paragraph reads better?

The first is straight, boring description. The second economically exposes everything that's needed in the scene, plus it lets us know a little about the detective, because the scene is told from his point of view.

You want to describe things as they relate to your story—and lists can be fun!—but you don't have to catalogue the world. This is freeing to realize.

Just focus on: What else is going to happen?

> *But it all has to make sense, right? What about Hemingway saying, "The first draft of anything is shit?"*

First, he did *not* mean that if you begin with crap, dung, *merde*, shit, you will without much effort end up with something far better.

Second, he did not mean that it's OK to start with a weak premise.

He meant that your first execution of your ideas must be as unfettered as possible. Which will result in—yes!—rather some shit. False starts, pretentiousness, clunky images, clichés. Fine. Get them out now. They won't contaminate your good stuff.

*How do I rough it up?*

Get loose, physically as well as mentally.

If, as I do, you write your first drafts longhand, consider your pen a paintbrush. Hold it relaxed in your hand and move it from your shoulder, not your fingers. Your whole arm will move freely, and you'll pour out the words as well as banish carpal tunnel to hell.

CHISEL IT IN STONE:
LEGIBILITY IS OVERRATED.

The common wisdom taught in writing workshops is: Don't stop to revise. But let's be honest, sometimes you really do see another possibility right away, and you should be free to pursue it.

I recommend **overwriting** as you go.

If, in a single moment, you think of two different ways of saying something, just write both, one after the other. Later you'll decide which is better.

Draw a box around a phrase, stack two competing adjectives one atop the other, make notes in the margin. I use the margins for research notes, too, like "what's position of Sirius over L.A./August?"

Fresh sheets are not just for motels. Use paper! If you want to go off on a new tangent that's longer than a sentence, rip off your current page and start a fresh one rather than crowd a new thought into a crevice on the page you're already on. If you feel guilty using fresh paper liberally, remember you can always reuse paper in other ways, not to mention recycling. Writing on your computer uses natural resources, too. If it's worth writing, it's worth doing well.

### RECEPTIVITY

Don't fight to write. Good writing flows from receptivity, which works much better than force.

And for the love of God, don't wait for a new thought to fully form before you put it down. More often than not, as soon as you write the first shard of that new thought, it'll work itself to fullness as you go. And that's the magic we all seek, isn't it?

If you want to add a word or a block of text, be free. Circle stuff, draw arrows, loop one piece of text into the middle of another, or alongside another. And keep going. If it's obvious instantly that one version of a word or sentence or graph is better, strike out the bad one and go on without looking back.

Will you mainly compose on your keyboard? Make the return button your best friend: set off a new idea by hitting one or two carriage returns.

Let your fingers splash on the keyboard. Let typos stand, keep going.

> CHISEL IT IN STONE:
> FEW GREAT ARTISTS COLOR INSIDE THE LINES.

Try writing faster than usual, not thinking. Take whatever comes without judging it too much. If you do this you'll soon find your own ways to be loose and free.

Why is it so important to suspend judgment when writing? Because that freedom opens you to the surprising stuff that you never saw coming. The stuff that makes you smile as you sit there in the coffee shop, your mug of joe cooling because you've forgotten to take a sip in fifteen solid minutes.

When starting a writing session, beginners often feel they must jump off to an excellent start, when all they need is to *start*. In this, there's no difference between me and you.

Often it takes me some real slogging through crap to produce decent writing, especially if I've laid off for a while. But I never despair, having learned that if I just keep going, I'll get someplace worthwhile.

*How do I face my second draft?*

If you've practiced slovenliness with a liberal hand, you'll be delighted at how much fun your second draft will be. Second draft, by the way, simply means the pile of pages you end up with after making your original pile of pages better. I'll talk more about that later.

After I've got a chapter or two roughed out, I go from my handwritten pages to my laptop, where I edit and rewrite as I go, adding new text and striking what—I can clearly see now!—doesn't work.

Thus I establish the simple rhythm that works for me: a couple of days writing longhand, then a day at the old laptop.

Some authors work through their entire manuscript in longhand before sitting down to type, and that's dandy, too.

Many beginning writers cling to every word they've written because, well, they've struggled to get that much out. But if you practice looseness and receptivity when writing your first draft, you will quickly realize that you have a *surplus* of good writing to sort through. You will know joy.

I just took a spin through a couple of my old *Writers at Work* volumes (The *Paris Review* Interviews). Along with George Plimpton's interview of each Famous Author, the *Review* reproduced a page from a draft of one of his or her manuscripts.

I studied some of those draft pages:

Cynthia Ozick: Her handwritten draft page is a beautiful mess, with almost more strike-outs than unscathed text.

Ralph Ellison: He used a typewriter, then marked up his pages with a ruthless hand.

Ernest Hemingway: His handwritten page from "The Battler" shows only one cross-out. However, between that and the published story, the passage shows subtle, significant differences.

Joan Didion: Her typewritten draft page is marked up with clear, bold lines, with circles and carats.

*What's a carat?*

This: ^

It's a proofreader's mark indicating insertion. When used below the line, it points up, when above the line it points down.

During the course of writing several novels, I realized that the days the truth shone brightest were the days my pen flowed the freest and messiest across the pages. And I was rewarded with longer and longer satisfactory passages. This is now my standard modus operandi.

It's beautiful to know that giving up control ultimately rewards you with what you seek the most: concise, insightful work.

## ACTIONS

Take six minutes to prove to yourself that lack of tension makes you a better writer.

- Rub your hands together to warm them. Shake out your hands, not hard. Let them dangle from your wrists. Loosen your wrists. Let that feeling of relaxed readiness flow from your hands into the rest of your body. This is what I do before writing or doing anything else that requires dexterity, like playing my mandolin on a streetcorner or the drums in the symphony I belong to.
- Do a little writing. I encourage you to do this longhand, for the best connection between your hands and the words you write. Gather your writing materials, find a comfortable place to sit or stand, and describe what you see when you hold your head level. Even a seemingly blank wall has characteristics. Write for five minutes. How does it go?

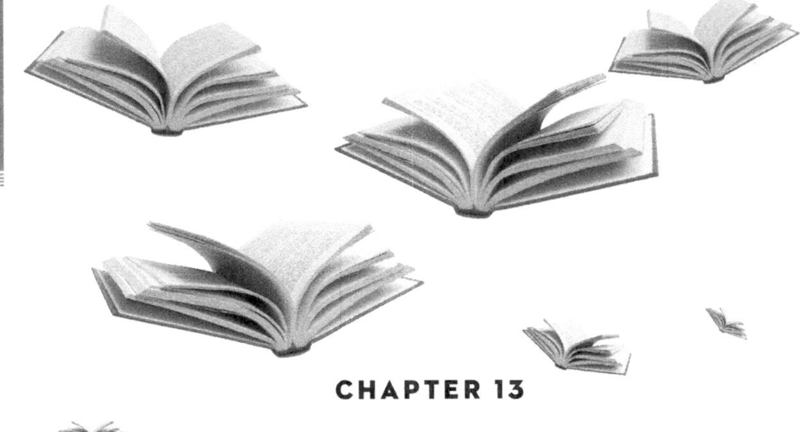

CHAPTER 13

# Writing With the Masters

Students learning to draw are often assigned the task of copying the works of great masters: DaVinci, Rembrandt, Rubens. Why? Because doing so makes you appreciate and understand drawing at a deeper level than just looking. There's a richer connection between brain, eye, and hand than between brain and eye alone. Ask any artist; they can attest it really works. After practicing this method while learning to draw, I wondered whether the same technique could help me as a writer. What if you literally copy out—either longhand or on a keyboard—a passage of a great work, and see what happens when you begin your own writing session?

> *Wait, wait, wait. A couple of chapters ago you said I should write with my own original voice, not try to mimic some famous author.*

Yes! And you should also learn to write well. I'm not talking about mimicry. I'm talking about an opportunity to teach yourself all about great writing. Stick with me.

As I thought about this, I remembered listening to a symphony conductor and composer talk about how he developed his talents. When he was young, he said, he earned money being a copyist, this being in the days before photocopy technology was commonplace. Music students were recruited to transcribe orchestral music from a single handwritten score to the forty or so individual instruments that made up the ensemble. More copies would be needed at any time.

Think of it: For every violin I part needed, perhaps five or ten copies would be required, and the same for the violin II parts. Every other part would have to be written out at least once: the first, second, and third trumpet parts; the timpani; the harps; the cellos, and all the assorted woodwinds. It represented a lot of work for those college kids.

One might expect such work to be mind-numbing: I mean, dude, just sitting there *copying* somebody else's work?

To the contrary, this conductor said; copying out music that somebody else had written—especially a master like Beethoven or Mozart—was fascinating, educational, and inspiring.

"Oh," he said, remembering, "I see how the clarinet doubles with the violas here, and I see how the chord progressions in the basses and the trombones work against each other here to create tension, and I see how they resolve with each other *here*, to relieve the tension."

He credited that experience with making him an acclaimed artist in his own right.

*Copying the masters*, I thought. *It works in drawing; it works in music.*

I was sure other writers must have tried it, but I didn't know any. So I gave it a go.

After experimenting on myself, then on a group of twenty-two amateur writers, I'm convinced that **Writing With the Masters** is a terrific tool for excellence. I found that copying the opening of a chapter from a classic work—say the opening of Book II, Chapter Eight of *A Tale of Two Cities*—for fifteen minutes, then turning to my own work, made me feel exceptionally focused and loose: the perfect frame of mind for writing. Also, somewhat to my surprise, I found that copying a great passage is the closest way to *read* that passage. And when we read with fine attention, we learn exactly what good writing is.

My human guinea pigs experienced much the same thing. Quotes:

- "Suddenly I could see the structure of the writing."

- "I never would have gotten as much out of just reading this piece. I never knew how much was there."
- "You realize every word has a purpose."
- "I even learned how the author used punctuation."
- "When I turned to my own work, I wrote with much more focus." (That's exactly how I felt.)

It's easy. It yields results immediately. Here's how.

## WRITING BLAST: WRITING WITH THE MASTERS

- Gather your writing materials.
- Find a comfortable place.
- Enter garret mode.
- Choose a work of fiction or nonfiction that you like.
- Start at the beginning, or select a place anywhere in the book, even the end if you feel like it.
- Read a page or two.
- Go back and copy down the same passage word for word. Do it longhand or on the computer, whichever you prefer. I like longhand. Spend about fifteen minutes, or go longer if you feel like it.
- Pause and reflect.
- Move to your own writing.
- How does it feel?

This is a practice you can use to sharpen your understanding of good writing, deepen your own skills, and kick-start your next writing session. It's not about writing *like* somebody else; it's about writing *as well as* any great author—by learning how great authors do it.

Do a stormwrite on a subject relevant to your book, then do a Writing With the Masters session, then do another stormwrite. Difference?

Needless to say, you can't plagiarize; that is, you can't pass off some other author's words as your own. Not only is it illegal, it brings bad karma. Writing With the Masters is for educational purposes only.

Unlike booze or heroin, you cannot overdose on Writing With the Masters. I encourage you to Write With the Masters at least once a week, or anytime you feel you need some help.

Since I first started working with students, I learned that Joan Didion, one of my favorite writers, helped teach herself how to write by copying Ernest Hemingway's work. Very cool, since I love Hemingway, too.

Below are a couple of passages, with a bit of commentary to get you going, that you can use.

Opening of *Pop. 1280* by Jim Thompson. This is a comic noir novel from 1964. *The New York Time*s called Thompson "the best suspense writer going, bar none."

> Well, sir, I should have been sitting pretty, just about as pretty as a man could sit. Here I was, the high sheriff of Potts County, and I was drawing almost two thousand dollars a year—not to mention what I could pick up on the side. On top of that, I had free living quarters on the second floor of the courthouse, just as nice a place as a man could ask for; and it even had a bathroom so that I didn't have to bathe in a washtub or tramp outside to a privy, like most folks in town did. I guess you could say that Kingdom Come was really here as far as I was concerned. I had it made, and it looked like I could go on having it made—being high sheriff of Potts County—as long as I minded my own business and didn't arrest no one unless I just couldn't get out of it and they didn't amount to nothin'.

This is great. You read it and you can miss half of it. The main thing I got when I copied this was the structure. The paragraph lets you in on the whole framework of the story, and you realize what to expect, and you're already relishing what's going to happen.

Translation of this graph: I'm not a very well-educated guy; no fancy airs, that's for sure. No fancy intellectual *or* moral airs. I'm a pretty nice guy, don't wish any harm on anybody. I'm the top cop, and I understand *exactly* how things work. I've got it cushy as long as I don't rock the wrong boat.

Well, *guess what's gonna happen*?!!! The paragraph all but tells us: This sheriff has got a tough choice coming up, quite the challenge. Just what it'll be, we don't know, and just how he'll handle it, we can't wait to see! Will his fondness for his own comfort trump what's right? Or no?

Here's the passage I mentioned earlier, Book II, Chapter Eight of Charles Dickens's *A Tale of Two Cities*. The chapter is titled "Monseigneur in the Country." It's not Dickens's best known, but it is quintessentially Dickens.

> A BEAUTIFUL landscape, with the corn bright in it, but not abundant. Patches of poor rye where corn should have been, patches of poor peas and beans, patches of most coarse vegetable substitutes for wheat. On inanimate nature, as on the men and women who cultivated it, a prevalent tendency towards an appearance of vegetating unwillingly—a dejected disposition to give up, and wither away.
>
> Monsieur the Marquis in his travelling carriage (which might have been lighter), conducted by four post-horses and two postilions, fagged up a steep hill. A blush on the countenance of Monsieur the Marquis was no impeachment of his high breeding; it was not from within; it was occasioned by an external circumstance beyond his control—the setting sun.
>
> The sunset struck so brilliantly into the travelling carriage when it gained the hill-top, that its occupant was steeped in crimson. 'It will die out,' said Monsieur the Marquis, glancing at his hands, 'directly.'
>
> In effect, the sun was so low that it dipped at the moment. When the heavy drag had been adjusted to the wheel, and the carriage slid down hill, with a cinderous smell, in a cloud of dust, the red glow departed quickly; the sun and the Marquis going down together, there was no glow left when the drag was taken off.
>
> But, there remained a broken country, bold and open, a little village at the bottom of the hill, a broad sweep and rise beyond it, a church-tower, a windmill, a forest for the chase, and a crag with a fortress on it used as a prison. Round upon

> all these darkening objects as the night drew on, the Marquis looked, with the air of one who was coming near home.
>
> The village had its one poor street, with its poor brewery, poor tannery, poor tavern, poor stable-yard for relay of post-horses, poor fountain, all usual poor appointments. It had its poor people too. All its people were poor, and many of them were sitting at their doors, shredding spare onions and the like for supper, while many were at the fountain, washing leaves, and grasses, and any such small yieldings of the earth that could be eaten. Expressive signs of what made them poor, were not wanting; the tax for the state, the tax for the church, the tax for the lord, tax local and tax general, were to be paid here and to be paid there, according to solemn inscription in the little village, until the wonder was, that there was any village left unswallowed.

I love this passage. We're shown how the people live in poverty (and why they do), and we're given a fabulous foreshadowing with the Marquis being 'steeped in crimson' from the sunset. He glances down at his hands (red in the same dramatic sunlight) and comments, "It will die out directly."

Dickens shows us what is going to happen with subtle irony: Red is the color of blood; blood is what will be shed by the lakeful in the coming revolution; and the complacent aristocracy is not long for this world.

The privileged man is riding in style through a land of poverty … Well, I wonder who's going to rise up and demand change? And how might that soft man in the carriage respond to such a challenge? With what level of bravery might he meet his fate?

Dickens is a great one to copy for learning sharply drawn characters, also for dialogue; Patricia Highsmith is terrific to copy to learn how to build suspense; John Steinbeck excelled at portraying landscape and any settings, really; Flannery O'Connor for earnest grotesqueness; James M. Cain for tight yet poetic action.

You'll learn basic and advanced skills from copying the writings of any accomplished author. Copy passages from your favorite books and your development as a writer will *bound* along.

Here's a nonfiction example, from *Black Boy* by Richard Wright.

> The house was quiet. Behind me my brother—a year younger than I—was playing placidly upon the floor with a toy. A bird wheeled past the window and I greeted it with a glad shout.
>
> "You better hush," my brother said.
>
> "You shut up," I said.
>
> My mother stepped briskly into the room and closed the door behind her. She came up to me and shook her finger in my face.
>
> "You stop that yelling, you hear?" she whispered. "You know Granny's sick and you better keep quiet!"
>
> I hung my head and sulked. She left and I ached with boredom.
>
> "I told you so," my brother gloated.
>
> "You shut up," I told him again.
>
> I wandered listlessly about the room, trying to think of something to do, dreading the return of my mother, resentful of being neglected. The room held nothing of interest except the fire and finally I stood before the shimmering embers, fascinated by the quivering coals. An idea of a new kind of game grew and took root in my mind. Why not throw something into the fire and watch it burn? I looked about. There was only my picture book and my mother would beat me if I burned that. Then what? I hunted around until I saw the broom leaning in a closet. That's it ... Who would bother about a few straws if I burned them? I pulled out the broom and tore out a batch of straws and tossed them into the fire and watched them smoke, turn black, blaze, and finally become white wisps of ghosts that vanished.

The passage, from early in the book, starts out sounding kind of mundane. A child's boredom; so what? But as soon as young Richard thinks, *Why not throw something in the fire and watch it burn?* you realize you're about to get hit hard. This is a good one to copy out.

## Writing With the Masters on Your Own

The authors that I mentioned in Chapter Five, Fact or Fiction? are good to use with Writing With the Masters. Just go to your shelves or to the library or to a bookseller, and pick up a couple. You don't need a whole lot of books to benefit tremendously from Writing With the Masters. I might add that a vast number of classics are available to download for free, because they're in the public domain. That means their copyrights have expired (if they had any to begin with), and anyone can print them, give them, sell them, whatever. (But you cannot pretend you wrote them.) Google 'public domain books' and start browsing.

If you find an author who really inspires you when you do Writing With the Masters, feel free to stick with that author for a while and do lots of reading and copying, like Joan Didion did with Ernest Hemingway.

Writing With the Masters can, by itself, take your writing skills to new levels. It's one more arrow in your quiver. Nock it, shoot it, watch it fly!

## ACTIONS

- Write With the Masters! Do it, enjoy it. Let me know how it works for you. Let me know if you fall in love with a specific passage or passages.
- Try an especially long session of Writing With the Masters. Choose a whole short story, perhaps, by a good author, or a full chapter from a novel or work of nonfiction.
- Enjoy the hell out of this. I love it.
- Write on your book.

CHAPTER 14

# Keeping Your Workshop:

## How to Physically Organize Your Manuscript and Materials for Best Benefit

Writing a book is a project.

Projects involve stuff.

Stuff takes up space.

Space is finite. (I believe even Einstein thought so.)

Therefore, your stuff needs to be organized. Even if your stuff is almost entirely digital, that is, on your computer—*especially* if it's mostly digital—you need to organize it.

Stuff that you might accumulate while writing a book:

- notes written on paper
- digital documents (files on your computer)
- maps
- travel brochures
- photographs
- sketches of people or environments
- drawings or diagrams of places and things

- people dossiers
- books
- e-books
- magazines
- newspaper clippings
- lists of websites, URLs, entries in online resources such as Wikipedia
- USB flash drives
- your manuscript pages, handwritten and/or printed out (they will accumulate as you go)
- your supplies: notebooks, pens, toner/ink cartridges

If your novel is set in a particular city, for example, even if you've lived there all your life, you might find yourself browsing used book shops, spotting titles on the city's past, and deciding to pick up one or two. Books of photographs are great to help you get to know your subject better and to deepen your knowledge of certain eras in history. (Some of my novels are set in Los Angeles, and I have a cubby full of snapshots I took for research around that city before I got a digital camera.)

You might find yourself talking to longtime citizens, asking for their memories and writing them down. This is called doing an interview, and that's all there is to it.

You can definitely be a slob and still get your book done. You can have crap lying all over the place. Go ahead, let your pygmy goat herd roam.

However, mess will hinder you. There's nothing wrong with going slow, but if you have to dig through the same pile of junk every time you want to find something, you'll waste time and become susceptible to discouragement.

If you can, segregate your book project. A shelf or two is fine. A drawer in a file cabinet is fine, a $15 file box from the office supply store is fine. A garret of your own? Sublime!

If you have lots of books to deal with, you can pile them in one place against a wall. You need only a few square feet for all of this.

Get a supply of plain file folders. Label them clearly with a black marker or a label maker. Keep them in alphabetical order in your file drawer. The better you keep like stuff with like stuff, the easier you'll lay your hands on it and the more at ease your heartbrain will be.

For instance, you could have a file that says, 'Plot Notes,' one that says, 'Secret Societies Info,' one that says, 'Faces,' etc.

## The Great Secret of Organization

Lots of people start out with a good system, tidy and neat. Two weeks later it's a mess.

What happened?

They didn't reorganize, adapt, or rearrange as they went, and most important, they were not decisive about keeping organized.

And that's all you have to do: If something doesn't fit, don't leave it in some random place that eventually becomes a random heap, which eventually becomes ten random heaps, which eventually becomes a hellhole.

*Be decisive.*

*Deal with it now.*

*Do not take the monkey.*

When I worked in an office with lots of people, we used the term 'monkey' for any problem another person came and wanted to give you. I've noticed, over the years, that people love to convince you that their monkey is really your monkey. My secret motto became: *Do not take the monkey.*

And it should be yours, too. Give away any monkeys that don't belong to you. Act on monkeys that require action in order to disappear, like returning overdue library books or refinancing your home to save money.

Throw out most pieces of paper that come your way, especially if you can easily get another copy if you ever want it.

File what you want to keep. Put it in a file folder, label it, and put it in your file drawer.

That's it.

## Digital Stuff = Stuff on Your Computer

Since agents, editors, and publishers almost invariably want materials in Microsoft Word files, get comfy with MS Word (for short) or Word (for shorter).

Start a new folder named for your project. I like to use all caps to emphasize that yes, this is my freakin' book!

Say the title of your book is THE MOROCCO MOTORWAY MURDERS.

Start a file called:

MOROCCO MOTORWAY MURDERS master file.doc (or whatever suffix is the current one for MS Word).

Or, to save space:

MMM master file.doc

This will be your book. From now on, use your title or its abbreviation as the first word or words of every file related to your book.

My files for this book are named like this:

YGABIY master file.docx
YGABIY outline.docx
YGABIY content notes and sidebars.docx
YGABIY master image list.docx
and so on.

The .docx suffix just means the file has been saved in the most current Microsoft Word version at the moment.

If your book is fiction, or if it's nonfiction about people, you can make digital dossiers using their names or category:

MMM dossier JB Petrovich.doc
MMM dossier minor chars.doc

## How to Keep It Straight as You Go

Create new files liberally. Label and relabel them as needed, and as explicitly as possible.

For instance, when I send a new manuscript (digitally) to my agent, she'll often make comments using the 'track changes' edit mode (this is done by going into the 'Review' or 'Tools' section and using buttons on the task bar at the top of a Word document when it's open) and then she sends it back.

For instance, say I send her a document named:
YGABIY outline.docx

When I get it back, she might have renamed it:
SIMS – YOU'VE GOT A BOOK IN YOU.docx.

I would probably save it as:
YGABIY outline Cameron's comments.docx

Any time there is a change, it is important to note that in the file name, or your most recent version could get lost in a sea of YGABIY files!

## Formatting Your Manuscript

To format something is to arrange it in a certain way. Standards have evolved in the writing world and here they are.

Make your title page look more or less like the sample on the next page. Make your chapter beginning pages look more or less like the sample following that. Use a serif font.

*What are serifs?*

Serifs are the bitsy tips and tails on letters like the ones in most print books. Fonts that have them are called serif fonts.

Sans-serif fonts are fonts without serifs (the word sans is French for 'without' or 'minus'). Argument rages on the Internet on the life-and-death issue as to which kind of font, if either, is easiest to read. It seems sans-serif is easier to read on a computer screen, while serif is easier to read on paper; something having to do with resolution and edges and word shapes. For print, I recommend Times New Roman because it is a familiar standard and looks like the type in serious books. I use it. When on line, I like Arial.

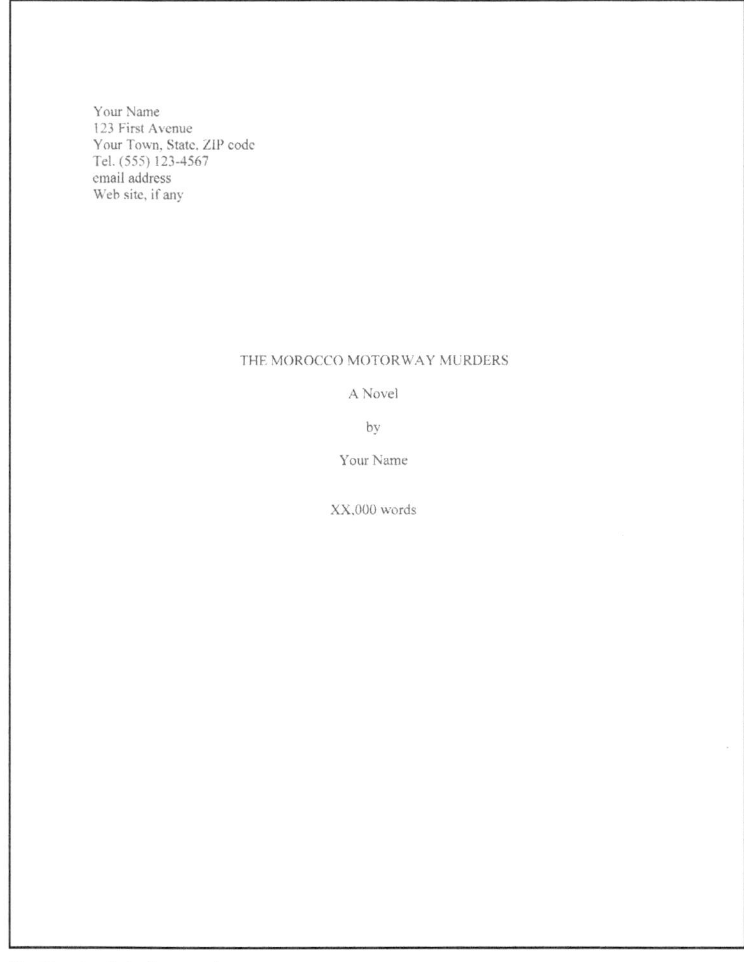

Your Name
123 First Avenue
Your Town, State, ZIP code
Tel. (555) 123-4567
email address
Web site, if any

THE MOROCCO MOTORWAY MURDERS

A Novel

by

Your Name

XX,000 words

Pretty straightforward.

Use first-line indent, automatic text wrap, automatic page breaks, and space-and-a-half between lines.

Publishers want everything double-spaced, but during the writing process when you're printing out copies for yourself to read and make better, narrower spacing will save paper. Single-spaced manuscript pages save the most paper, but they're hard to fit handwritten marks, additions, and notes into.

YOUR NAME / MOROCCO MOTORWAY MURDERS 2

Chapter 1

I never thought about testing the brakes before we set out that day.

The car was a rental, of course, and Lyle had picked it up last week. It had sat in the garage of our villa since then.

More text, your story, more text in nice paragraphs.

"Dialogue! Dialogue!" said Lyle.

I shook my head. "Dialogue."

There was nothing more to be said, so we packed a big picnic lunch, plus several bottles of wine, and set off. The first stop was supposed to be at Maria's house.

And so on.

Text and dialogue, text and dialogue.

Plenty of story, tons of terrific drama, conflict, everything your heart desires in a wonderful story. Characters that seem real! Reviewers will rave, your family will be tremendously proud, and who knows but what you'll be richnfamous one day!

Your margins should be an inch all around, and that's about it.

**Be sure to put a header on every page, as shown here.**

Space-and-a-half works best for me.

If you decide to submit your manuscript to agents or publishers, just 'select all' and change the formatting to double-space. Save as 'MY TITLE for submission.doc' or suchlike.

## HOW TO SAVE YOUR EYESIGHT

Even if your eyes work great, anybody can feel a bit of strain after a long session staring into a computer screen. To prevent this, I use the little magic slider-thing in the lower bar of a Word window to make my documents larger on the screen. Slide it from 100% to 130% or more and see the happy difference.

I like to put a little symbol at the ends of my chapters, usually a diamond. (Found under 'insert,' then 'special symbols.') I put it one or two spaces after the last period in the chapter. Just for fun. My publishers always take them out, but I cling to this idiosyncrasy.

When I come to the end, I change my font to small caps and skip a couple of lines, then center those magic, intoxicating words between two hyphens, like this:

- THE END -

Ain't that purty?

As someone whose first writing job involved an IBM Selectric typewriter and whose second writing job involved large-format floppy disks and the need to give print commands in DOS—no idiot-proofing, no automatic backups, no 'undo' buttons—I learned to save my work like mad. Even though current word-processing software executes backups periodically and automatically, I still hit that 'save' button like a hamster tapping for seeds.

These days I also use an online backup system; there are a bunch of these. I use Carbonite.

There's also this thing called DropBox, which is handy if you want to access your files on different computers.

Today one of my hyperintelligent nephews tells me that the Earth's magnetic poles might reverse soon (they do this from time to time), and when they do, there will be widespread extinctions, huge climate change, and mass hysteria in the human community. But more important, we'll lose a whole bunch of our data wherever the hell we've stored it.

I print out everything.

Because you never know.

## ACTIONS

- Create a digital folder for your manuscript and any support materials for that project.
- Scout around for an appropriate physical space for your notes, printouts, supplies, and support materials. Remember, you don't need much. Claim it. Clean it. Pitch your camp in it.
- Write on your book.

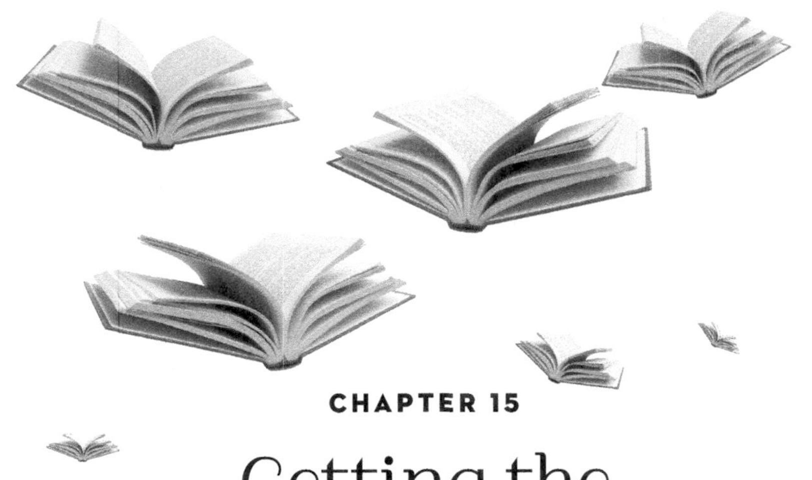

CHAPTER 15

# Getting the Names Right

This is a chapter for fiction writers, but I encourage writers of all sorts to read it in order to develop your ear for names and their rhythms. Besides, even if your book is nonfiction, you might want to fictionalize—that is, change—some names to protect the innocent.

I remember the first time I really thought about character names.

The auditorium was dark except for a pool of light at the center of the stage. One of my all-time heroes, Joyce Carol Oates, was giving a guest lecture at my school, Michigan State University. As her pictures suggested, she was a waif, standing there so pale behind the microphone, with a voice like a small stringed instrument.

I was an intense young writer of short stories, and to this day I remember part of her lecture word for word.

She spoke about her deep feeling for her characters and about her commitment to creating just the right name for every one. I thought of how her characters stuck into me like darts, and I realized that some of their power came from their names: the creepy Arnold Friend in "Where Are You Going, Where Have You Been?," the doomed Buchanan in "Wild Saturday," the primeval Sweet Gum and Jeremiah in "The Death of Mrs. Sheer."

Getting the names right required patience, the National Book Award winner said. Sometimes at night in her sleep a character she had invented but not yet named would appear before her and stand in silence. Oates extended her thin white arm, hand cupped. "And I ask, 'What is your name? Tell me your name!'"

Since then, I've taken character naming very seriously.

Professional authors know that a fitting name for a character is a precious gift to readers. Some names resonate as miniature poems, whether masculine or feminine:

Dracula (*Dracula*, Bram Stoker)
Holly Golightly (*Breakfast at Tiffany's*, Truman Capote)
Atticus Finch (*To Kill a Mockingbird*, Harper Lee)
Becky Sharp (*Vanity Fair*, William Makepeace Thackeray)
James Bond (*Dr. No* and others, Ian Fleming)
Scarlett O'Hara (*Gone With the Wind*, Margaret Mitchell)
Mr. Skimpole (*Bleak House*, Charles Dickens)
Mrs. Gummidge (*David Copperfield*, Charles Dickens)
Little Toot (*Little Toot*, Hardie Gramatky)
Cinderella (folktale, timeless)

Like Oates, you're rarely going to come up with that terrific name instantly; you'll have a character that demands to be born, and you'll have to start writing him or her (or it) without a name. In such cases, I use 'Evil Cutie' or 'Brother A', until I can really work on a name.

I'm against using nonsense names as some authors do for ease of typing during their draft phase. 'Jiji', for instance, uses just the first two fingers on your right hand, in the central part of the keyboard, and it could definitely save you keystrokes during the course of a long book, especially if your person ends up being 'Charlotte Summerington'. However, there is more to writing than saving keystrokes. Every character's name interacts with you as you write, melding with your ideas and feelings for the character. You don't want to stay dissociated from your people for any longer than necessary.

The work of Charles Dickens is great to study for character names. He wrote his first novels as long magazine serials; their character-packed success depended on every name being quickly and easily distinguished in the reader's mind—and held there from one month to the next. Contemporary British authors must have inherited some of his DNA, because they tend to be terrific character namers too (examples forthcoming).

In fairness, I should mention that Dorothy Parker wasted little time naming her characters, using the phone book and the obituary columns. An author friend of mine wanders cemeteries searching for interesting names!

If you think about it, character names come in two basic breeds: those with carefully crafted meanings and those that simply fit a character like a silk suit, impeccable, perfect. We'll look at both kinds, along with strategies for creating them; first, I'll get into 'meaningful' names, which pull back the skin of your characters and can be analyzed quite like literature itself.

## Ironic Names

Large chunks of the plots in Alexander McCall Smith's best-selling 44 Scotland Street series concern the difficult life of Bertie Pollock, a five-year-old (at the outset) Edinburgh schoolboy. Two of his schoolmates are lads named Larch and Tofu. Though minor characters, they're there for a distinct purpose.

The names interact in a savory irony. Tofu and Larch's names obviously have been bestowed by parents with finely tuned ideals. Political correctness abounds: one boy's name is a vegetable paste, the other a tree. Yet the characters, we learn from their actions and words, are as shallow and phony-hearted as their names are sophisticated.

McCall Smith gives us, by contrast, the simple, direct, honest Bertie. He is worth more than Tofu and Larch put together, but he is saddled with those schoolmates. His is an ordinary, unpretentious name; Pollock is a common fish. Bertie, then, is the humble everyman who must endure the idiotic, self-serving vanities of others.

But for pure triumphal irony, can anything top the Veneering family, of Charles Dickens's classic *Our Mutual Friend*? Such a vaguely grand name for a vaguely grand family. Simultaneously, of course, their name clues us in that they are nothing but surface. And we enjoy watching them try—and fail—to live up to their banal aspirations.

Ironic names are easy to create: Just think of your character's opposite qualities and brainstorm liberally. Let's say you've got a clumsy guy who lives with his parents and aspires merely to avoid work and download porn. You could give him an ironic name (i.e., one that describes heroic strength) like Thor or Victor or Christian or even Pilgrim. Or you could give him a first name that's actually a family surname, like Powers or Strong.

New authors who want to use ironic character names should strictly limit themselves to one per story or novel.

## Symbolic Names

We love symbolic names—sometimes. Carson McCullers, in *The Heart is a Lonely Hunter*, manages a good one with John Singer, a deaf-mute who essentially acts as the one prophet in the story. Harry Angstrom, the serial hero of John Updike's *Rabbit* books, has, I think, a particularly good symbolic name. First of all the name has the word angst right in there. Second, as you'll remember from science class, an *angstrom* is a teeny tiny unit of length. An allegory for a man who feels his life is too small—and who by his actions shows that he also might be a bit insecure about the length of a certain part of his anatomy?

But symbolic names are treacherous shoals for authors. Far too many novels (first or otherwise) feature bad guys named Grimes and heroes with some form of *truth* or *justice* incorporated into their names. Also I've seen too many heroines with the word sun in their names, more detectives called Hunter or Archer or Wolf than I can count, and multitudes of good guys with the initials J.C. (Jesus Christ). This latter was evidently too alluring even for literary giants such as John Steinbeck (Jim Casy in *The Grapes of Wrath*) and William Faulkner (Joe Christmas in *Light in August*).

Here's the key: Symbolic names work only if they're not heavy-handed. Challenge any symbolic name with the question: Could a twelve-year-old see the connection during a first reading? If yes, trash it! Keep looking for something subtle, based on your characters' deepest traits, or use another approach like the following.

## Connotative Names

A connotative name suggests without being explicit.

For instance, in Ernest Hemingway's short story "The Short Happy Life of Francis Macomber," the handsome hunting guide is straightforwardly named Richard Wilson, while the client he cuckolds has the fussy name of Francis Macomber. (A fair number of pantywaist-type characters in literature bear the name Francis; Scout's nauseating cousin in Harper Lee's *To Kill a Mockingbird* springs to mind.) In the end, however, Macomber achieves true heroism (albeit brief!), while Wilson is stuck with Macomber's sexy, monstrous widow, Margot.

Another example: Draco Malfoy in J.K. Rowling's Harry Potter series. Here we have the root suggestions of *dragon* (*draco* is Latin for it) and *malformed*, *malice*, and *malfeasance*. A great many other Rowling characters are perfectly named.

You can make up connotative names by asking yourself the following questions as you consider your characters: What expression is on his face when he looks in the mirror in the morning? If she were an animal, what would she be? If this character were a building or a political party or a piece of furniture, what would he be? How is her self-image at odds with reality?

## Phonetically Suggestive Names

Dickens again. In his masterpiece *Bleak House*, he tells the story of the mother of all lawsuits, 'Jarndyce vs. Jarndyce.' The suit drags on and your flesh creeps as that name hammers at you throughout the book: *Jaundice, jaundice, jaundice.*

Ayn Rand's despicable character Wesley Mouch (weasly mooch) from *Atlas Shrugged* is a pretty good example of a name that sounds like an epithet.

Here's an example of a way to think a phonetic name through. What if we had a coach who gambled on his basketball team? Well, it's about winning and losing, and it doesn't matter which if you can make money betting either way. Winning, Winton, Win, Lose, Fail, Failer.

How about Winton Fayhler (win failer)?

## Names Not of This Earth

For science fiction or fantasy characters or creatures, the cardinal thing is to make them readable and pronounceable. Even if you were never into comics, you might remember Jor-El, Superman's dad.

By contrast, if you name your hero Lohrates, your reader will spend the book going, "Lor-AY-tees? LOW-rates? La-RATS?"

A hard-to-read name is an excuse for a reader to put your book down.

Jean Auel did a good job of naming her prehistoric characters in her Earth's Children series (*The Clan of the Cave Bear* et al.): Ayla, Ranec, Broud, Durc, Jondalar.

If you feel wedded to a particular unusual name, at least let the reader know how it sounds by having a character pronounce it for another, or have your narrator do it.

Writers of sci-fi tell me they use foreign-language dictionaries to come up with names. For instance, you could name your shape-shifting monster Modir-Rettr, which is Old Norse for *mother-in-law*. (Roughly.)

You can also work wonders by changing one or two letters in a common name or a word, or you can add a hyphen or initial. Mess around and see what sounds cool.

## Just Plain Perfection

What of names that have no hidden meaning, but just play off the ear like powerful verse?

Anna Karenina (*Anna Karenina*, Leo Tolstoy)
Howard Roark (*The Fountainhead*, Ayn Rand)
Dr. Frankenstein (*Frankenstein*, Mary Shelley)
Blanche DuBois (*A Streetcar Named Desire*, Tennessee Williams)

Such names are the holy grail for authors. You know them when you see them—the rhythm, the grace, the style!—but defining them is almost impossible. Fortunately, it's also irrelevant. All we need are ways to generate those lovely combinations of consonants and vowels.

## A Good Name Template

Judging by successful character names, it seems a strong first syllable in both first and last names works well, regardless of number of syllables. (Harry Potter, Jo March, Robinson Crusoe.)

Here are a few methods you can use to generate pure, plain, good names.

### *Collar Them in Your Dreams*

Awaiting inspiration is perhaps the most organic way to name your characters, though it could take some time. Seriously, though, often you'll be working with a character and their name—complete, perfect, incontrovertible—will simply pop into your head. It can happen while you're writing or weighing plums at the grocery or drifting in dreamland. Accept these pieces of luck as your due. Expect them.

### *Books at Home*

Remember phone books? Leaf through yours and try putting different first and last names together. Phone books, however, are often limited regionally. If you live in a small town in Minnesota, for instance, you're likely to find a whole lot of Johnsons and Olsons but not so many Garciaparras and Hoxhas. I keep a couple of baby-name books handy when I'm in the early stages of an outline or draft. I also save commencement programs.

### *The Web*

You can surf the Web and find helpful reference sites that list first names and surnames by national origin, and you'll find sites that tell you name meanings. You'll also find assorted sites that offer help generating names. Browse around.

### *The Original Web*

But for real inspiration, I suggest going over to your local library, where you'll be amazed at the wealth of name stuff you'll find in the reference department. Besides general encyclopedias, which are rife with names from all eras, you'll find encyclopedias on every specialized subject from military history to music, sports, radio and television, steamships and railroads, law enforcement, crime, and more. All of these books are crammed with names.

The real paydirt in your library is in the genealogy section. Here you'll find books packed with names from all over the world, along with dates. Cities and other place names, too. You might even get ideas for characters right out of those books—or whole plots, for that matter. That's the serendipity of browsing, the fostering of which physical libraries are still unsurpassed.

If you feel a prolonged blank regarding a character name, there comes a point when you just have to choose. Call her Mary and get on with it. There also may come a point when, after you've named a character—even long after—that character informs you of her correct name. It just pops into your mind. Be open to things like this happening. If that character pulls up a chair and says, "My name's not Mary, dammit! Can't you see that I've been Yvonne all along?", well, my advice is to listen.

Whenever you're pursuing character names of any sort, heed common sense and do the following:

- **CHECK ROOT MEANINGS.** It's better to call a character Caleb, which means 'faithful' or 'faithful dog,' than to overkill it by naming him Loyal or Goodman, unless you do so for comic purposes. Some readers will know the name's root meaning, but those who don't might sense it.
- **GET YOUR ERA RIGHT.** If you need a name for an 18-year-old shopgirl in 1930s Atlanta, you know enough not to choose Sierra or Courtney, unless such an unusual name is part of your story. Browse for names in the era you're writing. A depression-

era shopgirl who needs a quick name could go by Myrtle or Jane; it will feel right to the reader. Small public libraries will often have local high school yearbooks on the shelves. Those things are gold for finding name combinations from the proper era.

- **SPEAK THEM OUT LOUD.** Your novel might become an audio book or an e-book with text-to-speech enabled. A perfectly good name on paper such as 'Adam Messina' sounds unclear aloud: Adam Essina? Adah Messina?
- **LARGE CAST?** Distinguish your large cast of characters by using different first initials, of course, and vary your number of syllables and places of emphasis. Grace Metalious (a great name right there) demonstrates this in her blockbuster *Peyton Place*, as do any of the successful epic-writers like James Michener and Larry McMurtry.
- **USE ALLITERATIVE INITIALS** to call special attention to a character: Daniel Deronda, Bilbo Baggins, Ratso Rizzo, Severus Snape.
- **THINK IT THROUGH.** You might notice that in most crime fiction the murderer rarely has a middle name or initial. Why? Because the more you expand the name, the more likely there's a real person out there with it. That person might see your story and become upset, file a suit, or come after you some night with a bayonet.
- **CHECK 'EM AGAIN.** When writing my novel *The Actress*, I wanted a name for a Japanese-American criminal defense attorney, and the name 'Gary Kwan' burst upon me. I loved the name and without further consideration used it in the book. Only thing was, as soon as the thousands of copies of hardcovers were printed and shipped to stores, I heard from a reader who pointed out the simple fact that Kwan is a *Chinese* (not Japanese) surname. I cursed loudly and decided a) that I would *always* check name origins, and b) that Gary Kwan had a Chinese grandfather who adopted a Japanese orphan who became Gary's father. Or something.

## Getting the Other Names Right

You may need to invent names for places, towns, companies, restaurants, schools, fantasy creatures, and sci-fi weapons.

Be open to the fact that inanimate entities have 'characters' too, not just people and pets, and that you can have fun with them.

Jonathan Swift deliberately used clunky, impossible-to-pronounce place names in *Gulliver's Travels*, his parody of the breathless, condescending travel narratives of his day (as well as an inquiry into the roots of human nature). Besides the universally known Lilliput, he wrote about Blefuscu, Brobdingnag, Balnibarbi, and Glubbdubdrib. The names are meant to be confounding, as if he were saying, "Since the more exotic-sounding the better, what do you think of *these*?" He must have been onto something, because his book has been in print without pause since its debut in 1726.

You can place all your characters in a solidly real city, like Arthur Conan Doyle's London, or you can invent whole towns, like the fictionalized Santa Barbara known as Santa Teresa in the works of Ross MacDonald and Sue Grafton.

Most authors need to mix at least some fictional names with the real. When I needed a name for a fictional company in Detroit for a subplot in my novel *Holy Hell*, I could have just flung something down, but the company was part of the story and I would refer to it several times. After some trial and error I came up with Hastings Benevolex, which sounds like it could be any of the countless automotive support businesses in the Detroit area and also conveys a sort of technocratic smugness.

Use the same brainstorming technique for discovering names for your places and things as you used for your characters. What is the personality of this place or thing? What words relate to it? What adjectives? How do your characters feel about it?

Write down the words that occur to you and extrapolate from there: Combine fragments, look to your own past, your own likes and dislikes, and let random stuff bubble up.

Naming characters and places just right is a challenge, but I think you'll find the fun in it. Study the names great authors come up with, let your mind loose to play, do your research, and above all, trust your ear.

## ACTIONS

- Do a mini stormwrite and jot down the names of people you've known and have never forgotten. Friends, sports heroes, politicians, movie stars, criminals, anybody. Do they have great names? Do you think their names might have contributed to their fame or infamy?
- Play around with the names you've come up with so far. If you've got a character without a name, start a list of possible names and have as much fun with it as possible. Visit your library and go on a name hunt in the reference section.
- Write on your book.

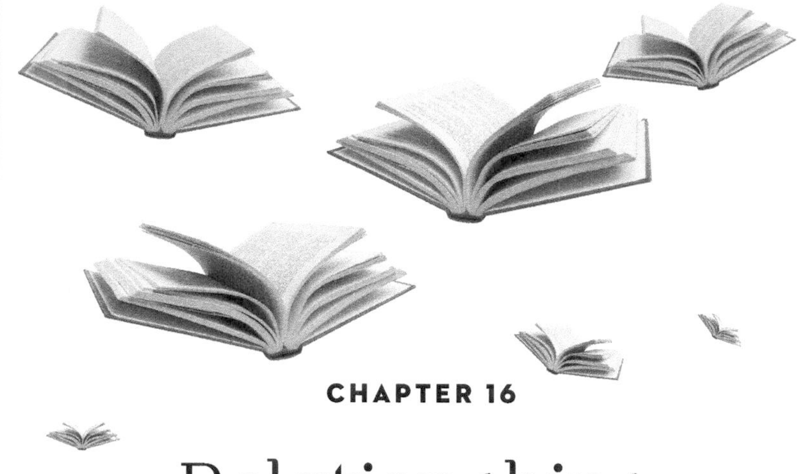

CHAPTER 16

# Relationships:

## The Key to Writing Compelling People

It might strike you that this chapter is mostly for fiction writers, but I encourage nonfiction writers to read it, too, particularly if you're writing a memoir or biography. Why? Because when you think about people as a novelist does, you will understand them better. This will help you bring deeper life to any writing you do.

The very first novel I, aged twenty-something, wrote is unpublished and will stay that way. An ensemble coming-of-age story of four teenagers, its weaknesses are legion: tame storyline, thin action, unimaginatively rendered settings, hackneyed themes. I will say the dialogue wasn't bad.

Having now written a bunch of novels, I look back on that manuscript and realize that underlying the shortcomings I just mentioned is its principal flaw: poor character development. The kids just don't pop.

I've been pleased to read reviews of my Rita Farmer Mysteries that praise the characterization. And I've been struck by the number of professional reviewers who cite the realism of my characters' relationships. I'd been working on writing convincing fictional relationships for years, somehow instinctively knowing that that could elevate my novels above the crowd.

In doing so, I've discovered a rich channel toward realism.

While plot is important, good characters can make or break your book. And if your characters relate convincingly to their world and to one another, you'll give yourself the best chance of success.

Let's consider, to start, the categories of relationships we might write:

- Romantic (with its countless subcategories: Boy Meets Girl, Psycho Worships Unattainable Celebrity, Old Couple Renews Love in Time Warp …)
- Parent/Child
- Sibling/Sibling
- Aggressor/Victim
- Rivals (Equal Adversaries)
- Best Friends
- Boss/Employee
- Caregiver/Cared-For
- Detective/Criminal
- Good Cop/Bad Cop
- Slave/Master
- Human/Environment
- Human/God
- Human/Pet
- Casual Acquaintances
- … and so many more.

Everybody has relationships. Even a hermit in a hut has relationships. Consider his world: You know he has feelings about the fire in his hearth; for sure birdsong has an impact, however subtle, on him; certainly he considers the possibility of strangers approaching.

In your writing—as in your life—you want to take relationships beyond the obvious. Like description, relationships can lapse into cliché. Think of the hero and his wisecracking sidekick, the frustrated housewife and the handsome next-door neighbor, the befuddled father and his precocious child, the renegade cop and the stupid chief. The list goes on and on.

So, when you create your characters, go ahead and give them meaty biceps or thin shanks, blue eyes, hemophilia, courage, a ranch, neuroses, penchants for vegetarianism or anarchy or Lawrence Welk or scuba.

Do this until you know who they are.

Then, explore who they are beyond themselves.

Here's how.

## Make Them Stop and Think

Introspection is the easiest and clearest way to develop your characters' relationships. Make your people think about their relationships, make them challenge their own thoughts and feelings. *I love him, but why? I hate her, because…? I can't be at peace until…? I must do this task for whom?*

Shakespeare was arguably the first master of introspection, via his incisive soliloquies. As storytelling evolved into modern drama and fiction, authors exploited different ways to reveal their characters' inner workings.

An entertaining example is Michael Chabon's novella *The Final Solution*, which merges the Holocaust with British-style crime busting, starring an elderly Sherlock Holmes (though the character remains unnamed through the whole story). You'll remember that Arthur Conan Doyle's original Holmes never reveals himself at all; we come to know him only through the eyes of Dr. Watson, the first-person narrator of all the Holmes tales.

By simply choosing to tell *The Final Solution* in third person, Chabon gives himself complete license to the great detective's brain and heart, portraying him as less self-assured than he used to be—though no less sharp. Holmes, we see, is a particularly introspective hero, beset by doubts and petty worries, struggling with old age and the threatening minutiae of contemporary life he'd been sheltering himself from. Most important, we see how hungry he is for human connections: *Will they like me, will they understand me? Who am I against? Who am I for?* These questions motivate him throughout the story.

When working on your own material, take a little time to tell your readers what your characters are thinking about the others.

Let's say you are writing the story of a father and a son. Let's get heavy and say the son is considering whether to kill his own father, in order to stop him beating up his mother. How juicy is that? What kind of agonies would he go through, if the act were premeditated? And if it weren't, what kind of hell would he experience afterward?

Instead of having the son stand next to a tree and tell the ladybugs his troubles, you could write something like this:

> Roger Jr. fingered the five-dollar bill in his pocket and decided to buy the breakfast burrito instead of two Hostess fruit pies, same price. As he paid the zit-faced clerk, he wondered if he would meet his father in Hell. If, after tonight, a bus ran over him, Roger, Jr., would he go to Hell instantly or would there be some kind of processing period? Would the pain of being dragged under a bus be worse than waking up in Hell? Do they drag people under buses in Hell? Would his father be the one to drive the bus, even? Drive the bus around and around the lake of fire or whatever. Roger, Sr. would rightly go to Hell for what he'd done—for what he'd done for so many years, over and over—but maybe he could work his way out someday. After half of infinity, maybe. Whereas Roger, Jr. would stay in Hell forever because he'd committed a murder. "You're *still* the dumbest one in the family," his dad would say in Hell, one more time, crookedly, what with half of his face blown off. Let's at least be sure to blow off the full face tonight.

## Give Them Strong Opinions

I think some aspiring writers are reluctant to give their characters strong opinions. Why is this? Maybe because we identify too much with them and we don't like to seem overbearing! Well, being overbearing is a flaw, to be sure. But in fiction, flaws are good! Give them flaws that can be fatal. My character Rita Farmer tends to lose her temper. Her anger flares and builds, and before you know it she's doing something she'll regret. On the other hand, her anger can save her—if it comes up at just the right time. And her anger has much to do with her opinions.

In the opening pages of Ernest Hemingway's *The Sun Also Rises*, the main character Jake Barnes does nothing but tell all about another character, Robert Cohn, giving opinion after opinion. From the way Jake describes Cohn and his accomplishments, we learn some things about Cohn, but we learn a lot more about the way Jake thinks, and we see right off that Jake despises Cohn. Soon we also see that Cohn and Jake are friends, at least of a sort. We sense that they may become rivals. Why? We want to keep reading to find out. Why is it so important for Jake to prejudice us against Cohn at the beginning? Perhaps Jake is envious of Cohn. If so, why and for what?

Reread that book and you'll see that much of its power comes from the feelings the characters have for—and against—one another. We identify with their love, and we are appalled by their callousness. We are also educated by it. *This is how some people live.* Is it shallow or deeper than it really seems? Desirable or undesirable? We hold ourselves up to its mirror.

In your own work, remember that every narrator has a personality. Let that narrator's opinions inform his or her character. And by all means, let characters gossip among themselves. An exchange as simple as this young adult situation can paint a sharp little picture:

> "Jeanette has zero self-respect," said Wendy, shoving two skinny sixth-graders aside so she could be first in the cafeteria line.
>
> "Yeah," agreed Dani, crowding behind her, giving an extra shove to one of the littler kids, then looking to Wendy for approval. Then, after a pause, "I saw her making out with Tony after the game Friday."
>
> Wendy whipped around. "Why didn't you tell me? He told me he went home!"
>
> It wasn't true, but Dani did stuff like this over and over. She didn't know why, except that it felt good to get other people in trouble.

## Sacrifice Them

Make one character sacrifice something for another. Countless spiritual scriptures, myths, classics, and modern tales exploit the heart-clutching moment of a character dying to save others, or for a cause. There's Jesus on the cross, Charles Darnay in Dickens's *A Tale of Two Cities*, and war heroes portrayed by authors too numerous to count, though I'm partial to James Jones.

Equally compelling can be a character merely *risking* his or her life for another.

For example, in Margaret Mitchell's *Gone With the Wind*, Scarlett O'Hara puts everything at stake by remaining in Atlanta as Sherman's army advances, in order to help her sister-in-law Melanie Wilkes through a nearly fatal childbirth. The day drags on, it's hot as hell, Melanie writhes in pain impossible to relieve, Dr. Mead is busy with thousands of wounded soldiers, most everybody else has fled Atlanta, and the Yankees are coming. Scarlett doggedly mops the pain-sweat from Melanie's body as the fear-sweat from her own soaks her dress. Margaret Mitchell could have cut this scene without affecting her main plot too much, but quite the opposite, she positively *hammers* us with it. Why? Because *it is a test of Scarlett's character*, pure and simple.

Granted, Scarlett had promised Melanie's husband, Ashley, she would look after Melanie while he was away fighting. But at the risk of her own life? After all, Scarlett wants Ashley for herself. How easy it would be to let Melanie and the unborn baby, well, sort of die!

No. We need to know that Scarlett wouldn't abandon Melanie even under threat of annihilation, because we need to know that Scarlett isn't merely a hard bitch who always gets what she wants. If that was all there was to her, she'd be a fine stereotype in a soap opera, but she wouldn't be an immortal character. We would not love her; we would not root for her in spite of her flaws.

Making one of your people willing to die for another, and putting him or her in position for that to happen, can cause your readers to curse their alarm clocks in the morning.

## Add a Hypotenuse

Make triangles. Did you notice something about the relationships I listed earlier? They are all dyads. Most relationships start out that way, but too often new writers stay stuck on dyadic relationships to the exclusion of more complex ones. Consider F. Scott Fitzgerald's *The Great Gatsby*. Gatsby and Daisy's relationship is memorable, but it's only so because of the huge hulking reason they can't be together: Daisy's husband, Tom Buchanan.

A lesser author than Fitzgerald might have skimmed over the character of Tom. Sure, you'd introduce him, but why spend much time on him? The very fact of his existence, plus the fact that Daisy took a moral and legal vow to be true to him, should be enough.

And it would have been, for a dime novel of the day.

But it wasn't enough for Fitzgerald. He enlarged the character of Tom by giving him a relationship with the narrator, Nick Carraway. Do you remember this? The two men had known each other in college. The relationship wasn't much to begin with, but it intensifies throughout the novel, and it gives readers a deep look into Tom's character. Through Nick's eyes we see Tom's strength, his selfishness, his cruelty, and—in a powerful moment when Tom, baffled, exposing his core, tries to win Daisy's heart back from Gatsby—his tenderness.

Sexual obsession is a terrifically handy tool for the writer: Human emotions are not rational and our relationships are not rational. Sexual attraction is the great motivator of millions of bad decisions—and sometimes, of course, of salvation.

So, consider adding a sturdy hypotenuse to your two main characters and see what happens. The hypotenuse doesn't even have to be human. The third party in a love story can be an animal, a career, an addiction, a call to adventure, an obligation, anything that gets in the way of the cozy dyad you've set up.

## Leverage the Group

When I was a retail store manager (prior life), I learned that the two games that groups like to play the most are Ain't It Awful and Kill the Leader. (Negativity and primal resentment rule!) People behave differently in groups than they do individually, the most obvious and horrifying example being a mob, which is capable of violence far beyond the natural inclination of most individuals. Why is this? The mob acts as both a shield and an excuse. The relationships between individuals in a group—whether a clique of three or an organization of thousands—are never static, but endlessly varied, shifting, and fascinating.

If you are a writer, you are a student of human nature. If you've been focusing on individuals up to now, go deep into groups and see what commands your attention.

Three works that use group dynamics to gripping effect are the novels *A High Wind in Jamaica* by Richard Hughes, *The Help* by Kathryn Stockett, and the play *Glengarry Glen Ross* by David Mamet.

In the first, a group of children fall into the custody of pirates, and the relationships between them serve to illustrate that there really are no rules in this haunted world, and moreover, that the veneer of civilization is thinner than most of us can bear to admit.

In the second, we have three protagonists, each with her own tribal affiliations, which overlap and clash throughout the book. Essentially each character takes on the question, "Why do people do what they do?" The book demonstrates that while groups can greatly influence individuals, the right individual can exercise great power over a group.

Mamet's play reinforces all of the above messages while presenting an absolute spectacle of testosterone-fueled ruthlessness, set in a Chicago real estate office. Competition for money and success drives the men to cruelty, to lying and thieving as one aligns himself against the other, pairs align against individuals, and the group alternately pits itself against the boss, then casts itself in profane servility to him.

One small, subtle moment from the play (which was slightly expanded in the film version) shows how even a passing reference to a relationship can deepen a character and help define motivation. Levene, a struggling salesman, is desperate to get better customer leads, and in pleading with his boss, he finally says, "My daughter..." and trails off.

That's it. No more manipulative words beyond that. Just the simple mention of a relationship—a family obligation, the obligation of a father to a daughter, the obligation perhaps freighted by some special, unnamed circumstance about the daughter—helps the audience understand where Levene is coming from. It shows that he is needy, and it shows that he is so pathetic he isn't above exploiting his own pain.

How can you use group dynamics to deepen your work? The key to remember is that in a group, relationships and alliances are ever changing, depending on circumstances. And we know circumstances never remain the same, so mix it up, stir it around. Figure out how the underdog might transform into a tyrant, or how a fun little secret can become a public threat.

## Befriend Ambiguity

If we wish to write clearly, how can ambiguity be OK? I think Patricia Highsmith is just about the best there is when it comes to harnessing ambiguity in relationships. In her Edgar-winning novel *The Talented Mr. Ripley*, the relationship between the two main characters is sexually nebulous, and the same goes for *Strangers on a Train* and others.

This was, no doubt, due in part to the mores of the time, but this strangely developed ambiguity worked very well to make things feel unsettled, ulterior. Tom Ripley murders Dickie Greenleaf out of a twisted sense of possession, if not love. This is so much deeper and more compelling than if Ripley had murdered Dickie for gain in cold blood, a shallow friendship being their only connection.

In your own work, resist the urge to overexplain relationships. Everybody instinctively understands that there is more than meets the eye. In every adult, there is a bit of a child. In every cop, there is a bit of a criminal. In every sadist, there is a bit of a masochist. In every human, there is a bit of a beast and a bit of a god. This is a deep truth that can help you create characters that are overwhelmingly genuine.

## Never Underestimate the Power of a Grudge

Mythology and folklore are chock-full of motivational grudges, as is life. All of us have probably cherished a grudge against somebody for a while, fantasizing various retribution scenarios, but what kind of personality *acts* on a grudge to the point of destructive vengeance? A sort we know too well from true-crime books and 'Most-Wanted' kinds of TV shows: a person whose self-esteem is lower than whale crap, but whose ego is as big and fierce as Kilauea.

Recently I was studying the mythology behind Richard Wagner's opera epic, *Der Ring des Nibelungen*, a.k.a. *The Ring Cycle*. It all begins with an ugly dwarf, Alberich. (Must all folklore dwarves be ugly?) Alberich tries to seduce the Rhinemaidens, but they spurn him. Spitefully, he grabs the lump of magic gold they're supposed to be guarding.

When later the gold, from which he has crafted a powerful ring, is taken from him by the god Wotan, does Alberich simply say, "Ah, heck, what difference does it make? That gold wasn't mine to begin with, tra-la-la"? Of course not! He's furious, and he rains down curses, and from that point on he's committed to ruining everything for just about everybody. Dig it: Alberich's grudge fuels the entire twenty hours of *sturm und drang*! What's more, in our dark little heart of hearts, we can relate to that! Which is one reason *The Ring Cycle* keeps getting staged to packed houses the world over.

Grudge-holding characters have fueled popular fiction as diverse as Edgar Allan Poe's short story "The Cask of Amontillado," Stephen King's *Carrie*, and Dan Brown's *The DaVinci Code*.

Take a look at *Carrie*. King downplays the quality of this, his first novel, but it continues to fascinate and terrify readers (in enviable numbers). Teenaged Carrie is taunted by her classmates for being odd. She's dominated by her warped, religious-nut mother. The other kids push her to the limit, not knowing that along with her menses, she's developed telekinetic powers.

Why is this story so believable? Because Carrie's eventual murderous rage is believable. And it's believable because King pushed his imagination further than it had gone before. In devising ways for Carrie's schoolmates to torment her, he put her into situations of intolerable shame and degradation, culminating in the pig's-blood drenching at the prom. You read that, and even though you're basically a mild-mannered person, you find yourself whispering, "Kill them, Carrie, kill all those bastards!"

Your readers are going to expect any grudge you create for your characters to be as powerful as Carrie's. So do what Stephen King did: Create a person with a sensitive spirit, then make him or her suffer injustices that would shrivel your stomach.

Then sit back and enjoy the fun.

> CHISEL IT IN STONE:
> GOOD WRITING DOESN'T FLINCH.

## The Energy of Strangers and Acquaintances

If you own a car and are at all like me, you can drive for hundreds of miles without reacting to the other idiots in their cars. Somebody cuts you off in traffic and you shrug or even smile indulgently at the poor jackass. But then one day something inside you is different. Somebody zooms too close and your anger surges beyond all reason. You want to run down that dirty, rude, stinking dog and flatten him into the pavement. You want to bump his vehicle off a plunging cliff.

You want him to die.

You don't even know his name.

Yes, a chance encounter with a stranger can be powerful enough to change your life. Just think what you can do in your fiction, with a little planning and imagination.

Similarly, acquaintanceships can bolster your characterization. An acquaintanceship can serve to illustrate a character trait, or it can foment enormous change in a whole cast of characters.

Good examples are found in Jim Thompson's noir novel *The Grifters*. In the first pages, the character Roy Dillon chisels some money out of a shopkeeper, a stranger. But the shopkeeper catches on and beats him up, setting off an entire chain of events surrounding Roy's recovery from the beating. In a later situation, Roy befriends some servicemen (making their acquaintance), for the purpose of conning them out of money.

A smile comes to my lips when I think of the blackly funny *The White Tiger* by Aravind Adiga, who won the Man Booker Prize for it.

The narrator, Balram Halwai, zooms around India trying over and over to break free of the miserable circumstances of his life. All the while he meets new people. He is used by them and he uses them, with very little personal affection on anybody's part—yet each circumstance is pivotal in some way.

Let your characters approach others, glance off them, then continue on different trajectories.

## An Ancient Symbol Holds the Magic

By now I think you know what all this advice boils down to: Let the yin-yang symbol be your guide. You've seen this circular symbol made of equal parts black and white, with a drop of black in the white, a drop of white in the black. No relationship is clear-cut or one-sided. Leaven the love with a little fear, or maybe even hate.

I believe that if you spend some time thinking about relationships, you'll discover opportunities to develop your characters further than you ever imagined. Because characters *are* us—people. Relationships reveal the various roles we play, the ever-changing masks we all wear, and the yearnings that expose our hearts.

### ACTIONS

- List out a few of your people. What are their relationships? Write them down. Sometimes relationships are more than one way—a parent and a child, caregiver and cared-for, could also be friends. How might these roles interact? How might they foster conflict? Get to thinking about relationships and how you can change and enhance them. Make notes as you go.
- Answer these questions: Who is the steady one in your story? What might happen to upset that person? Who is the loose cannon? How might these two interact? Make notes. Just think about this stuff, heartbrain open; let it point you toward writing richer people.
- Write on your book.

CHAPTER 17

# The Source of Great Dialogue: Your Own Ears

Dialogue—the words people say—is a huge component of good writing. Because fiction or nonfiction, no matter what you write, you're going to write stuff that somebody said. The more convincingly you do it, the more you will awaken your readers' heartbrains and bind them to yours.

More than anything, I want to help you *understand* dialogue so that you can begin to think about dialogue as professional writers think about it—as a component of writing that's alive and totally your servant.

First off, let's get in the mood.

## WRITING BLAST FOR DIALOGUE

How We Talk:

- Gather your writing materials.
- Find a comfortable place.
- Enter garret mode.
- Pick one and write about it:

- The first time you found yourself in serious trouble for something you did. Lying, fighting, shoplifting, speeding, perhaps?
- An argument you took part in. Siblings' spat, lovers' quarrel, barroom debate, for instance?
- Have you ever been involved in a proposal of marriage, either the asker or the askee?

- What happened? What was said? Write down the words that were spoken as best as you remember. Just write everything as naturally as it came out, without worrying about grammar or sounding stupid or anything.
- After this incident, were you like, "Yeah, but I shoulda said…" Write that too. Just add it on.
- Write for as long as you like.
- When you're ready to stop writing, stop.

**TRY THIS:** Read what you just wrote aloud. If you can, read it aloud to somebody else, or better still, have somebody else read it out loud to *you*.

How does it make you feel? Are you engaged with what was happening, does your heart move a little bit?

I thought so.

Does any of it sound fake or weak?

I thought not.

Why is that? Because you wrote something that was totally real to you. You wrote honestly and without strain to make up something. You weren't trying to force anything. You were in flow.

This is a key thing. You now know you can write realistic dialogue. If your book is fiction, when it comes time to make up dialogue for your characters, simply be as relaxed and energetic as you just were a moment ago, and **let it come as if it's already happened and you're remembering it.**

If you're writing nonfiction, just be easy and natural when you're writing what people say. Genuineness is better than precise grammar.

Great dialogue:

- sounds real
- fits each individual character
- develops character
- moves the story forward

We'll get at all of these aspects, but first, I'll tell you something professional authors think about a lot.

## The Great Paradox of Dialogue

Authors must write dialogue that comes across as real. Yet why does actual speech sound so dumb when transcribed onto the page?

Here's an example.

> **SHE:** Did you remember to pick up milk? Because Chris had his friends over and they—
> **HE:** Yeah.
> **SHE:** —and like I said on the phone I'm going to make pudding, and I need four cups for the recipe.
> **HE:** Yeah.
> **SHE:** Yeah you got it?
> **HE:** I put it in the fridge.
> **SHE:** What?
> **HE:** In the fridge.
> **SHE:** I'm sorry, I didn't hear you.
> **HE:** It's OK. Is anything the matter?
> **SHE:** No. Everything's fine.
> **HE:** I have to get ready for bowling.
> **SHE:** I think Chris is getting less allergic to sesame seeds. He ate a McDonald's bun in the car with Anders and his mom, and he was fine.
> **HE:** Still, I wouldn't feed them to him because—
> **SHE:** I'm not. I totally agree.
> **HE:** I'm gonna eat, then I gotta get out of here about seven.

Fascinated yet? Me neither.

The reason real speech sounds so dumb on the page is that most of what people say is *really boring*!

Why? Because our lives are not like novels or movies. Most speech is self-referential, repetitive, unnecessary, and mundane.

However, there's gold in it. Real people say unique, remarkable things, especially when they're talking about something they feel strongly about, or when they're talking about a memorable event, like you just did in the Writing Blast above. Those things are like gold nuggets in the fine gravel of a miner's pan. The words and phrases that make your ears perk up, make you laugh out loud, make you cry, or make you seethe with anger are dialogue gold—keep an ear out for anything that makes you *feel.*

The gravel you sift out of your pan is the brainless dreck that people say and forget. It's our job to pan for the gold.

## Special Note on Dialogue in Nonfiction

It's really OK to put lots of dialogue into your nonfiction material. In fact, passages of dialogue break the monotony of monster paragraphs of description and explanation. If you're writing memoir, do your best to remember conversations, then write them. Be as fair and accurate as you can.

Other types of nonfiction benefit from passages of dialogue, too. If you're writing a how-to book, it might be fun to include conversations you've had with mentors or competitors.

Let the people talk.

## Starting to Listen

Real people don't speak words alone. They use tone and cadence to get meaning across.

The word *Oh*, for instance, is endlessly flexible.

Like this:

- "Oh," he grunted.
- "Oh!" Cassie couldn't believe her luck. "Oh!"
- All at once he understood. "*Ohh.*"

You can see the difference on the page, and you can almost hear it. Notice that here we combined the word with punctuation and narrative to add context to the dialogue and achieve different effects. More on punctuation soon.

In plays, you'll see dialogue that might read awkwardly but comes to magical life in the mouths of actors and actresses.

Not long ago when I read a play by the extremely talented Martin McDonagh, *The Beauty Queen of Leenane*, I kept noticing the word 'so' at the end of characters' lines, and I was like, I guess that's an Irish-ism. And it sort of is, but sometime later I heard myself say 'so' at the end of sentences sometimes, like, "I already ate, so." Which is a trailing off with a precise meaning: "So I won't go along to lunch with you guys."

And I heard myself say that and a bell was ringing in my head, and I remembered those plays where sentences ended in 'so,' and I realized, "I *do* that, it's a *modernism*, it isn't totally just an Irish-ism." And I understood another little thing about realistic dialogue there.

Tennessee Williams was a master of dialogue; I recommend reading his plays. Here's an excerpt from *Cat on a Hot Tin Roof*:

> **MAGGIE:** One of those no-neck monsters hit me with a hot buttered biscuit so I have t'change!
> {Water turns off and Brick calls out to her, but is still unseen...}
> **BRICK:** Wha'd you say, Maggie? Water was on s'loud I couldn't hearya...
> **MAGGIE:** Well, I !—just remarked that !—one of the no-neck monsters messed up m' lovely lace dress so I got t' —cha-a-ange...
> **BRICK:** Why d'ya call Gooper's kiddies no-neck monsters?
> **MAGGIE:** Because they've got no necks! Isn't that a good enough reason?
> **BRICK:** Don't they have any necks?
> **MAGGIE:** None visible. Their fat little heads are set on their fat little bodies without a bit of connection.
> **BRICK:** That's too bad.
> **MAGGIE:** Yes, it's too bad because you can't wring their necks if they've got no necks to wring! Isn't that right, honey?

William Inge was also pretty good with dialogue, and while I'm on the subject of plays and great dialogue, I must tell you to read *Who's Afraid of Virginia Woolf?* by Edward Albee. Raw, wrenching, startling—it's just terrific.

You know that every word you write must serve a purpose, whether to move the action forward or to develop a person.

But dialogue, unlike every other aspect of our craft, is an opportunity to do both at the same time. Reading plays really helps you see that.

Reading screenplays is also a fun way to learn more about good dialogue. They're available in libraries, in bookstores, and on line.

## How to Tune In and Get Good

People talk for different reasons.

They talk in order to:

- communicate neutral information
- give warning
- demand
- complain
- manipulate
- grieve
- process stuff
- keep from thinking or feeling
- keep from listening
- express hurt
- fill silence
- declare love
- boast
- lie

Here's an example of a miner's pan that has at least one gold nugget in it. This is an exact excerpt from an interview I did while putting together an oral history project for a symphony orchestra I was a member of a few years ago.

*Wait, what exactly is an oral history?*

Simply the spoken memories of a person or persons, recorded. The recording could stand on its own as an audio version, or it can be transcribed into written form.

This is a female musician talking. A cellist, in fact.

> I remember Leo Sunny, when we were in France, on a symphony tour, and we were sitting in this restaurant, a hotel restaurant. You could always count on Leo to have his violin, and he would always serenade with his little gypsy songs, just wandering around, just this little infectious smile, who could resist that—just serenading everybody, kind of a little bit out of tune and then oh, he would serenade us when we were in the airport when we were sitting waiting, he would serenade us at the airport and also hotel lobbies while we were waiting for the luggage to be packed up. Out of sheer nothing else to do, he'd try to cheer our spirits up, keep us preoccupied. Anywhere, you could count on it.

A piece of gold from this excerpt is the phrase, "Out of sheer nothing else to do." You know? It's so real, so informal. I might someday have a character say, "Out of sheer nothing else to do," or not. If that cellist had *written* her memories of Leo Sunny, I guarantee you she wouldn't have written, "Out of sheer nothing else to do," she would have written something more formal. She'd probably have left it out altogether. Which would be a loss, which is why oral histories are so rich.

Another piece of gold in here is "kind of a little bit out of tune." Informal, kinda funky, totally real.

If you ever have the chance to do an oral history project, jump at it. If you go and ask people questions and let them talk into your microphone and you transcribe it, you will learn tons about natural speech. Unfortunately, while speech-to-text programs are freeing writers from the task of transcribing, the same programs are robbing writers of the highly educational duty of transcribing.

If you're doing a nonfiction book, consider recording some interviews for it. You can even interview yourself! You'll get real words you can use.

As you develop your ear and eye for natural speech, you'll sort through the gravel and you'll immediately pick out the gold, and you'll use it.

Now when I say "use it," I don't necessarily mean insert it into your fiction or nonfiction word for word—though you could, depending on your needs. What I mean is to use it to inform yourself as to how people talk.

Read oral histories when you can. I recommend Studs Terkel's *Working*, which I'm not sure is still in print, but that one is really good for developing your ear. There's another one I have on my shelf called *The Life Stories of Undistinguished Americans*, edited by Hamilton Holt, which is filled with compelling examples.

I'd also recommend reading 9-1-1 transcripts if you can handle it emotionally. You can find these on line. Just Google 9-1-1 transcripts, or Google some famous murder case that had a 9-1-1 call, and you'll see how people talk under life-and-death stress. In some of them, the emotion comes through, and in some it doesn't.

As a writer, you should also develop sensitivity to ambient speech, which is the speech that goes on around you, not necessarily involving you. How exactly do you develop sensitivity to ambient speech?

## Eavesdrop!

It's simple:

- Watch out for opportunities.
- Listen.
- Make notes!
- Look for context.

First, be very aware of your environment, not merely as it relates to you. When something interesting starts to happen, don't turn away out of politeness; get closer. Be a good witness.

Next, tune in to the speech around you and simply listen, really listen. Coffee shops are the cliché place to eavesdrop, but there's good reason for it. Often two people who haven't seen each other in a long time meet at a coffee shop and talk their heads off, or two people with something important to discuss will go to a coffee shop.

For about a year, I did a lot of writing at a particular Starbucks in my town. Once in a while I would see a certain type of couple: a young man sitting drinking coffee with a much older woman. Their conversations were quiet and exceptionally intense. And I saw this over and over, with a different young guy and older woman every time.

And I started to wonder about it. And I started to quietly, stealthily eavesdrop. I started to look at the bigger picture, and I realized that that coffee shop happened to be a few doors down from an armed forces recruitment center.

And I realized that these young men and … their *mothers* had just been to the recruitment center. And they came out and saw the Starbucks and decided to come here and talk it over.

And the faces I saw and the conversations I overheard were too intimate to recount here, but they informed me as a writer. I haven't yet used a conversation like that in one of my books, but all of it is inside me somewhere. It adds to my experience as a person and as a writer. Being a good listener, being a sponge, will help you tremendously as a writer, too.

Practicing being sensitive to the human interactions around you is what you need to do.

Third, make notes. This is huge. How many times have you heard something imperishable, but when it came time to recount it, all you could do was weakly paraphrase? Keep paper and pen handy at all times. It's tremendously helpful to scribble down the pieces of dialogue you hear.

Fourth, look at the bigger picture. You want to gain context. Let yourself draw commonsense inferences. Yes, that young man looks like he's trying very hard to be confident. The mother, look at her, she's scared, but she knows the Army might be the best place for this kid. Why? Maybe because he's got lousy posture and a potbelly and this town has a 25 percent unemployment rate. Might be the best thing.

And that could be a story idea right there.

Reality TV is good for learning dialogue, if you can stand it. I got a good line from a reality-type program on bad drivers: "When my husband George is in the car, he becomes very *argumental*." Well, can't you just hear her talking about her kids and the new Diamonique anniversary band that she guilt-tripped George into buying her last month? Can't you imagine her throwing together a tuna casserole while talking to her sister on the phone about the sister's latest bout with Crohn's disease?

Documentaries are good, too, the ones where ordinary people are allowed to talk at length. I'm a fan of Michael Apted's social documentary series ("7 Up," "14 Up," etc.).

As you listen to conversations, you'll realize that dialogue consists of two things:

- content; that is, the words they're using, and
- delivery

Here is a key point for authors: *One is as important as the other.*

As you listen, focus on *how they're saying it.*

Developing your ear for actual speech will let you use the vernacular for your own purposes.

> *What does vernacular mean?*

Simply the everyday speech of a region or group.

My neighbor told me the other day that he had once again, with the greatest determination, picked up *The Adventures of Huckleberry Finn* by Mark Twain, and he was going to read it if it killed him.

Why was he having such a hard time with it? *You* know: the dialect, of course. Twain was totally faithful to the regional vernacular and dialects, both white and black, of the old South, and it requires a bit of work to make your way through it. Once you get it, though, you get it and you enjoy it.

> "Huck, does you reck'n we's gwyne to run acrost any mo' kings on dis trip?"
> "No," I says, "I reckon not."

Today readers don't have much patience for dialect, so my baseline advice is minimize it if you need to use it at all. Furthermore, readers are extremely sensitive to stereotyping. So this is a tricky area for authors.

If you do decide to use dialect, sprinkle little bits of it here and there to suggest it and let the reader use her imagination to fill in the picture.

Ah! Here's our Cockney friend to illustrate:

> "Glad to 'elp, gov'ner, it's the first house on the right."
>
> versus
>
> "Glad to 'elp, gov'n'r, it's the first 'aouse on the royt."

Cockney is a variation of British English. The second example is actually more accurate than the first, but it gets to be a li'tle much after a woyle.

Here's an example of a common American accent:

> "Elizabeth, your cah has to be moved. You can't pahk on the street overnight."

That example has two words that were changed, to indicate, oh, a Brooklyn or a Boston accent, I guess. You could probably get away with just one and still be successful.

Use your best judgment, and remember, less is better when it comes to accents and dialect.

Your chief goal as a writer of dialogue is to absorb the way people talk and make it your servant. In the next chapter, you'll learn much more about creating dialogue.

## ACTIONS

- Get out and do some eavesdropping. As I've said, coffee shops are great locations for this. Also buses, shopping centers, carnivals, barber shops/hair salons, emergency rooms. Be sure to make notes.
- Get a copy of a good play or a screenplay and read it. Try reading some of it aloud. Notice how ungrammatical much of the dialogue is, and notice how real it sounds. As you read, mark the lines that move you the most. Turn those lines over in your mind and feel their power. Let 'em soak in.
- Write on your book.

CHAPTER 18

# People Will Talk

Now for the nuts and bolts of making your people sound real. I'm a big believer in stormwriting at every opportunity and especially when writing dialogue.

If you're writing along and you feel you need some dialogue but you don't know what your characters should say, do some stormwriting.

## First Stress-Free Guideline to Stormwriting Dialogue

Ask: What do I need in this scene?

Do they even need to talk here? If they do, what needs to come clear? What needs to happen?

Shed your author skin while writing dialogue.

If, for instance, you're writing a scene in which two little children are lost in the woods, you might think about the dynamics between the two—who will be the leader, who the follower? You might think about the logistics of their situation, and you might fall into the trap of making *them* think and talk that way.

**Two Kids in Woods, Version I**
Joyce looked at the sun and said, "It won't be light for long."

"How will we find our way home?" asked Terrell.
"I don't know. If I had a compass I bet we could find our way."
"Mom and Dad must be worried."

That's not all that realistic. The kids are gonna be kids. They're going to focus on themselves and their immediate feelings, their immediate surroundings, and in a time of stress they will likely engage in magical thinking.

**Two Kids in Woods, Version II**
Terrell said, "I'm hungry."

"Well, we don't have anything to eat," said Joyce, turning away from the tears in her little brother's eyes. "Let's walk this way."

Terrell squatted on the trail. "Look at this caterpillar! I think he's trying to show us which way to go."

Joyce thought that if she could close her eyes and stand still for long enough, she'd stop being lost.

Which brings us to the...

## Second Stress-Free Guideline to Stormwriting Dialogue

Become the character.

Open your heartbrain and write from there. Become the person you're writing about. What do you need, what do you want, what are you afraid of? What do you want to say, what do you want to avoid saying, what will you say instead?

Seek the heartbrain of your character. Go deep into your characters' fears. This works for both fiction and nonfiction. Even a how-to book can be made more interesting if you riff on fear, like "When I walked into the bank for my first business loan, I was so scared I thought I'd have a stroke."

Also remember that people talk *around* issues a lot. It's our job to cut through that. (As writers and as humans, I might add!)

CHISEL IT IN STONE:
THE THING THAT IS HARDEST TO SAY IS THE THING THAT MOST NEEDS TO BE SAID.

Fear is the most primal emotion there is, and a whole lot of behavior and thought springs from it. Sometimes people don't even know they're afraid, and that's a potent thing for a writer to realize—and exploit.

The third and last guideline is my favorite:

## Third Stress-Free Guideline to Stormwriting Dialogue

Be irrational.

I hope you smiled. Because you know exactly what I mean. Humans don't always act rationally, and neither should your characters. There's always a bit of randomness in the things we do every day, the decisions we make, the things we say.

Abandon literalism in your writing of dialogue. People talk in elliptical ways sometimes; that is, they try to get at something indirectly, maybe because they haven't formed a clear thought in their own mind yet. They trail off, they pause, they stop talking while they think, they feel dissatisfied with something they just said, they try to say it over, with better meaning. Show your characters doing this from time to time.

Sometimes we talk things out in order to think them out. Let your people do this, too.

Professionals constantly ask themselves while writing, "Do I even need dialogue here?" If you're uncertain whether dialogue is necessary at any point, try dropping it altogether and add some action instead.

For instance, two characters who are having a conflict could have a shouting match—or they could have a silent fistfight—or they could go through a whole weekend not talking! Imagine writing that. Now that's a challenge I could sink my teeth into.

Although I'm against hard-and-fast dos and don'ts, especially don'ts, here's one:

Do not permit your people to say what they're going to do and then show them doing it. Why? Because it's redundant.

Redundancy = Reader boredom!

Say you have a character who says, "I'm going to make a pan of lasagna and take it over to the house after the funeral." You don't have to show him cooking the pasta, draining the tomatoes, etc. Simply cut to the arrival with the lasagna. Or just cut the dialogue in the first place

On the other hand, when a character says one thing and does another, you have something to show.

> Zoe watched Jim zip his jacket. "Where are you going?"
>
> "To the police station. I'm going to turn myself in."
>
> Zoe let out her breath; she hadn't realized she'd been holding it. "They'll arrest you, of course."
>
> "I'm ready."
>
> Fifteen minutes later Jim stood at Lt. Halsey's desk. "I want to take that deal after all."
>
> "Yeah?" The detective sat back, waiting.
>
> "Immunity for the name, right?"
>
> "Right."
>
> "It was my sister Zoe who killed Senator Carson, and I can prove it."

Do you notice that in this sample, there are no tags like 'he said' or 'she muttered'? You don't need them all the time.

But sometimes you want them. What are some of these tags?

Common dialogue tags:

- said
- asked
- told
- answered
- replied
- remarked
- repeated
- insisted
- yelled

- barked
- snarled
- cried
- sneered
- droned

and many more.

You can never go wrong with plain old *said*, though I do like to use different tags once in a while, when appropriate. Be advised that way too many detectives *bark*, way too many villains *snarl*, and way too many second wives *pout* their words. I kind of like *droned*, which you don't see every day.

You can break a long sentence by putting your dialogue tag in the middle, like this:

> "When I was a boy," he began, "we never thought twice about jumping off that riverbank, especially during spring flood."

Mix it up by putting dialogue tags at the beginning of some sentences, at the ends of others, and in the middle of longer ones.

And as you observed in an earlier example, you don't need to use tags all the time, especially when you're combining dialogue with action. Which, by the way, is a great way to break up long passages of dialogue and make the conversation more interesting.

Two people sitting in a room talking is an unnecessarily boring setting. Why not put them in fencing outfits and make them have a go while they're talking? Obviously fencing would have to be part of the plot, but I'm just saying. At least make them take a walk or a drive. By having them interact with their environment, you can develop their characters. I always remember the opening of John Steinbeck's *The Grapes of Wrath*, where Tom Joad, fresh from prison, catches a ride with a trucker.

During their seemingly inconsequential conversation, a bee flies into the open window of the truck cab. The trucker carefully cups his hand around it and guides it out again. A few minutes later a grasshopper flies in, and Tom squashes it. We are to understand differences between the two men. The whole time they're talking, and the whole time we're learning about Tom from dialogue and from the action.

So, when you have a lot of dialogue to deal with, i.e., you need the characters to reveal a lot of info in a short period of time, break it up with some action—any action—smoking a cigarette, planting shrubs, shooting practice—and you'll be fine.

## Adverbs and Their Cruel Abuses

We've talked about dialogue tags, now we need to talk about adverbs—a.k.a. the 'ly' words:

- he said menacingly
- angrily
- coolly
- fearfully
- cheerfully
- ironically
- quickly
- slowly
- sorrowfully
- …ad infinitumly

New authors tend to abuse adverbs. Professionals, however, have learned that when it comes to adverbs, less is more. Some writing coaches advise not to use them at all, because they want you to *show* readers that the assailant is menacing. But I say, use adverbs only on occasion, because then when you *do* use them, they'll have more impact. Avoid using them as a way to hotfoot it over showing the reader what's going on.

Here's what I'm talking about. Which is better?

> "You don't know me at all," he said angrily.
>
> versus
>
> He slammed the table. "You don't know me at all."

The second example is better, because it *shows* you his anger. "You don't know me at all," is essentially a neutral sentence. Context is what brings it alive.

## How to Portray Emotion in Dialogue

Smart professionals know that mixing dialogue with bits of action is an excellent way to portray emotion. Here's another example, with the narrator giving the clue:

> She groped for a response. "I—I'm sorry you feel that way."

The words themselves aren't so hot at portraying emotion; it's the business that comes before or after them that helps get the feeling across to the reader.

Swear words can get emotion across.

> "Who the hell do you think you are?"

We get a pretty good idea of just what emotion is on display here.

You can have a character betray impatience by being sarcastic.

> "Now, we'll never see Cleveland again."
> "I'm devastated."

So far, we've talked about developing your ear for dialogue, and we've talked about generating dialogue, and just now we talked about some basic techniques. Let's go further.

## How to Give Each Character a Distinctive Voice

This is the single most important goal for you as a writer of dialogue. Why? Because agents' and editors' most common criticism of amateur writing is—and you know what I'm going to say—"All the characters sound the same."

Kiss of death, right?

The main thing is to make your characters speak in individual ways. Which is a challenge, because you're writing all of your characters, and you're only one person.

It would sound fake if you made every character say *everything* in a different way from every other character. There's not a lot you can do with, "Turn left at the next light." But one thing you can do is to use dialogue markers.

## Dialogue Markers

Quick little labels that help characterize how your people talk are dialogue markers.

The key is to place them intermittently, not constantly.

What are the basic dialogue markers?

Well, we want to give your people different and distinct **vocal characteristics**. What are their *voices* like? The way you describe a voice can go a long way.

- "But I love you," he said in his hoarse voice.
- Her voice lilting, she protested, "But I love you."
- His baritone voice broke as he murmured, "But I love you."

This works as a once-in-a-while thing. Obviously you're not going to write 'his hoarse voice' every time the character speaks. But using it judiciously, once in a while, works.

Describe the pitch and timbre of a person's voice early on, shortly after we meet him or her. Then bring it up again, every now and then, to remind the reader of it, so the reader will supply that gravelly voice on her own as she reads.

*What are those words you just used, pitch and timbre?*

They represent sonic characteristics.

**PITCH** is the frequency of a sound; that is, how low or high it sounds.

**TIMBRE** (pronounced 'tamber') is the distinctive tonal quality of the sound. For instance, I just described a voice as being *hoarse*. The timbre of a flute, for instance, could be described as smooth and airy compared to that of a *bassoon*, which could be described as throaty or dark, or even hoarse, come to think of it.

Human voices are just as varied. When you get close to a big, barrel-chested guy and he talks, you can almost feel the vibrations. A high-pitched voice, such as that of a nervous child or woman, can be like needles shooting into your eardrums. Notice these things. Let your *people* notice these things.

You can compare human voices to those of birds, animals, or nonanimate things. For instance, I write a character in my Lillian Byrd crime novels, a butchy female, whose voice the narrator, Lillian, describes as, "like rocks grinding along a fault line." She doesn't simply say, "Her voice was rough," or even gravelly, which I wanted to surpass.

Here's another example that shows how you can use just one word of narrative to characterize a voice:

> He addressed his elderly neighbor, as usual, in a deferential bellow. "Good morning, Mr. Rinaldi!"

He wouldn't just yell, "Hiya, Pops!" The descriptive word is *deferential.*

## Other Ways to Illustrate a Voice

A metaphor is a figure of speech that uses one object or concept in place of another, to suggest alikeness. A simile (pronounced 'similee') is also a figure of speech, but it compares one thing to another.

An example of the difference:

> **METAPHOR:** His voice was a jackhammer: "Do it, do it, do it!"
> **SIMILE:** His voice was as insistent as a jackhammer: "Do it, do it, do it!"

Metaphors tend to be more direct and, in my opinion, fresher. Why do I even mention the words metaphor and simile? Why do I distinguish between them? To build up your knowledge and make you aware of your options as a writer, and also so that you know what the hell literary professionals mean when they use the words.

Other examples, to get your juices flowing:

> Her whisper was like fine snow drifting down his neck. "I'll never tell..." (simile)

> He talked on, his voice silk and flowers. "I've never felt about a woman the way I feel about you." (metaphor)

> "Devin!" Her voice made him jump like a firecracker. "Don't touch that." (simile)

Did you notice that in that last one, the simile really refers to Devin rather than the voice? We need not be rigid about any of this stuff. Have fun and let your imagination loose!

Now, as to what your people *say.*

## How to Give Your People Distinctive Verbal Markers

*Verbal* markers (what they say) are different from *vocal* markers (how they sound when they say it).

### *Contractions*

You can have a character use different habitual contractions, like:

> "I'm gonna watch in case they come back."
> "You guys'll take fifty percent."

When it comes to "Yeah" and "Yes," it rarely works to have a character say "Yeah" all the time; most of us use both, depending on the context. Like this:

> "Do you know where the remote is?"
> "Yeah, here."
> Versus
> "Would you like to go on a free cruise?"
> "Yes!"

### *Elisions*

Characters might *elide* sounds or syllables, meaning eliminate them, like this:

> "We're gonna go swimmin' after school."
> "Prob'ly she'll divorce him."

### *Idiosyncrasies*

A character can use a certain idiosyncratic construction habitually, like "Yessiree!" or "I'm obliged to you," instead of thank you and "Oh, you bet," instead of you're welcome.

### *Interjections*

An interjection is a common dialogue marker. In speech, an interjection is an abrupt exclamation that conveys emotion.

> "Holy hell!"
> "Oh, my word!"
> "Mercy me!"
> "Dammit, Jim!"
> "Oh, no way!"

One of Dickens's characters in *David Copperfield* keeps saying, "Oh, my lungs and liver!" The White Rabbit in Lewis Carroll's *Alice's Adventures in Wonderland*, says, "Oh, my ears and whiskers!"

A contemporary character might say, for example, "Get outta here!" or "Well, I'll be a …" Fill in the blank with something fun. The cliché is "Well, I'll be a monkey's uncle" or "I'll be damned," but you can think of something unique to your character. "Well, I'll be a barbecued barracuda." Something. Take liberties with common clichés and expressions, and make them into your characters' own.

### *Slang*

Slang is nonstandard vocabulary.

> yeah
> megabucks
> reefer

*Yeah*, actually is slang. *Megabucks* is slang. *Reefer* is slang for a marijuana cigarette. I find habitual slang to be useful as a dialogue marker.

**Habitual emphasis** is a cousin of slang, I feel, and can be a marker in itself. That is, a person can be shown to be intense, or overly dramatic, simply by using italics. Like this:

> "I *told* you, but you didn't *list*en. I can't *believe* they left us behind."

Of course any person can emphasize a word here and there, either out of irritation, as above, or another emotion, and you'll use italics to show it.

But you can have a character who talks this way a lot, and that will distinguish that person as a drama queen or an especially intense personality.

### *Idioms*

Idioms differ from slang in that they are expressions that are not understandable or don't make sense if taken literally:

> hit the ceiling
> totaled
> put all your eggs in one basket
> a piece of cake
> to make a silk purse out of a sow's ear

The phrase "to hit the ceiling" is an idiom. "When he found out I totaled the car, he hit the ceiling." Totaled used this way is slang for "declared a total loss by the insurance company." To literally hit the ceiling, you'd have to find a ladder or stand on a chair, make a fist, and pound on the plaster.

All languages have idioms, not just American English.

Make up your own idioms. For example, in a scene in *The Actress*, I needed a Japanese-American character to scold another character. I wanted him to use a Japanese idiom, but I didn't know any, so I made one up. The line goes: "I leave you on your own for one day, and you drop your whole fish box!" So far no one has said, "Where the hell'd you get that fish box thing?"

If an off-the-wall construction occurs to you as you're writing, don't cross it out just because you've never heard it before. Keep it and look at it again later.

You can distinguish a character by having her or him talk more formally than anyone else. Someone who makes a point of not using contractions might be trying to show their high class or esteemed education—this of course betrays insecurity and informs readers about the character. A perceptive reader will see this.

(Note here: **Always** write for a perceptive reader. Don't ever dumb your writing down, even if you're writing for children. *Especially* if you're writing for children.)

## Profanity and You

Since we've touched on profanity, we might as well discuss it.

You have four choices with profanity:

- Don't allow it at all.
- Allow some or all of your people to use it in a limited way, including mild swear words like *hell* and *damn* (this is what a lot of authors writing in the young adult genre use).
- Allow some or all of your people to use it as far as they want to take it, including the f-word and whatever other vulgarisms the characters might need to express themselves.
- Or use fake profanity (which I will explain).

The fact that authors are divided on the subject of profanity is not surprising because *readers* are divided as well. Some really big tough-guy authors such as Lee Child, author of the Jack Reacher series, use no profanity in their books, and lots of readers don't even notice it. Why? Because Lee, for instance, doesn't even write *dammit* which would call attention to the fact that he's not using *god damn it*. And he's certainly not going to have his characters, who blow each other's brains out at the drop of a hat, say *darn it*, for the same reason. This is important to remember if you want to omit profanity entirely.

On the other hand, Tom Clancy, another tough-guy author, uses lots of profanity, and he sells lots of books. I use profanity in most of my books.

You can have a character who habitually uses profanity in contrast to others who don't. That in itself is a good **individualizer**.

What is fake profanity? Well, I really mean nonprofane words used in places where you'd expect to see profanity or a vulgarism. This can work if you want to call attention to the fact that the character's sensibilities are too refined to use profanity, even in an extreme situation. I referred to *darn it* earlier.

Here's another example: You have a police veteran who, in the midst of a shoot-out, gets hit. He yells, "Fiddlesticks!" If you want this to be funny, or to call attention to his unshakeable squareness, fine.

Otherwise, use real profanity, or nothing at all. The police officer could simply scream, or he could yell, "I've been hit!"

## Keeping Track

In fiction, it's useful to keep a list of who uses what verbal and dialogue markers. You can expand on this list as you write, and refer to it when you need to refresh your mind.

Here's a sample. Can you guess which classic fictional character the following describes:

- Swears liberally, but no f-word
- "For Crissake!"
- "That kills me."
- "No kidding, I really do."

It's Holden Caulfield, from *The Catcher in the Rye* by J.D. Salinger. Salinger was *fabulous* at writing dialogue, and I believe it was because of his excellent ear. Study his books with an eye to dialogue and you'll see. No kidding.

## Vocabulary as Social Marker

Educated people tend to have larger vocabularies than uneducated people, and of course an educated person will usually be comfortable enough with language to use contractions, elisions, and slang when appropriate.

If you study speech habits, you'll find that in general, people of lower socioeconomic levels talk more than the upper crust. And you can use this to help distinguish your characters from one another, as well as to develop each character.

In my experience, it boils down to self-esteem more than social rank. Of course, self-esteem often comes with social rank, which is why the generalization holds. But the poorest monk is often a man of great dignity and few words, while an insecure member of the nouveau riche might chatter nervously all over the place.

These are subtleties that you can use, once you're conscious of them.

## The Engine Beneath the Words: Subtext

Writing compelling dialogue is about focusing on what's important. What is the kernel of this scene? What needs to be revealed, what needs to be concealed?

Who needs what?

This issue of what your characters need is one that professional authors go deeply into; they don't stop at the surface.

For instance, if a character is in need of support from another, that's one need. But what is beneath that need? Wanting support might mean the character is temporarily weak due to circumstances or it might mean the character is profoundly anxious and fearful, and has been for decades. Digging deep for your characters' motivations will help bring your dialogue to life. Because the dialogue will be about more than what shows on the surface.

In other words, you must have **subtext**.

Subtext is simply the real issues beneath the surface, the stuff people try to say without saying, the inner feelings that motivate their talking. Subtext is the bush people beat around.

The movies are great to study for subtext. "A scene should never be about what it's about," is advice every student in screenwriting classes hears again and again.

If it's about what it's about, it's dead.

**The exception is sex**. That's why so many authors and screenwriters have a hard time with sex scenes: Sex is about what it's about. Unless, that is, the story calls for conflict or ambiguity, because then you can do more.

If, for example, an argument crops up during foreplay, you have something more interesting going on. Will the couple get this resolved here and now so they can both wind up with some pleasure, or not?

## Subtext in Action

If you're unsure what subtext is, this example will instantly make it clear:

A thirty-year-old guy, who lives near his mother, comes over to see her.

"Mom, I'm going to start college in the fall."

"I thought you couldn't afford it." (Subtext: not happy for him)

"Well, I've been saving from my job. I can take three classes: math, biology, and writing."

"What are you going to do with that?" (Subtext: skeptical)

"I want to be an ichthyologist and study sharks."

"Well, there aren't many sharks around here." (Subtext: hints of fear, jealousy, and desire for control arise through a ridiculous objection)

"Right, I'll have to leave Abilene eventually and transfer to a school with a marine studies program." (Subtext: this is the news he needs to deliver, and he sticks to the point)

"I don't think that would be a good idea, honey. Why don't you study accounting? Then you could get a good job right here in Abilene."

"Well..." (Subtext: he doesn't agree but sees he may not get his feelings across)

"What if fish fail to keep your interest? I mean, honestly, fish?" (Subtext: another objection, this one quite weak)

"Fish are fascinating to me."

"Well, what if something happens to you? It's dangerous to go diving and things in the ocean. I don't think you realize that." (Subtext: subtle threat through another objection)

"I'll be OK. They have all these safety precautions." (Subtext: goals are researched, staying factual, sticking to the point)

"What if you run out of money? Don't think I'll be able to help you. Ever since your father died, I don't have anything extra, you know." (Subtext: another objection by eliciting sympathy, as well as another threat)

"I'll be OK. I'm keeping my job. This time, I'm really serious about getting a science degree." (Subtext: he's caved in to her objections before, but he's changed)

"Ohhh..."

"Mom, what's the matter?"

> "Suddenly I don't feel well. I think it's my heart." (Subtext: now we're really into passive-aggressive threat territory!)

On the surface, this conversation is about college.

But below the words, there is subtext. This conversation is not about college!

It's about the mother's fear of abandonment, it's about her attempts to manipulate her son, and it's about the son's growing independence. Will he give in to her? Will she step up her efforts to undermine him in an attempt to make him stay close to her? Will she segue into an outright guilt trip? ("Oh, honey, I can't believe you'd go away from me after all I've done for you.") That is the subtext. That is what's really going on.

If we wrote a scene about the guy talking to the college admissions officer about class availability, etc., that would be a scene that's 'about what it's about.'

But we wouldn't put that scene in our story. Wouldn't need to. You understand this intuitively; I'm making it explicit to bring it to your conscious attention.

The above sample contains only dialogue and no other business, but you could make things even more interesting by highlighting the subtext. For instance, the son could be fixing the computer for his mom, or the two could be out on a shopping trip, or they could be robbing a bank together, or they could be at a cattle auction (their town being Abilene and all). And the things they do in between their speech can help show the reader the nature of their relationship and what's really going on with it.

Give it a go!

## WRITING BLAST: SUBTEXT

With dialogue there is often disagreement. That's good, because:

Disagreement = Conflict = Reader Interest

- Gather your writing materials.
- Find a comfortable place.
- Enter garret mode.

- Here's a scenario for you: A married couple are on vacation. They've rented a large motor home and they're driving it across the country. The subtext: *Their marriage is in trouble.* He's talked her into going on this trip, thinking maybe they can work on their relationship. But vacations can bring their own stresses! No matter what happens, they can't agree for long.
- Write it for ten minutes. Let 'er rip.
- Check in with your gut as you go along. Let your heartbrain loose. Use **Yes and—** and **What if?** a lot.
- Have fun! Take it to the max!
- Write for as long as you like.
- When you're ready to stop writing, stop.

As you wrote, did you discover or invent more subtext? Like, the husband might be insecure about his job, the wife might want children. The husband is uncomfortable with the prospect of visiting her hometown because her childhood sweetheart still lives there. The situation escalates! I love writing stuff like this.

## A Peeve I Love to Pet

As you write your dialogue, do not have one character tell another character something they both already know, just so you can reveal it to the reader. The cliché is two cops in a squad car telling each other about the rap sheet of the guy they're hunting for. Figure out another way. Try something like this: Knowing that X was a high-profile financier, I said, … or simply let the reader infer. Readers are better at inferring than you might think.

## Phone Conversations

I get questions from aspiring authors about how to use phone conversations in their work. I actually try to avoid writing them in my fiction, but if there's no way around it, keep it brief and have your characters do their processing off the phone.

A phone conversation is a good thing to **summarize**.

> He told me he was breaking up with Clarice, which I'd expected, then he said they were going on one last Club Med vacation together. I gave him hell for that, but we hung up friends just the same. Let's see how much of a tan he comes home with.

That summary can be a phone conversation or an in-person one.

Another very effective technique is to intersperse summarized dialogue with real-time dialogue, especially if you have a long conversation going, with a lot of information to give to the reader. Like this:

> They discussed the kids for fifteen minutes, then Trent said, "I got another speeding ticket today from that same bastard cop."
>
> "Really? Was he in the same place?"
>
> "Yeah, behind those trees on Mill Road."
>
> "That so totally sucks."
>
> Trent changed the subject, but Leslie could tell he was going to stay steamed about that cop for at least a week.
>
> "So," he said, "would you like tickets for that Jets game?"

## Writing Complex Conversations the Easy Way

First of all, challenge yourself to see whether you need as many people in the scene as you think you do. If you have lots of characters who are there just for that scene, for instance, you might combine a couple into one. Leave out anyone who isn't essential.

Physically placing your characters can help the reader make a mental picture. Say you have a bunch of people in a drawing room discussing who the real murderer is. As soon as somebody talks or appears, make it clear where they are:

> "I think the butler did it," said Gen. Kassar from the window seat. Opposite him, at the door, the Fairchilds looked at each other and stayed where they were. Craig racked the billiard balls while Tyler got ready to break.
>
> Craig tossed the rack aside. "You can't be serious."
>
> Mrs. Marten laid her head on the divan's velvet arm. "Will you stop that rackety-yack?" she asked drunkenly. The

> footman fed a chunk of maple to the fire and wished he'd taken his day off like he'd planned. The flames intensified and he flapped his armpits discreetly.

Make sure you use vocal tags:

> In his sissy-boy voice Tyler said, "If I don't win, I don't play."
>
> The footman picked up the errant coal with his bare hand, grunting an apology as he threw it into the hearth.

You can also leave several characters hanging until you need them to talk or act. If you've placed them well, the reader will remember them when they speak up.

And simply use their names.

Readers do appreciate being reminded of who is speaking a little more often when a scene involves three or more people. It's not an intrusion; it's a help.

One of my correspondents recommends the dinner scene from Frank Herbert's *Dune* as a great example of a complex scene with lots of characters talking.

As you write dialogue, use any or all of the techniques you've learned in these chapters. Give your characters distinct voices and individual dialogue markers, and give them some business to do, and you'll be golden. Speaking of gold, here's:

## The Golden Test for Dialogue

Read it aloud.

Simple. I recommended this elsewhere.

How does it sound, how does it feel in your mouth and throat? Even better, read it into a recording device, then play it back and listen. Or give it to somebody else to read aloud to you. You'll instantly hear whether it sounds right. Your attention will be drawn to what *doesn't* sound right. Tinker until it's better.

I encourage you, going forward, to do what I do: Pay attention when you're reading the news or magazines whenever you come across an article that discusses a study about speech habits and patterns. You can learn a lot of little things that will help you. The same goes for material concerning body language and psychology, for that matter.

A good author is a student of people and the language they use. Watch, listen, write it down, search for context.

Simple. Live. Be aware. Go far.

## ACTIONS

- Do a Writing With the Masters session with some dialogue. Pick a passage that includes dialogue from a book you admire. Read it, and copy it. What did you learn?
- Write some dialogue. Set up a couple or three characters and set them to arguing. Why an argument? Because people who agree all the time are boring. Conflict is interesting.
- Write on your book.

CHAPTER 19

# How to Write a Chapter

Chapters, if you write decent ones and enough of them, will accrue into the book of your dreams.

What is a chapter, anyway? It's a chunk of writing that might be one scene in a novel or a few scenes put together. In nonfiction, a chapter might be a cluster of information all on one topic or a particular sequence of events.

## The Essential Truth of Chapter Writing

You do not necessarily need to *plan* chapters.

If you're writing nonfiction and you've piled like with like, your chapters will become evident as you write.

If you're writing fiction or narrative nonfiction, simply write the scenes, or episodes, that follow your hero's adventure. Write the events that occur. Carve off a bit of your Route 66 map and write it. You already know that a scene is an event where characters do stuff, think stuff, and where action occurs and change happens.

You can teach yourself how to write scenes by practicing Writing With the Masters often, for fifteen minutes at a time.

And you can write scenes using a humble tool like this one:

## A Simple Scene Blueprint

A person in your book:

1. sees something
2. evaluates it
3. reacts to it

This is a great little tool. It's a mini arc. You can use it over and over again, with every character or person, and no reader will get tired of it. This tool will help you make a compelling overall arc—that is, your major story line, whether fiction or narrative nonfiction. You show your hero going after something. He or she doesn't get it, gets defeated, then regroups and forges a new path to victory. Scene by scene, that's it.

**BUILD YOUR ARC**

Obey the voice of authority and build yourself an arc.

Then build another one. And another, and another, and another ...

In olden times, lots of authors used early chapters—whole chapters—to set up the story. They spent tons of time introducing people, placing them in time and setting, and filling readers in on the natural, social, and political local history. Plus the weather, oh yeah, we learned a lot about the weather.

Early plays, though, tended to be different. Actors got up on the stage and—well, they had to *do something.*

Which gives us the idea for what comes next.

## A Great Test for Fiction and Nonfiction

Imagine your people on a stage. What are they doing? If nothing, or if it's unclear what the hell's going on, stop and figure it out. Give them something to do. If you're writing fiction, set the people against one another. If nonfiction, figure out something to tell that would be interesting if played on a stage. Cut all the other crap and keep writing.

Because today's readers expect real story and real action right away, from page one on. And that's easy to do, once you know how.

The best way to *get* how to write a chapter is to read some good ones, then do a Writing With the Masters session.

Let's look at a few chapters from well-known works.

## Fiction Chapters to Learn From

*The Big Sleep* by Raymond Chandler
Chapter One

(Before I begin, I want to mention that if you're looking for some fiction that will knock you down with its precision, liveliness, and originality, read some Chandler. A contemporary of his, James M. Cain, who wrote *Double Indemnity* and *The Postman Always Rings Twice* among others, is equally good.)

Chapter One of *The Big Sleep*, told in first person by the narrator, Philip Marlowe, is short and simple. He describes his outfit as nicer than usual due to his impending meeting with the very rich General Sternwood, whose mansion he has just entered.

Marlowe comments on the mansion as he notices a number of things: a family portrait, a stained-glass window depicting a slightly kinky scene, a chauffeur who's visible through another window and is dusting a car.

As Marlowe waits to be shown to the General, a wild-child young woman drifts into the entry hall and aggressively flirts with him. The appearance of the butler chases her off, and Marlowe learns that she is one of the General's daughters.

### *What we learn:*

The chapter gives us just one scene: a man standing in an entry hall. It launches the hero and it launches the story. And the way it does that is by launching questions in the reader's mind:

What's the purpose of Marlowe's visit to the General? Might it have anything to do with that beautiful, feral creature that just dropped herself into his arms?

The General is rich to the tune of $4 million, Marlowe tells us. Riches are exciting in and of themselves, aren't they? Plus, intuitively we know that if somebody who is rich is also old, there might be an inheritance in the offing for somebody.

Chandler's writing is original and imaginative. Here are some samples from his prose: "...little sharp predatory teeth..." "...thinking was always going to bother her..." "There was a smell of cold sea..."

Simple. A few facts, a bit of intrigue, and we're off and running.

*The Handmaid's Tale* by Margaret Atwood
Chapter Twenty-Seven

The main character, a woman named Offred, goes out on foot to do her daily errands with her friend Ofglen. (Get the names: Of Fred, Of Glen. The women are property.)

This is a novel of a dystopian future where a warped and desperate theocracy is keeping fertile women in prisonlike communities, so that they can serve as surrogate wombs for women in the ruling class who have become sterile, presumably from various toxins in the environment.

Out of self-preservation, both Offred and Ofglen have managed to give the impression that they feel supportive of the regime, and they have been rewarded with a small amount of freedom. Now, as they walk, they speak covertly and frankly for the first time, and discover that neither of them believes in the system.

Suddenly a government van pulls up to the curb and agents jump out. They grab a nearby male pedestrian, subdue him, and abduct him.

### *What we learn:*

Again, one basic scene. A street. Two women. A quiet conversation, then a violent abduction.

The main character experiences a major emotional change when she learns she is not as alone as she'd thought. *My God, an ally.* What possibilities might open up now?

A second wave of emotion sweeps over Offred when she sees the stranger being beaten, then thrown into the government van. We expect her to feel terror and outrage, but she tells us she merely feels relief because she was not the victim.

This engages the emotions of the reader, who realizes that terror runs so deep in Offred that it has changed her. Instinctively we know that only a victim of long-term trauma and oppression—a person whose entire existence is a quiet fight for survival and integrity—would react that way.

We turn the page because we want to know how Offred will proceed. Her situation is perilous. The next abductee might be her. Will anything change?

Again, simple and powerful.

> *The Hunt for Red October* by Tom Clancy
> Chapter One

Some years ago I was in Ft. Lauderdale, Florida, for a large meeting of booksellers. A few brand-name authors were on hand as well. I remember strolling around the deep-water marina there, having fun gawking at the biggest yachts, some of them more than a hundred feet long.

I noticed a huge boat with a one-word name painted in tall letters across its stern. The name was OCTOBER. The letters were red.

It took me all of a second to realize who owned it and how he had paid for it.

This famous and widely successful novel is written in the third-person omniscient (where an unnamed narrator tells the story, shifting from one character's point of view to another's at will). In chapter one, we meet a Soviet submarine captain named Marko Ramius, who is taking his vessel out of port, en route to engage another Soviet sub on a military exercise in Arctic waters.

As the submarine leaves dock and makes its way out to sea, we learn a lot about submarine technology, cold-war Soviet military life and politics, and Capt. Ramius's background.

Immediately we sense, from Ramius' thoughts as he spars with the ship's political officer (a Party watchdog named Putin), that he is perhaps not as loyal a Soviet as he should be. We understand it explicitly when we're shown him thinking about his mother's death, which occurred giving birth to him during the siege of Leningrad, and which he considers the fault of the Soviet Union.

Ramius appears to be planning a surprise.

Amidst the minutiae of submarine operations, Ramius meets with the political officer alone in the wardroom and quickly kills him with his bare hands. He stages the death to appear an accident, then he produces new orders he has forged, and sets the sub on a course for Cuba.

***What we learn:***

Clancy lulls us with technical jargon and sinister hints about what's on the captain's mind, then hammers us with a brutal killing that points to much bigger things in store. We're hooked, all right.

This chapter is fairly complex, giving us action, history, a grudge, intrigue, a murder, and a whole lot of immediate questions.

Juicy.

Yet for its complexity, every sentence is simple and basic. Clancy weaves plot and explication together, but if you read closely, you'll see that he takes one thing at a time. This is an excellent chapter to do Writing With the Masters on.

Great lesson: If you have an idea of where you're going, you can have a lot of fun getting there.

## Nonfiction Chapters to Learn From

*No Shortcuts to the Top: Climbing the World's 14 Highest Mountains* by Ed Viesturs with David Roberts
Chapter Seven: "Nemesis: Annapurna"

This is a long chapter, almost forty pages, in which Viesturs, one of the world's foremost mountaineers, recounts his first two attempts to climb Annapurna (in Nepal), one of the world's tallest and most dangerous peaks.

Viesturs tells of the two expeditions chronologically, in quite a bit of detail, and also recounts the months between them. Both expeditions led to failure to summit for him.

***What we learn:***

Viesturs, with his co-author Roberts, simply tells what happened. He focuses on the most exciting stuff: a narrowly missed avalanche, a harrowing accident with a power saw at home between expeditions, a summit attempt that involved near-fatal conditions and resulted in a fractured team.

One might think that two accounts of failure in a row would be a letdown for the reader, but in fact the failures only set us up to be more excited to read about Viesturs's eventual triumph. We turn to the next chapter eager to find out how he overcame his failures and made it to the top.

And that right there is a great truth: In life as in writing, mistakes, misfortune, and failure are but stepping-stones to success, *if* we are humble enough to learn from them.

> *The Four-Hour Workweek: Escape 9-5, Live Anywhere, and Join the New Rich* by Timothy Ferriss
> Chapter Five: "The End of Time Management"

Timothy Ferriss, a business-efficiency and lifestyle guru, launches his chapter with the assertion that by doing less, you can get more accomplished. A startling claim! He follows up by discussing his own failures to manage his time well, and by showing how too many people use up their work time doing unimportant, nonproductive tasks. He lays out the logic behind Pareto's Law (a.k.a. the 80/20 principle, which posits that 20 percent of your output accounts for 80 percent of your results) and describes how he put it to use in his own life. Ferriss also discusses Parkinson's Law (work expands to fill the time allotted), then tells the reader exactly what to do to use those two laws and become more productive in less time.

### *What we learn:*

Ferriss begins with a bold assertion, gives us the theory to support it, demonstrates it, then advises how to apply the theory ourselves.

His is a very workable stress-free recipe that any how-to author can follow:

1. Make a claim (the bolder the better) based on your knowledge/experience.
2. Back up your claim with information, personal experience (which is almost always in scene form), and theory.

3. Show how readers can do it themselves.

(I adopted this recipe for the book you're reading, starting with the bold first sentence, "Writing a book is easy and fun.")

### *To learn even more:*

To learn even more and to feel supremely confident in writing chapters, do some longer Writing With the Masters. Pick a book you love, or a book that's a long-term success, and read a chapter of it. Afterward, copy out the whole chapter. Now do it for one or two more books. Chapter structure will find its way into your bones.

Remember, scenes *form* chapters. Speaking of scenes, consider the following off-the-wall thought.

I'm thinking of a conversation I had with a professional actress. I asked her how she prepares to act in film scenes, especially emotionally demanding ones. Somewhere I'd read that Marlon Brando had regretted overpreparing for a particularly wrenching scene in a film; he'd gotten himself so worked up before the first take that he found himself spent, with no fresh emotion to bring to it.

My friend nodded vigorously. "You can overprepare," she said. "I learned to let the moment bring the emotion to me. You have to count on the scene itself to give you what you need."

As always when talking with a fellow artist and craftsperson, I thought about writing. I thought about how the writing process is closely related to what my friend had said. If we dwell in the present, don't overthink, and keep in touch with our heartbrain, the scenes we need to write will flow naturally from our ideas.

> *I heard somewhere that I'm supposed to hook the reader. What exactly is this hook concept?*

A hook is simply a compelling event or piece of information. A compelling event is a mysterious murder at the beginning of a book. A compelling piece of information is that a decorated military captain just killed a government official who had never done him any harm.

Why? *That* is what we want to know. Why, why, why? And best of all: *What's next*?

A good story draws us in by our heartbrain; it engages our emotions. It does so by making us identify with someone in the story. It can happen over and over in a book. When we see a submarine launched from the point of view of a competent captain, we begin to identify with him. When he commits a murder, we feel shock just as naturally as if we'd seen it with our own eyes.

## Two Great Truths of Fiction Writing

1. The only reason to paint a calm picture is so you can disrupt it.
2. The only reason to paint a violent picture is so you can resolve it. (After, of course, upping the violence and amping the distress, etc.)

*How about hooks for nonfiction?*

The title itself can be your main hook for your nonfiction book, like Tim Ferriss's *The Four-Hour Workweek*. Arresting, interesting, attractive! The world abounds with great nonfiction book titles that hooked readers before they'd read a word of the book, let alone bought it. *Europe on $5 a Day* (a while back!). *How to Win Friends and Influence People. Black Boy. Feel the Fear and Do It Anyway.*

Chapter titles can be hooks. Declare your truth, then support it!

## The Secret to Ending Chapters With a Bang

The most important page turns in any book are the ones at the ends of the chapters. Why? Because readers tell themselves, "I swear I will turn out the light at the end of this chapter, because I am committed to going to yoga at 6:30 tomorrow morning."

An alarming 40 percent[1] of readers who put a book down before finishing it never pick it up again. Stuff gets in the way: kids, work, Columbo reruns, Facebook.

So you simply have to keep them reading to the end.

As a novice writer, I pondered chapter endings. How was I supposed to do it right? I couldn't throw in a car wreck or an assassina-

---

[1] *This statistic came to me in a horrifying nightmare several years ago.*

tion or a dangling hero or a miraculous cure at the end of every single chapter; that would be ridiculous.

The answer came to me in the middle of my first novel, *Holy Hell*:

You don't create heart-clutching moments in order to end a chapter. You end a chapter when you get to one of your naturally occurring HCMs.

More specifically, when you come to a point *just before* or *just after* an HCM, break your chapter.

This works every time. Realistically, of course, you don't have thirty-three huge HCMs in a book; you might only have five or ten. So in the meantime, break chapters at smaller HCMs or change points:

- a turning point (where something or someone is about to change)
- a jump in time or place
- a shift between characters' POVs
- a settling of the action
- a ramping-up of the action

These chapter breaks tend to be quieter, but no matter, you must still give your readers a compelling reason to turn that page. It doesn't have to be big: a pique, a prick, a whiff.

### *Here's an example of how to shape a chapter ending:*

My agent, Cameron McClure, is a demanding reader whose opinions I value. After reading my working draft of *On Location*, she sent me notes, including one concerning this chapter ending. The proprietor of a filling station in the storm-soaked Pacific Northwest is concluding a conversation with a visitor:

> "First Truck goes off without telling me, now Joey. The gas pump busts, and I'm here selling no gas. No garage work gettin' done either, I'm sure you notice. Turned away a brake job this morning."

Cameron wrote: "This isn't a good way to end a chapter—it doesn't feel over. You do such a good job with chapter endings, and making things feel wrapped up, yet throwing in some detail or aspect that makes the reader want to read on and know more, that this half-assed chapter ending really sticks out. Can you fix?"

(Side note: As an author, you must develop the necessary dermatological depth to be OK when your own agent calls your work half-assed.)

I pondered her request and realized that I could add a feeling of menace and uncertainty.

I left everything the way it was, but added this paragraph to close the chapter, consisting of internal thoughts of the visitor:

> When I went out, the moss on the bulletin board looked like it'd grown an inch longer since I'd gone in. The moss, I realized, thrived on the heavy moisture in the air, and the wood that hosted it was decaying because of the same. The wet giveth, and the wet taketh away. Yeah, that was written all over this place.

The day after writing that, I gave a talk in a bookstore about reading and writing mysteries, and I used this very thing as an example of working together with an agent: If the agent has good suggestions, you take them. I read the original chapter ending to my audience, then Cameron's criticism of it. Then I read the added paragraph, and listened as they collectively made a soft little 'yeah' sound.

For nonfiction, you can't go wrong dividing your material into short sections with snappy headings in bold type.

In any kind of book, your chapters can be very short or quite long. But as we all know, short stuff is more easily digestible in our ADD world. I've written some long chapters in this book with confidence, because I know that writers tend to have longer-than-typical attention spans.

*Should I put in photos or images?*

Readers love pictures, and human beings learn from images that demonstrate a point. If your nonfiction book will be better and more interesting with some photographs, diagrams, charts, or drawings, put them in. Your publisher will tell you how to prepare them. If you're going to self-publish, your printer or digital partner will tell you what to do.

Some novelists are putting in images and photographs, so if you feel like it, go ahead.

Above all, have fun choosing and producing your images. Walk around with a digital camera and see what happens. Grab a sketch pad and a big ol' marker and express what words can't say.

**LET THE POWER FLOW**

As you accumulate chapters, your book will take shape. You'll get a growing feeling of power.

And that's magic.

## ACTIONS

- Look at your book so far and identify the high points. That is, the emotional grabbers, the hooks, the best HCMs. Pick one and stormwrite on it, challenging yourself to make it even more exciting. Heighten the danger, take away something from somebody, inject conflict.
- Write with the Masters for fiction. Pick a passage by an author known for writing good suspense. Read it, then ask: How did this author build suspense in the scene? Then copy it, and ask the same question. You'll know more. (P.S. All good novels, whether romance, crime, or sci-fi depend on suspense, a.k.a. tension. There's always conflict, and the reader always wants to know what's gonna happen next!)
- Write with the Masters for nonfiction. Pick a passage by an author known for compelling work. Read it, then ask: How did this author convince me of her point? Then copy it, and ask the same question. Apply what you learn to your own work.
- Write on your book.

CHAPTER 20

# The Power of Lists

If you were in charge of a toddler who's gotten her room horribly messy and you want her to learn how to clean it up, you wouldn't just yell, "Clean up your room!" and slam the door.

Why? Because you instinctively know that such a formless directive will overload the child, who will stand in the middle of the room without the faintest idea of how to begin.

Instead, it might occur to you to suggest that she start by clearing a large space on the floor. You'd suggest she start piling things that are alike together. "Your blocks could go here, your dolls could go here, your cars could go here."

The child will instantly grasp what to do and will feel in control.

You wouldn't suggest too many steps at a time because, again, that would distract and overload her.

You'd want to explain how to do it, step by small step. "As soon as all the blocks are together, you can put them in their bag."

This way, bit by bit, the child can tidy up the whole room by herself—and have an idea how to go about it solo the next time.

There are two valuable lessons here:

1) **Don't overload, take it little by little.**

and

2) **Pile similar stuff together.**

*What does this have to do with us?*

When it comes to writing, we are all small children.

Every project is different. We are new to everything, all the time. What a glorious life! Every question that we pose for ourselves is new, everything we do is fresh.

It follows that if you overload yourself by trying to figure out the whole project at once, let alone *write* it all at once, you'll stand there with your hands on your hips, your heart sinking. With perhaps one small tear inching down your cheek.

**THE LITTLE LEADS TO THE BIG...**

...which is why writing about details can prompt your heartbrain to new scenes, new ideas. So write your way into something small, and let it get bigger, further, different, developed. Love your ideas. Let 'em loose, let 'em run, then chase 'em down!

Taking it step-by-step, without hurrying, but without dragging your feet about it, will give you the results you want: free, happy writing, in manageable hunks, that will add up to the book of your dreams.

The best way for a writer to avoid overload and pile like with like is unbelievably simple: Make lists. Because once it's down on paper, you don't have to hold it in your head. You're free to focus on writing one well-defined piece at a time.

Professional authors write lists all the time. Why? Because it's liberating, helpful, and fun.

### *Lists to help avoid overload:*

- Not happy with a character name? Get going on a list of possibilities. Throw in anything, no matter how dull or weird. Don't just think about it, write it down.
- Unsure of how your hero should respond after a particular setback? Play around with ideas; make a list.
- Wondering how detailed to make your book on wilderness camping? Write lists of the aspects, pieces, and information

you'd like to cover, then pick one thing to write fully. When you're done, calculate the number of words it would take to do the same for all of your items. Then you can judge if you need more or less material to cover the bases.

- Can't choose which anecdotes from combat training before your tour in Vietnam to put in your book? List them all, then sort through for the most powerful ones, the funniest ones, the saddest ones.

***Lists to help you pile like with like:***

- If your book is about knitting, pile the information on equipment together (needles, etc.) and do the same for materials (yarns), technique (stitches), and patterns. You'll soon have plans for coherent sections. Maybe add a section on troubleshooting. History. What's going on in the field today, perhaps.
- If your book is a family memoir, pile stuff about each person together, then arrange it chronologically. Voila your book.
- If your book is a novel, pile scenes and notes together according to your list of heart-clutching moments. Doing so makes writing so much easier.

The list itself can lead you to solve all manner of issues.

If you put each thing on a separate sheet of paper or index card, you can organize them any way that seems right.

## How to Leverage Lists

Let your lists sit for a bit. Go back to them. What stuff seems best? Reviewing a list often will trigger a new idea or a combo of two you've already written down or a twist on another one, and you realize *that's it*!

Then when you go ahead and write, it comes easily because you're free of doubt. You're free to have fun. So satisfying!

What of the leftovers? You're at liberty to save anything you won't use right now. Maybe it's a mundane idea or chunk of writing that you'll throw away eventually, but you don't feel comfortable rushing it to the trash heap. Put it in a folder (physical or digital) with other pieces you've saved from stormwrites and draft pages.

> **JUST WRITE IT**
>
> It can't hurt to sit down and write the scene that's going to go into the book. If you write them all, in whatever order, you'll have your book, and all you'll need to do is put them in a reasonable sequence.

## Lists Can Lead to Great Things

Another terrific benefit of list-making is that you might realize, as you go, that you have a bunch of material for a second book in the making. Your camp craft book might evolve into a book on making your own equipment and another on environmentally-friendly camping techniques. Your novel about a woman who finds romance behind prison bars might evolve into a series about the woman, her convict sisters, and the guards who love them.

*I hadn't even considered the possibility of a second book.*

There ya go.

You can vanquish a dry spell by starting any silly old list about a person, place, or thing that you're writing about. What does Character A hate with a passion? What kind of stores make up the shopping plaza in Chapter B? How many different jobs have I held in my life?

And, of course, a list can turn into an honest-to-gosh stormwrite before you know it. Remember your friends **Yes, and—** and **What if?** Write those chunks that suggest themselves to you, pursue those tangents!

### *Listing is so potent because:*

1. Even though you're not exactly writing your book, you're writing, dammit!
2. Listing helps you prioritize as well as organize your material.
3. It stimulates your mind at the same time as it helps settle and focus it on the full-on writing you're about to do.

4. It leads to stormwrites, chunks, and tangents that can become parts of your book.

## ACTIONS

- Make a list that will drive your book forward. If your book is fiction, think about your villain (or one of them). What does that person want and why do they want it? Let loose and make a list to see if new ideas are lurking beyond the ones you already have. If your book is nonfiction, make a list of obstacles. Past, present, or future. They might be obstacles that relate to a person or obstacles that could come up if the reader doesn't follow your advice.
- Make a list of the kinds of people who make up your ideal reading audience: young, old, pursuing certain careers or hobbies, in a personal hunt for growth, on a quest to find trouble. Whoever they are, make lists about them. Some authors try to focus on one prototypical reader.
- Write on your book. Write to your audience now and forever.

CHAPTER 21

# How to Write Unboringly About Yourself

A friend of mine who works in publishing is a new mother. She recently told me, "Half of my family is Mormon, so there's a lot of moms and a lot of kids. And all these moms write mommy blogs, and out of family obligation I read them. And they're horrible! They're boring. Repetitive, unhelpful, pointless. These women, if they're gonna write, they might as well write well."

A blog is essentially a memoir written in real time. Many people publish their blogs as memoirs.

(By the way, blog is a *portmanteau* word. We know that blog is short for *web log*, which is a diary that you post on the Web. A portmanteau is a large suitcase that opens into two more or less equal halves. Thus a portmanteau word is made up of two words—or pieces of them—that become a whole.)

Before blogs, there were letters. Remember letters? Many memoirs of yesteryear began as correspondence, a best-selling example being Betty MacDonald's *The Egg and I*.

You can blog or write a memoir about a specialized aspect of your life (I'm a mommy; I'm an economics professor; I'm a Civil War reenactor; I'm a bodybuilder; I'm an art curator). Or you can blog or write memoir about your life in general.

The latter has the greatest tendency to be boring.

If you write about a specialization, you can share and comment on anything you read or learn about the subject, in addition to writing about your direct experience. This kind of blog stands the best chance of becoming a successful book. There are numerous companies on line that will transform your blog into a book, basically by harvesting your selected postings from the Web and compiling them. Sport around and see who's doing what.

## Best Practices for Memoir and Blogs

Chapters in memoirs and blog entries have to be *about* something. Conflict, lessons learned via pain, an unexpected punch line: These all work.

To learn how to blog well, follow popular blogs. You will note that the best-loved bloggers:

- don't take themselves too seriously
- write about their mistakes/disasters/embarrassments, as well as their successes
- let loose with strong opinions that they back up with reason, facts, and real-life examples
- appreciate others in their field of interest
- refrain from belaboring any point or opinion
- strive to link their personal anecdotes with something bigger

As you rightly infer, the above points also go for a book-length memoir, especially the last one.

Besides having served as a contest judge for fiction, I've also done so for memoir, and I can tell you that the two most common weaknesses I see are:

- long strings of opinions and generalities with nothing to support them, and
- a failure to offer perspective on anecdotes.

To clarify, let's take my own sentence above where I mention that I've served as a writing-contest judge. If I simply told you that I've been a writing-contest judge, what's the point? It's merely a factoid, a microanecdote. But when I tell you that I drew from that experience and figured out two common weaknesses in amateur memoir, the microanecdote becomes a useful part of this chapter.

Here's a stress-free recipe for a successful memoir episode or blog entry:

- Tell an anecdote.
- Offer perspective by linking it to something bigger. (That is, take it from ground level to an eagle's-eye view.)
- Answer this question: What's the point? Basically, what is the lesson here, what did you learn, how did this incident affect you or change you?

As you can see, we are talking about arc!

A longer example will illustrate.

When I was in the fourth grade, I threw a snowball at a younger kid and made him cry. I felt pretty powerful and good about that, not having younger siblings to bash on.

The kid told on me and I got hauled into the principal's office. The scolding I got made me feel sorry, all right. Why? Because kids got away with stuff like that all the time. I'd gotten hit (in the face!) by snowballs bigger kids had thrown, but did I tattle? No way. Totally unrepentant for the crime itself, I was chagrined that I'd had the bad luck to select a little goddamn tattletale to throw my snowball at. (Anecdote.)

I realized that while bullying brings its own rewards—ah, that rush of supremacy!—it also carries risks. Risks that can be stupefyingly unfair, but still. (Introduction of a bigger topic: bullying.)

At no time did it occur to me to:

- deny the crime or
- cut the kid from the herd after school, give him a good shove and tell him that if he ever tattled on me again I'd kill him.

At that point in my life I realized that I was cut out to be neither a career bully, nor a career tattler. (Perspective.)

I could go further with this line and discuss how, for a tattler, there's never a guarantee that intervention will occur or help anyway. It can even make things worse. Even if a grown-up can help, who wants to be a weak sniveling tattletale? I could also explain how life's unfair. (A lesson. A gigantic, momentous, soul-rocking lesson.) Or how to avoid the bullies, outmaneuver them, or fight back if you have to. (Concrete thoughts on going forward.)

If I were to write this in full length, I'd put in more details about the kid, the consistency of the snow, what the principal said to me, etc. But the point is, the story doesn't mean much to the reader without the bigger picture tied in.

## WRITING BLAST FOR MEMOIR: INTERVIEW YOURSELF

- Gather your writing materials.
- Find a comfortable place.
- Enter garret mode.
- What are your peak memories? List a few.
- What is the very top, most positive one—your triumphant, hey-damn story? Write it, write about how you felt. What about the moment was so great? How were you affected going forward? Write as long and full as you like.
- Set it aside.
- Then write about a painful moment: a regret. Something you should have done but didn't do, or vice versa. If your dark side was involved, go into it deep and write about it. If your regret stems from an innocent mistake, press into the pointless guilt or shame you felt (or still feel!). Write it all. Go as long and full as you like.
- When you're ready to stop writing, stop.

Take a break, then read both pieces slowly. Which is the more interesting piece? Why?

## ACTIONS

- Play around with how you might organize your memoir: chronologically or episodically? Look at your placemat map and see what it tells you.
- Take an episode that you'd like to write about—or that you've perhaps done some writing on already—and do a stormwrite on it, bearing in mind "anecdote, perspective, lesson."
- Write on your book.

CHAPTER 22

# How to Write What You Don't Know

My friend, a Mafia hit man, waved across the room to a buddy of his, a bronc rider. The bronc rider fell to talking with two other cowboys. A hockey goalie lumbered in carrying a heavy equipment bag, and a disheveled sales manager made room for him. The witches had clustered together, and in the distance you could hear a crone's low chortle begin, then rise higher and higher to bone-chilling intensity. The witches stopped in midsentence to listen.

Hell's foyer?

Actually, it was the waiting room of a studio in Los Angeles where eight different television commercials were being cast. I'd come as a silent support to my actor friend Phil, but my main objective was to soak up the atmosphere.

Six months earlier, I'd decided to set a novel in Los Angeles, featuring a struggling actress as the protagonist. It was a daunting choice, since at the time I lived in the Pacific Northwest and had never acted in movies or television.

However, I had spent lots of time in Los Angeles, and I had acted in corporate videos and community theater. It was a meager base to be sure, but I've never been big on, "Write what you know."

Think about it. Most thriller authors have never committed murder or terrorism. Most science-fiction authors have never colonized outer space. Most literary authors have never met someone who thinks in complete, philosophical sentences. Most nonfiction authors are not the absolute, total authority on their subject. And yet the best ones write convincingly about all of it.

## Research = Stuff You Find Out

The main thing that keeps writers from tackling exciting material is lack of confidence. You know, "I'd like to, but."

> *Yeah, like I'd like to turn this cozy little beginning into an international thriller, but I've never even left Wyoming.*

First of all, you know a lot more than you think you know. For instance, you know from books, movies, and television that international air terminals typically bustle with people of all colors and nationalities, and you know that there are ticket counters and porters and people hurrying here and drinking coffee over there. You know that there could be a quiet teenager in a leather jacket carefully watching the passengers exiting the concourse.

The teen turns his head, watches a passenger in a chartreuse dress and stiletto heels walk by, then he sneezes and lets a magazine drop from his hand.

Across the lobby a woman wearing heavy black-framed glasses nods and sets off to follow Ms. Chartreuse.

So what if you don't know what kind of caps the baggage agents wear in Stockholm! If I were writing the scene, I might make up a uniform for them, including a blue stripe down the pants and a handsome billed hat with the airport logo on it.

If somebody were to prove me wrong, I'll simply say, "Oh, yeah, they must have changed their uniforms since then."

Similarly, it doesn't matter if you have no idea how diplomats talk to one another, how to build an undetectable letter bomb, nor the specifics of the secret accords recently conducted in Auckland.

Going further in the global-thriller vein, you know that international law enforcement agencies run the gamut from two-bit border guards to well-funded paramilitary outfits that never show a public face.

The logistics don't matter *that much* as long as they sound good. While it's nice to have friends in high/low/secret places, they're not a prerequisite to any kind of cool writing.

You can find out enough on your own. Moreover, getting good at harvesting useful facts will help your writing and improve your bullshit skills.

## Use the Procrastination Machine From Hell

Start with the World Wide Web. (Point of accuracy: the Internet is billions of computers and cables that talk to one another, and the World Wide Web is the information you find on them. So if you Google a word, you are searching not the Net but the Web.)

The Web has changed *everything* for authors. My gosh, if you want to know what a hubcap from a 1932 Pierce-Arrow looked like, you can find out in seconds on the Web. Google (or your favorite search engine) and Wikipedia are your friends.

You know very well why your computer is the procrastination machine from Hell. You find out what that 1932 Pierce-Arrow hubcap looked like, and then you go, gosh, I wonder what the rest of the car looked like or I wonder how they came up with the name Pierce-Arrow, and I wonder if my grandpa had one, and before you know it you have to abandon your writing time and start cooking dinner.

Also, you know that too much time surfing the Web will sap your wits. Guard against this. Use the Web to help you build iron self-discipline: Set aside time for research, then stick to it. The most successful professional authors do this. When it's writing time, write. Put a question mark, star or other symbol where you need to check a fact or flesh something out, and take care of them all later. Do try.

## Create a Free Clip Service

Whenever you're on the hunt for information on a subject of current interest—whether your book is fiction or nonfiction—do like scholars and journalists do: Set up Google alerts. Just Google 'Google alerts' and you'll find an overwhelmingly easy way to monitor news on just about anything on the planet. Every time something on your subject gets posted and Google indexes it, you get an e-mail with the link. Supercool.

## Read a Book or Two

Read nonfiction books on the subject you feel lacking in. You'll gain a boatload of information, plus you'll achieve insight into how the people you want to write about operate, what they do and think about. Read bios of politicos, spies, heroes, craftsmen, criminals. You'll see how real-life events start little then grow bigger and more complex as more people become involved and time wields its power.

To get historical facts and flavors right, newspaper and magazine archives (either on line or at the library) can't be beat. Be sure to notice advertisements, too. Court transcripts can also be relevant and fascinating, whether criminal or civil.

### YOUR FREE DEGREE

In Britain, they have an honest way to describe 'getting a university degree': They call it 'reading.' As in, "He decided to read law at Oxford." The core of education is reading. You can educate yourself to Ph.D. level and beyond by simply picking up a book that seems interesting to you, reading it, then following your interest to another book, letting that book suggest another to you, and so on. If you're really into a particular great author, for instance, and you've read everything by him, you can often find that person's collected letters. What a trove! You can see what they read and liked, and what they thought about it. And so much of this is *free* at your local library. What a wonderful thing about civilization!

## Dig Deep Into Your Own Life

For a writer, every experience is research. Our whole lives, from getting hit in the face with a ball on the playground to having a heart transplant, and everything in between, it all informs our work.

Here's an example. Say you decide to write a scene in which a person gets shot. In my first novel, *Holy Hell*, I wrote such a scene. Few of us have actually *been* shot, and congratulations if you have because in a warped way I'm envious, but you can write about getting shot convincingly if you do at least three of the following four things:

### 1) Draw on what you do know.

Your own experience is more valuable than you might think. If you've ever been hit in the face with a ball on the playground, well, you're going to be able to draw on that experience in portraying what it's like to get shot. You're going to draw on the feeling of total, complete shock—that deep jolt of getting smacked unexpectedly by a projectile. It stung. It felt like you'd been hit with a bullet!

Use your powers of reason and imagination to extrapolate from that experience. What would it feel like to take a bullet? Well, it's a smaller projectile, but it's going a lot faster, and it pierces your skin and goes inside your body, and maybe it comes out the other side, or maybe it stays in there. It would sting like hell. It would feel hot, because lead is hot when it comes out of a gun barrel. You know that for sure if you've ever touched a gun barrel just after it was fired.

### 2) Look into what other people report about their first-hand experiences.

This is great fun. You can start by searching on line and you'll learn a lot, but it's better to talk to somebody. See if you can track down a person who's been shot. A great place to start on this one would be your local police.

If the thought of just calling up your local police department—or any police department—daunts you, you need to get over it. See Call Reluctance and Crippling Tact later in this section.

### 3) Go after the experience yourself.

In the case of getting shot, you're obviously not going to do it just to gain the experience. But you can buy or borrow a gun and learn how to use it. You'll feel the recoil, you'll smell the gunsmoke—such a great smell! Exactly like when you used to shoot off caps, only more intense. (Paper caps in red rolls—yeah, baby.) You'll go out and shoot some targets. You'll try to hit a bottle, and when you do hit it, you'll be shocked at how fast it jumps. Bring plenty of ammunition, because you won't leave the gravel pit or wherever you went shooting until you've hit your bullseye a couple of times.

If you're going after some other experience, you can go get it. I needed to write convincingly about the wilderness in Washington's Olympic Peninsula for another novel, *On Location*. Well, I happened to be living in the area, but I didn't know what it was like to sleep on the ground near a rushing river in those mountains until I backpacked out and did it.

### *4) Whatever you don't have yet, make it up.*

If you've done a reasonable amount of the other stuff, what you make up will ring true. You can't just start from square one and expect to convince your readers. You might be able to do it for a while, but you'll be opening yourself to some real blunders.

Say you want to know what the inside of a nuclear bomb looks like, because you need to represent it on the page. It has to sound convincing, but face it: You're not going to get a look inside a nuclear bomb casing tomorrow afternoon.

*Neither are my readers!*

You're catching on beautifully.

You might be able to see pictures of the insides of *old* bombs, like Fat Man and Little Boy, and they'll be helpful, but they're not going to be current.

Current atomic devices are top secret, so learn what you can, then use common sense and your imagination to take it from there. What might be different today in a bomb? Well, you can bet the electronics are smarter and smaller. And with the addition of new fictional details, you can bullshit your way convincingly through the scene:

> The guts of the bomb were now open to his scrutiny. As the detonation sequence began, Agent 008 focused on the

> microchips, which were shielded, for fail-safe reasons, behind a thin titanium screen about the size of a credit card. Microchips are delicate. If he could somehow disable one … perhaps something as small as a scratch. Yes, that might do it. Nothing to lose at this point. He snapped the clip off his Montblanc Meisterstück and, using it as a miniature crowbar, went to work.

Or maybe you need a recipe for the perfect poison and have no idea where to begin. Make one up! You can invent something by inventing someone who invents it. In this case, you could create a character who's a chemist and have that character develop a poison that's as lethal as cyanide, as innocent-smelling as strawberries, and as traceable as water.

Be bold!

For my novel about an actress in Los Angeles, I searched online for acting techniques. I read about Method, Stanislavski, Boleslavski, Stella Adler. I reminisced about my own acting experience. I bought maps of Los Angeles and looked at Google satellite images of specific locations. I read books on courtroom law, because that figured into my plot as well.

But then there came the point when no guidebook or Wikipedia entry was going to tell me the ethnic makeup of the checkers-playing regulars at West Hollywood's Plummer Park on weekday mornings (or even whether there *are* checkers-playing regulars) or what a hock shop on Melrose Avenue smells like or how a young actress chasing stardom talks about her craft.

## Sometimes You Gotta Pack the Duffel

My budget was tight, but in order to feel good about writing my book I had to go to L.A. and explore some things in person.

In doing so, I found out a lot about finding things out, which all hold true for fiction and nonfiction.

I gave myself a scant week in Los Angeles to nail down hundreds of details, sensations, and impressions that would make the narrative voices in my novel confident and authentic. So I planned carefully, first finishing a detailed synopsis and character sketches. Next I made a master list of things to find out about, and started telling my friends and family what I was up to.

Because my actor buddy Phil was allowing me to crash at his place for a couple of nights and letting me tag along to auditions, I didn't want to press him to open his black book for me if I could help it. As luck would have it, my niece told me that one of her girlhood chums was working in Hollywood, soon to appear in a movie "with a Baldwin in it." I got in touch and was granted an interview.

On the plane I went into human sponge mode, eavesdropping on other passengers' conversations and reading the inflight magazine, which told me where the groovy people eat, drink, and play in L.A. (Thus I knew to avoid those places because they'll be overrun by the ungroovy who've read the same magazine.)

## Persist and Be Shameless

Gatekeepers would not stop me, I vowed, and I found that persistence and shamelessness pay off. Every morning I jotted out an agenda. If my main crime occurs in Beverly Hills, which of Los Angeles's courthouses would try the case? *Talk to someone from D.A.'s office, check out courthouse. Cruise Beverly Hills, note house styles, distances of houses from curbs, outbuildings.*

One morning I decided I wanted to talk to an insurance investigator, because insurance fraud was a subplot in my outline. I phoned the headquarters of a big insurance company, carefully explained who I was and what I wanted, and after three transfers and forty-five minutes of hold music, got nowhere. I opened the phone book, called a local insurance agent at random, and had a wonderful talk about insurance fraud, investigation techniques, and multimillion-dollar settlements.

Subsidiary lesson: **Do not start at headquarters**. There's too much of a cover-your-ass mentality there.

Even people who seem totally unapproachable will talk to you, if you inquire nicely. At the courthouse I walked into a trial in progress, sat down, and made notes as to the configuration of the room. During a recess I approached the stone-faced, prisoner-wrestling deputy behind the rail.

"I was just wondering where the prisoners hang out during breaks," I said. He hitched up his gunbelt, smiled, and told me about the holding cells, the layout of the building, the surrounding police departments, and the L.A. county lockups and their histories.

It's magic to just ask!

(It bears particular mention that courthouses are public places. If you're a citizen, you're entitled to walk in and hang out in any open courtroom.)

**HOW TO ASK:** You always want to introduce yourself courteously. "I'm Elizabeth Sims, and I'm an author, although you probably haven't heard of me because I'm not very famous—yet. I'm writing a novel, a piece of fiction, and I'm using some aspects of [fill in the blank: police protocol in Los Angeles, for example], and I want to make sure I've got some details right. I don't want to take much of your time. Do you think you could help me, if I run a few details by you right now?"

In this usage, *detail* is code for *question*, like this: "If a murder happened in Santa Monica, would the local police handle the investigation from beginning to end, or would they call in detectives from downtown L.A.?"

## A Word Is Worth a Thousand Pictures

Sure, tourists are expected to take photos of the Hollywood sign and the tar in the tar pits. When, however, you start taking pictures of people minding their own business in a park or bar, or the exterior of a government building, you draw uncomfortable attention to yourself.

But you can, as I did, sit quietly with a small notebook, look around as much as you like, and make detailed notes and sketches. Moreover, the act of writing it down forces you to pay attention to the world of sight, sound, texture, and smell.

## Multitask, Multitask

While waiting to meet the film actress, Jennifer, for lunch, I studied the clothes and hairstyles of the other diners. She had picked an eatery popular with film folk. I saw Phil's screenwriter neighbor I'd met a day earlier when I borrowed his dog for a walk in the Hollywood Hills. (During that walk, I took note of the posh new houses being built next to the old ones, the vegetation, the cries of the raptors overhead, the way the breeze felt coming through the canyon, the way the sky over the city looked as dusk turned to night.)

Jennifer's exquisite looks and utterly self-assured manner made me feel as ravishing as a three-legged donkey, but I plowed into my list of questions. We frankly discussed everything from her strategy for developing acting skills to sidestepping the updated tricks of today's casting couch to the one menu item we both craved but would not permit ourselves: a huge plate of fried potato-plus-yam planks, tossed with fragrant herbs and delivered steaming to the table of two hunky guys next to us.

## Be Open to Serendipity

Accidental contacts can turn gold. While strolling in West Hollywood one evening after dinner, I bought a pack of cigarettes on impulse. After smoking one, I realized I didn't really want them, and gave them to a street guy. Another man came up to me and said, "As a smoker, I want to thank you for what you just did." We started walking together, and it turned out he was a psychiatrist for the California prison system. We talked about crime, punishment, human weakness, and human evil for half an hour before exchanging phone numbers and saying goodnight. How cool was that?

By the end of the week and 500 miles on the PT Cruiser I'd rented, I'd filled my notebook with information and sketches, and carried much more in my head and heart. New plot twists had come to me, and I realized I'd gotten answers to questions I never knew I'd had. It wouldn't all find its way into the novel, but all of it would inform my writing. Keeping my senses open every minute had been the key.

When I got home, I let fly on the page with verve and confidence.

And guess what happened? Right! The novel I wrote, *The Actress*, featuring struggling actress and amateur sleuth Rita Farmer, garnered me a two-book hardcover deal with a major publisher as the first in a new suspense series.

**** BOAST ALERT****

Shortly after my agent made the deal for me, she was having coffee with one of the editors from another publisher who had read my manuscript of *The Actress* and liked it—wanted to buy it—but couldn't get her marketing board to agree with her.

My name came up, and this editor said again, regretfully, how much she'd liked the book. And she said, "Elizabeth *was* an actress in Hollywood before she became a writer, right?"

And my agent said, "Well, I *think* Elizabeth has had a little acting experience, like company videos or something, but no, she never was a struggling actress in Hollywood. No."

The editor said, "Oh my gosh, I can't believe it! I was an actress in Hollywood. I tried to make it for two years before I gave up and came to New York. It was *just like that.* It was *just like* how she wrote it. That's amazing."

When my agent related this conversation to me, I have to say, it made my day. I felt validated. I was like, *yes*, I am a professional, and I know what I'm doing.

The thing is, it wasn't that hard!

My boasting here is to make a point: If you take reasonable care with your research, your writing will resonate with authority. It will ring true to you, and it will ring true to your reader.

****BOAST ALERT ALL-CLEAR****

## Everything Is Research

You can take a detail, one detail, and build from there. I remember being in Las Vegas on business, and one of the things I had to do was visit a construction site and talk to the construction boss. And it was summer, and it was about 112°F in the desert, and I got out of the rental car and went up to the contractor's trailer.

And you've seen these trailers, it had an air conditioner stuck on the outside, and there were three steps up and a thin steel railing. I was wearing street shoes and the ground was uneven, and when I got to the steps I grabbed the railing. And the temperature of that railing was unbelievable; I almost needed medical treatment for my scorched hand. That was when I really felt how life-threatening the heat of the desert is. And I used that hot railing and the sound of all those window air conditioners in Las Vegas when I wrote *Lucky Stiff*, the third in the Lillian Byrd series.

Mind you, those details were essentially irrelevant to the plot. But they helped hold my readers to me. It helped them feel that the story was alive.

## Call Reluctance and Crippling Tact

I've noticed that many writers suffer from the twin maladies of Call Reluctance and Crippling Tact, especially when it comes to research.

How to recognize Call Reluctance:

When you need to make a simple phone call and you keep thinking of excellent reasons to put it off, or you wait until the time zones mesh exactly right, then forget to make the call and have to wait until tomorrow to do it, then you have a typical case of Call Reluctance.

The way to get over it: Don't dick around.

Just pick up the phone. It's like killing a spider over your kid's bed. Don't think about it too much, don't hesitate, just do it.

Decisive action, I might put in, is a strengthening practice in general. The more you 'just do something' right now, stop thinking about it and planning it and just do it, the less your anxiety will be the next time.

> CHISEL IT IN STONE:
> COURAGE BUILDS ON ITSELF.

Crippling Tact occurs when you really need to ask a question that you suspect the other person won't like and you shrink from it. For example, if the Mayor comes into the City Council meeting with a black eye and tape over his nose and nobody says anything, that's Crippling Tact. Somebody has to ask!

Crippling Tact, unfortunately, does not strike the sexes evenly. Many more women than men suffer from it. Cultural reasons, I suppose.

And you just have to get over it. The secret to getting over it is to realize two things:

### *1) People love to talk about themselves.*

They get excited to tell you stuff they know, things that have happened to them. Even bad, uncomfortable things, like getting burned out of their house or having cancer, or even getting caught in a scandal.

I learned this when I was a reporter for a weekly newspaper in suburban Detroit, years ago. That was terrific training for being an author.

I learned to talk plain and ask questions directly. Don't try to beat around the bush or try to find out something without really asking because that just confuses people and wastes time. It is amazing what people will tell you if you ask bluntly and neutrally; that is, without putting any judgmental inflection in your voice.

### *2) Nothing bad will happen to you if you ask somebody a question they don't want to answer.*

All that will happen is they say no, and if they look at you with an insulted air, you just say, "I beg your pardon," sincerely, and go onto the next thing. Or leave.

By the way, when you're out and about, *always* open a door that looks interesting to you. Just walk in. If you're not supposed to be there, simply say the magic words, "Oh, I was just looking for the bathroom."

## An Ancillary Note on Being a Good Person

Aspiring writers sometimes ask me about writing about living people in their memoir or other nonfiction. Fiction writers want to know how thickly they should veil a real person they're going to fictionalize.

I discussed this initially in Chapter Five, **Fact or Fiction?**, but I'd like to add:

A great many books have been written for the sake of revenge or spite. If that is your sole motivation, put down your pen and seek counseling. Notice I say "sole motivation." Revenge alone will not create a good book. First and foremost you have to have a desire to write something great. Revenge, if desired at all, must be secondary.

If the person is a national public figure, pretty much anything is fair game, though in my opinion you should avoid cheap shots and go for something substantial. What's a cheap shot? Calling a politician *stupid*. What's substantial? Examining that politician's path to poor judgment via fictitious situations.

As for individuals you know personally, realize that it's pretty much impossible for a victim of nastiness in your book to retaliate in kind. Consider how you might feel about your book and that person ten years from now. Will your beef still be so important? Consider this as you write.

Even if you don't intend any harm with whatever you're going to write about a person you know (typically in a memoir), it's honorable to let that person know that they're going to appear in your book, and even to let them read in advance what you've written about them. If there's a problem, better try to work it out now rather than later.

If you need more convincing on this, I leave you with two words: *nuisance lawsuit*.

## ACTIONS

- Interview yourself about your book. Write questions and answers. It's great practice, and you'll use the interview when it comes time to publicize your book.
- Walk up to a stranger and ask a question. Anything: "Where did you get your glasses? They're very stylish." Or go up to a police officer and ask something about the burglary rate vs. the assault rate in your neighborhood these days. Or ask what kind of locks the police recommend for your type of dwelling. Feel the fear ebb.
- Write on your book.

CHAPTER 23

# Living With Your Book and Driving It to Completion

Learning to write well and freely is fun. Getting going on your book is fun. Feeling inspired is fun.

Feeling burdened is not fun. Wondering if you'll ever get to the end is not fun. Doubt takes many forms and comes from many places: a vague feeling of anxiety, a disparaging comment from an acquaintance, the sudden thought *Maybe I can't, after all.*

Doubt sucks.

Sometimes doubt creeps in when you're in the midst of your project. You're not sure what to write next. Days and weeks, even months have gone by, and you have a pile of pages and you're not sure if you've got something good or just a stack of dirty paper.

The right attitude to take here is: So what?

Just believe this: You're doing fine.

No deep, dark neurotic crap lives inside you and tries to hinder you from doing your work.

*Not even a little?*

No!

Doubting yourself, or feeling 'blocked' (hate that word with me, please) is not something that happens. It is not mysterious. It is not a force.

Like I said in Chapter Twelve, it's merely the monster under the bed, which, of course, you create yourself. You get scared to set your bare foot on the floor, and the fear can keep you from taking that first step.

But it's all your own doing. And undoing it doesn't require you to lie on a shrink's couch or pay money to do a firewalk or barter with a shaman to make you whole.

No incantations are needed.

Focusing on trying to get over being blocked is just another block.

Writing is all you need to do. Sure, you'll hit challenging patches along the way. Don't call them 'hard.' A challenge is a challenge. You have the skills and strength to make it through.

## The Little Bitch or Bastard on Your Shoulder

Sometimes writers split in two. Not like schizophrenia, which seems to be a half-and-half sort of thing, but a little piece of you breaks off and perches on your shoulder and becomes this little bitch or bastard that yammers about how everything you do is no good, especially writing.

I'm about to share with you two great secrets about how to deal with this. It has taken me decades of trial, error, work, and study to figure out these two things.

Resistance won't work, tricks won't work.

## The First Great Secret of Writing Freedom

**The way to destroy a writing demon is to welcome it.**

"Hey, little bitch/bastard, come on! Do your worst!"

The correct philosophy here is exactly that of judo: not resistance, but acceptance. A judo move in response to an aggressor does not begin with resistance. No: Accept that opponent, take him in close to you, then convert that energy to what *you* want. Which is to pivot gracefully and slam him to the mat.

Because only if we say, "Hey, you little shit, bring it on!" will the enemy show his face. That face really turns out to be nothing: blankness. How easy to take down a nonentity! Facing the worst, pouring as much light as possible on it, *not* shrinking away in fear: *only* this, and *merely* this, will reliably vanquish your demon. It works fast, too.

If a writing demon thinks everything you write is no good, invite him to be specific, make a list, use **Yes and—** and **What if?**

Turn those negative feelings into opportunities to explore your work deeper than you already have. Turn the dark into light.

Know why demons are shadowy and vague? Because light kills them. Because, in reality, they're weak and insubstantial. Frank evaluation of them from your honest self is your light. Face them with acceptance, give them your full attention, and watch them evaporate.

What's left is pure energy for you to use. *You* use it. Write like a bitch! Write like a bastard!

How to do it? Go sloppy, rest your mind, relax your body, especially head and neck. Dwell in your gut.

Go deeper into whatever is bothering you. The good stuff lies there. Just stay with it and be patient.

### DRY WRITING

Sometimes we writers need a word for "not at my best." Let's use the word *dry* instead of *blocked*. Because *blocked* connotes an obstacle, while *dry* is a simple, natural state that can easily be changed by adding a little moisture. For a writer, nourishing moisture comes in the form of acceptance, belief, and the pursuit of zest.

## The Second Great Secret of Writing Freedom

**Being at a loss is fun.**

When you have no idea what should come next, you get to enjoy a no-holds-barred stormwriting session.

## THE NO-HOLDS-BARRED STORMWRITING SESSION

This stormwriting session is similar to the original one in Chapter Six, except it doesn't tell you to put a subject or idea at the top of your blank page. You just start with a blank page!

1. Gather your writing materials.
2. Find a comfortable place.
3. Enter garret mode.
4. Close your eyes or stare off into space or doodle brainlessly with your pen for a couple of minutes.
5. Focus your heartbrain on what's happening with you right now. What have you been doing, what have you been thinking about? Any worries in there? Problems, issues in life, work, love? If so, what are they?
6. Write on those questions. Just tell the paper what's going on with you.
7. Throw down anything and everything. Do you feel like you've been chasing your tail? Write about it. Upset by the high proportion of idiots in the world? Write about it. Use plenty of paper. Write line by line if you want, or go off and group words together and connect them with slants and circles or leave them orbiting alone, whatever feels right.
8. When you feel ready to stop, stop.
9. You will feel better after you get all of that crap down on paper.
10. Take a break.
11. Now move forward with your writing project. At the top of a fresh page, write a basic idea or situation you've been working with.
12. Write on it! Throw down any thoughts that come.
13. Using **Yes, and—** and **What if?**, let each item suggest a new one. Welcome tangents. Write on them as long as you want (even for pages and pages!). As you work, if your gut suddenly jumps or your heart starts to beat faster, listen and follow.

14. Keep going, don't stop to criticize or censor. Open your heart-brain's throttle wide. Plunge in. Write down anything and everything that *might* come next. Anything that *could* come next. Doesn't matter: Write down every idea even if it seems ridiculous or awful. If you do this with a feeling of open exploration, you will come up with a good idea of what should come next.
15. When you feel you're ready to stop, stop.
16. Take a break.
17. Come back and look over what you've done. Look for patterns and anything that pops out as important or thrilling. Fresh, amazing stuff will be there. Explore that material some more or set it aside for further stormwriting sessions.

You've just blasted through a dry spell. Going forward, commit to the experience. Put your ass into it! The fact is that so-called writer's block is nothing but impatience with the process, trying to force it rather than let it come. The answer is to give up control not just in your writing, but in your life. You can't control anything anyway, and if you give up trying to do so, you'll learn more.

I once had a student challenge this technique, saying, "It's all well and good to just vomit out everything you can. But how am I supposed to get from vom to good writing?"

The answer is a paradox: The more honestly and thoroughly you vom, the sooner your material will sort itself out. The chaff will be obvious—and there will be wheat.

Understand that as a writer you are by nature a bit of a mystic. You take the creative journey others fear to take, and you return with something no one's ever seen before. You can't force it, but when you shift into a place of nonjudging receptivity, you'll be amazed at what you get.

## NO HOLDS BARRED

"No holds barred" is a term from the fighting arts, mostly wrestling. It denotes a match in which no holds are considered unfairly advantageous. In writing, no holds barred means giving yourself permission to write and think without stricture. No judging, nothing off-limits. Take it to the mat!

## Your Book as a Presence

In talking with my author friends, I can tell that some of them consider their book—whichever one they're working on right now—a cranky, unpleasant companion they're chained to, like a smelly convict. Some of them even seem to regard their book as an enemy: something to be avoided or conquered. When they finish it and send it off to their publisher, they feel as relieved as if they've come to the end of a horrible ordeal.

I sigh to hear this, because this pain is so unnecessary, so self-inflicted. When I send a book off, I feel wistful and a little sad. Like I'm saying goodbye to a friend!

Other authors feel the same way I do.

Many authors agree that a good way to live with your current book is to not spend a lot of time thinking about it. Attend to it when it's time to write. Rest assured that your subconscious has adopted the project anyway, and your subconscious mind is a lot more powerful than your conscious mind. Gratefully take the gifts it gives.

Choose to see your book as a dear, wonderfully quirky companion. Somebody who requires a bit of understanding, a bit of forgiveness from time to time, but somebody who can make you see things in a totally different light, somebody who's a real kick to be around!

Not everything about your book will present itself at once. Sometimes a problem, question, or issue has to sink into your subconscious for a while. Given a little time, your intelligence-that-lies-deeper-than-your-frontal-lobes (that is, your deep natural wisdom, a.k.a. your heartbrain) will come up with what you need for your book. That intelligence is always working on it smoothly, effortlessly, invisibly beneath the surface.

## Growing Pains and Pleasures

Your talent will develop and change over the course of writing your book. Is this a surprise?

You might not recognize it as growth at first. You might feel discombobulated and maybe even a little angry sometimes. What can cause this anger? For one thing, that idea you thought was so great three months ago now clearly seems not. Invariably, that's because another (better) idea has presented itself, or is about to.

So you'll have to go back and change some stuff. Welcome any growing pains that come your way. The pain is temporary. Be patient and stick with it, see it through and reap the rewards of your growing talent.

## Review as You Go

To get through the middle of your book and drive it to the end, be patient and persistent. Review your three touchstones (Truth, People, Map) frequently: Are you on course? If so, great. If not, change your course or change your map! Harmonize!

If you feel your middle is dragging and you're anxious to get to the cool stuff you've lined up for the end, cut straight to it. Take up that cool stuff and write it. Maybe you don't need any more middle. Seriously.

## Taking Breaks

Sometimes putting your project down for a few days or even weeks can help you bring a fresh eye to it. But beware the siren song of break-taking, which can turn into procrastination, which can turn into no book.

Better to rely on persistence and the sheer benefit of writing regularly as a way through any threatening dark grove.

I'm in favor of mini breaks. After every hour of work, take five or ten minutes to get up, walk around, fetch some water or other healthful beverage, shake out your shoulders, close your eyes, then set your eyes on a distant point for a good twenty seconds.

Trust the process and don't try to force anything.

Results will come in their time.

They will come.

## Nearing THE END

As you get closer to the end of your book, keep an eye on your map.

### *If Fiction:*

Your story should be building to its climax, its great finale. Exciting things will be happening; your hero will be gaining competence, facing dangers, and vanquishing foes.

Don't hurry through this! Let your readers enjoy this wonderful stuff; let us smell the pine trees, hear the ricochets, taste the lips of that long-lost lover.

If you've built convincing characters and worked out a believable, suspenseful story but things fall flat at the end, it's because you haven't gone far enough. Some authors take their foot off the accelerator toward the end, either because they're tired or because of an unnecessary sense of restraint. Whatever the case, you must ramp up the emotion.

Now, you don't want to be cheap, but be advised that exploitation works. Readers expect to be knocked out of their socks, and it's OK to strive to satisfy that expectation.

So juice it up. A good way to do it is add passion, violence, or both.

*The Great Gatsby* is memorable not only because Jay Gatsby fails to attain the object of his obsession, but because he gets shot to death in his pool.

Every romance story from *Pride and Prejudice* to *Sweet Savage Love* ends with love, love, and more love, therefore if you're writing a romance, adding passion is a no-brainer.

If you've got a thriller or mystery, or even a literary novel, violence goes a long way toward making readers feel excited and, ultimately, satisfied.

If the police come to arrest the bad guy, make it a shoot-out. If your tragic hero dies, make him die horribly. If your heroine is happy at the end, make her happy and rich. If your novel already ends with a bang, make it louder!

What I'm trying to say is this: Keep your eye on your map, but when you're almost there, throw it away.

Yes!

The best endings are a bit wild.

And by now, you know what can take you there.

Yes! Luke Skywalker turns off his computer guidance system and vanquishes the Death Star by following the Force. They called it the Force back then because they didn't have the term heartbrain.

Let your heartbrain be your guidance system and see where it takes you. Nothing is so exciting as this. You might wind up just where you were planning to go all along, or you might follow one last weird vector off the map and be astonished by the results, and so happy.

### *If Narrative Nonfiction:*

If you can end with an exciting episode, do so! Another good way to wrap up is to write the last of your episodes, then close by writing about what was learned.

Great question to address at the end of a memoir: If I could live it over again, would I do it the same way? What have I learned? What is my legacy?

Other narrative nonfiction would be served well by some commentary along those lines; that is to say, reflection.

### *If Other Nonfiction, Including How-To:*

Readers want to take away lessons and inspiration from every book they read. Your last sections should prompt them to do that.

I suggest:

- Recap your book in micro.
- Tell the top two or three things you hope to have gotten across.
- End on a note of encouragement.

## A Note on Celebration

After you write THE END, it's time to celebrate.

Actually, you should be celebrating all along. Mind you, I'm not saying you should glorify each good writing session with a night of drinking and casual sex with strangers. (But hey, don't let me run your life.)

Be alert for opportunities to celebrate or commemorate. Overcoming a challenging issue, getting to the end of a major section or significant chapter, arriving at the end, getting published.

When you get to the end, take time to experience it. How does it feel? Quiet, loud, joyful, a little sad, maybe sort of numb with "I can't believe it."

It seems right that a proper celebration should involve a change of scenery and special food and drink (not necessarily alcohol or even caffeine). You don't need excess or depravity. In fact, your celebration will mean more to you and be more respectful of your work if you approach it with some thought.

Lay in whatever delicacies you enjoy (and can afford).

Go out and get some fresh air. Take a car or bus or train ride. Or get out for a good walk. Or go to a museum or sporting event. Go alone or with a friend.

Have a grand day out!

Then come home and as evening falls, relish your treats and feel how much you deserve them.

I am serious about this! Writers tend to downplay their ambitions and achievements. To hell with that.

Take time during your celebration to reflect on your journey. Think back to where you were at the beginning of your book. What were your doubts, fears, or hesitations? Where are those nasty little things now?

> *They're like, gone. Or practically gone.*

Right. Do you sense something familiar going on here? Let's see, you started in a comfortable place. You realized a challenge was taking shape, that is, you had a strong creative urge to write. You thought, *Nah, that's too much of a stretch*. Then the challenge grew stronger and more insistent until finally you decided to give it a go. A helper materialized, in the form of this book. You set off on your writing adventure. You made progress. Sure, there were tough patches! But you learned from your mistakes, you challenged the demons that wanted to discourage you, and you accepted that writing isn't hard if you let yourself create freely and look for the fun in it. In the end, you produced your book! And now you return to the familiar world a changed person. You've learned what it takes to write a book, and now you know it isn't nearly as scary as you'd thought at the beginning. You're holding your book in your hands.

You're a hero.

## ACTIONS

- Spend a few minutes getting to know the little bitch or bastard on your shoulder. What's that ugly, worthless troll all about, anyway? Welcome it. See it for what it really is: nothing to fear.
- Give some thought to celebration.
- Write on your book.

## CHAPTER 24

# Now What?

## The Making-It-Better Process

I detest the word *revisions*. It sounds boring, it sounds like work. To me it actually has a breaking-rocks-in-a-quarry-under-the-hot-sun feeling to it. I think that's because it carries connotations of school and abstruse processes that are difficult for ordinary humans like you and me to grasp.

*Abstruse?*

Yeah, it's a good word to drop into conversations once in a while. It means deliberately hard to understand, obscured. The word *obtuse* is often used in its place, but that's wrong. Obtuse applies to a person who is dumb, sometimes willfully so—a person who just can't or won't grasp the meaning of anything complicated. However, people are using obtuse to mean abstruse so much that both words will eventually be taken to mean the same thing. Our language is going to hell, I tell you.

But to the point—you've finished your book, you've celebrated. Now we're going to demystify revisions—the simple process of making your book *better*.

As you've written your original material, you let good enough be good enough. That's because as we're writing, we can't always tell what's good and what's bad.

During the writing of your book, you've almost certainly gone back and read what you've written. You've made tweaks and notes, you've cut some here and added some there. But now you have a complete manuscript, so you must look at the whole work with a new perspective.

Revise = re-vise = to see anew.

(You see the root of the word vision in there.)

To make your book cleaner and better:

**1) DO NOTHING.** A healthy revision process always begins with downtime. Set your book aside and put your mind on other things for a few days or weeks. This could be an extension of your celebration time. You need this breathing room from your book. More to the point, your book needs breathing room from *you*.

**2) PRINT OUT A FRESH COPY.** Even if you're steadfastly digital, a printed copy gives you a more intimate connection with your words. Some kind of neurological shift happens between looking at something on a screen and holding it in your hands, being able to riffle back and forth quickly through the pages. Being able to literally grasp the whole project at once. Read it away from your computer.

**3) OBTAIN A PENCIL OR A COLORED PEN.** I like to use a mechanical pencil with a 0.7mm lead width or, if I'm feeling fierce, a gel pen with green ink. That green ink just looks so zingy.

**4) GET A FEW DOZEN SHEETS OF FRESH PAPER READY.**

**5) READ THROUGH YOUR MANUSCRIPT.** I love to do this in my garret places, especially my favorite coffee shops, where I can sip and read and really get into it. Try it. As you go, you'll immediately find things to change. Anything from typographical errors (a.k.a. typos) to some weak way you phrased something to a general feeling of uh-oh.

You might see that you need a little more explication here, and a little less there. Maybe there's something in section nine that you already said in a different way in section two, and you'll cut one of them. You'll notice a cliché, and you'll set about to either cut it or create a cool new version.

In short, you will just go through and naturally improve your work. Write directly on your printout and use extra paper if you need to write something to insert later.

Label your insertions. Write *Insert A* where you want your inserted material to begin, and write *A* at the beginning of the stuff to insert. Go on through the alphabet using *B*, *C*, *D* and so on. For every new section I revise, I start with *A* again, and I always circle my capital-letter labels to make them stand out.

Most of us begin revisions by thinking *I'll cut or rewrite stuff that seems weak*. Change your mind to this: *Is it bedrock? Is it bone and gristle? Is it a hard, clear gem*? If not, it goes.

Or you rewrite it until it is one of the above.

Ask not: "What is weak?" but: "What is excellent?"

On the other hand, too much scrutinizing and amending will sap the vitality of your original writing. Most aspiring authors fall victim to this from time to time, causing needless pain, delay, and, frankly, stunted results.

Go ahead and make whatever changes you feel are necessary, but don't obsess over anything. Far better to leave something be than to randomly mess with it.

> *What about that feeling of uh-oh? It's like I know something's wrong but I don't know what to do.*

When you come up against a vague, troubling problem, take a breath and do what professionals do:

- Calmly evaluate the problem.
- Decide whether it really *is* a problem.
- Work out a solution.
- Implement it.
- Move on.

Did you pick out the key phrase in that list? It's 'a solution.' Not 'the perfect solution,' but 'a solution.' There is no single best way to solve a writing quandary. There are lots of fine ways, and professionals know that.

## Here's How to Handle Common Problems

**PROBLEM:** My action here drags.

We've all been there: You've got an action scene that's starting to bore even you. Granted, your story is moving forward, but it feels cumbersome. This can happen in fiction or narrative nonfiction.

**SOLUTION:** Don't pile it on; tighten what you've got.

You could spend hours—days!—trying to inject more life into a scene, but a professional's instinct is just the opposite. We'll *tighten* first; usually a quicker pace will do the trick.

One very easy—and surprisingly effective—way to tighten prose is to turn full sentences into fragments and to use one-line paragraphs. (Remember me talking about fragments?)

If you start with this, for example:

> The thug was much taller and heavier than Jamal. Looking up, Jamal thought: *If I don't think of something fast, we're all dead meat.* There was the pool cue propped against the table, his only available weapon. He grabbed it, wound up as the big man began to react, and swung. It was with a tremendous sense of satisfaction that everybody in the bar heard a crunching sound.

Turn it into something like this (and be sure to drop the 'dead meat' cliché):

> Jamal looked up.
> A giant.
> Without thinking, he grabbed the pool cue and swung it, eyes closed.
> A satisfying crunch!

You shouldn't try to write a whole book this way, but rat-a-tat passages like this will bring variety and movement to your writing.

**PROBLEM:** I'm afraid I've got too much exposition here, yet I have to communicate all this to the reader.

You're at a turning point in your novel, and you have one character revealing information to another, or he's making connections in his head. Puzzle pieces are falling into place—or your omniscient narrator is explaining a lot of stuff to the reader. And it doesn't feel natural.

**SOLUTION:** Turn narrative into dialogue.

Most aspiring authors underestimate the modern reader's ability to infer, generalize, and make connections. A professional's first instinct is to cut exposition, but when you've sliced away all but the essential and you're still looking at an amateurish block of text, turn it into dialogue.

Figure out which of two characters should talk first. Give them some back-and-forth, something to disagree about. Create a little conflict while delivering your basic facts. If the character is solo in the scene, give her an internal argument. I've done this in some of my books, having ripped off the technique from Erica Jong in *Fear of Flying* (who probably ripped it off from Shakespeare—all those soliloquies...)

Here's an example. Say you have a character who's figuring out a complicated murder.

You could write this:

> I was starting to understand what was going on. I knew who killed Tim, but Otto didn't know I knew. The whole thing was tied into the bank robbery, and although the police suspected it had been an inside job, they were clueless beyond that. The more I pondered the whole thing, the more upset I got. What the hell should I do? I know it had to be Otto. But he was so ruthless. What if he decided Selma or Johnny were threats to him?

This block of text is not bad, but not terribly lively for the reader to plow through.

Or you could write this:

> **ME:** I ought to confront Otto with what I know about Tim's death.
>
> **ME:** Wait a minute, shouldn't this be a matter for the police?

> **ME:** To hell with the police! They don't know Otto worked for the bank five years ago. Plus—
> **ME:** You're getting upset. Stay cool.
> **ME:** I'm cool, OK. I just want him to know I'm onto him, and if he tries anything with Selma or Johnny, I'll be in his face.

From this dialogue, the reader can infer a raft of information in an entertaining way.

**PROBLEM:** I have a complex plot, but now that I look at it, I'm afraid my wrap-up seems fake. How do I make the final unraveling seem natural?

You're proud of your plot, and you want to show the reader that you've thought of everything. This one's as tight as a drum! But now it feels like you're ticking off boxes on a checklist, and the effect is artificial.

**SOLUTION:** You don't have to wind up every loose end.

Readers will know they're in good hands if you pay off your suspense. This is key, and it bears repeating: Suspense is the most important aspect of a book to build and bring to a satisfying climax and conclusion. This holds true in any genre; even the most sedate literary novels are built on a foundation of suspense: *Doggone it, what's going to happen next*? Whether it's Mrs. Dalloway and her flowers or Hannibal Lecter and his fava beans.

It follows, then, that not every loose end needs to be tied up. This is an instant fix! Granted, some highly successful authors commonly tie up their loose ends meticulously—Harlan Coben comes to mind—but others make a point of not doing so, like Elizabeth George.

Especially if you're launching a series, leaving your readers with a little bit of *hmmm*… is a good thing.

Example: If you have a minor character who dropped out halfway through the book, the reader will either have forgotten about her by the end or understand that that particular loose end is irrelevant.

Challenge your impulse to wrap up everything with a bow, and you might achieve a more natural result.

**PROBLEM:** My book is too long, but I don't know what to cut.

**PROBLEM:** My book is too long, but I don't know what to cut.

Prospective agents and editors tell many authors on the brink of getting published, "I love this book, but it's too long. If you can cut it by about 10,000 words (or whatever terrifyingly high number), I think I can sell/publish this." They don't want any *specific* cuts at this point; they just want the manuscript to better fit a common format.

Or you might simply realize that a 400-page book on the best lunch places in Waco is overkill.

**SOLUTION:** Microedit your way to success.

You can spend lots of time rereading your manuscript and painfully strategizing what hunks to cut, but an excellent way to quickly trim it to size is to cut one word per sentence. This technique is pure magic. And it's incredibly easy.

Or you can divide the number of words you need to cut by the number of pages you have, and come up with an average words-to-cut per page. This is a job that you can do in the interstices of your day; you don't have to find large spans of time for it.

As a former newspaper reporter and editor, I got good at cutting excess verbiage early in my writing career. But every so often I challenge myself to cut one word per sentence. If I can do that too easily, I know I've gotten sloppy.

**PROBLEM:** But what if I feel like the whole thing stinks!?

Every author is stricken, at least once per book, by Creeping Rot Disease. CRD begins as a dark feeling that takes over your mind and spirit when you least expect it. You look at your manuscript and the feeling creeps over you that all you've done is foul a perfectly good stack of paper. *It's lousy. It's not original. It's nothing anybody would look at twice. I'm wasting my life. I'm a fool.*

**SOLUTION:** Take a longer break!

Believe me, when CRD strikes, you are in plentiful, excellent company. Terrific authors have drunk themselves to death trying to self-medicate against CRD.

I talked about the value of 'letting it sit,' but if you're close to finishing your book and CRD has grabbed hold of you, it's most likely that you didn't get enough time and space away between writing the end and starting revisions. Turn off your computer, close your notebook, cap your pen (because the problem is not with your manuscript, it's *you*), and do something completely different:

- Walk outside. Note the first great-looking tree you see. Hang out with it for a while.
- Go get some *good* coffee.
- Phone a friend and spill your guts.
- Prepare a minipicnic lunch and open the window.
- Make a sketch of a simple object, like a bowl or a bottle.

Do anything to break the stream of negative thoughts.

Now square yourself and get back to it, working in harmony, looking for fun.

Here are two more stress-free techniques to make your book better.

## Go Back to Your Touchstones

If something's wrong with your book, and you can't put your finger on it, get quiet, open your heartbrain, and listen. If a little thought or an urge comes up, let it grow, make friends with it.

Next, focus one at a time on Your Truth, Your People, and Your Map. Go back to the material you wrote about all of them: your Statement of Truth, your dossiers, your Map or the stormwrites that you used to make it. Then, ask the question: Has this to do with my Truth? Pause and think. My People? Ditto. My Map? Ditto. Make notes as thoughts come to you.

One of those touchstones should prompt an idea. "Ah! This scene needs another character to get all nervous and set everybody else on edge too." Or "I know—I'll add a paragraph that tells how a basic generator works, then the rest of my chapter on home electricity will make more sense, even to a novice."

## Go to Beta

The most time-honored way to gain perspective is to borrow another set of eyes. To beta test—a term from the computer world—means to try out a not-final version on volunteer end users. The ideal beta reader is someone a) you know is a discriminating reader and b) who cares about you. That is, someone who at heart wants you to succeed as a writer.

When it comes to soliciting feedback, the main, open-ended question to ask is, "What did you think of it?" Make it clear that you want to hear it straight, good or bad. Needless to say, *be receptive*. You don't have to agree with everything, but don't waste time defending or explaining your work. A useful response is, "Thank you, I'll think about it. What else?"

Sometimes you'll hear vagueness like, "It was different!" or "I really liked it," or "I don't know, I couldn't get into it." Such feedback is essentially worthless.

Help your beta readers by asking directed questions, questions that get them to comment on specific aspects of what they've just read.

Let's say you're in doubt about a particular scene or chapter. Ask:

How did you feel when you read this scene?

What did you like about it?

What didn't you like about it?

Did you ever get bored? Where?

What part made you feel the most emotion? How come?

I coach my beta readers in advance by saying, "I'm going to want to know wherever you went over a bump." That way they're free to say they were uncomfortable with a scene or felt something didn't work without fearing that I'm going to expect a step-by-step dissertation. Then I bear down with follow-up questions.

Readers love stories that make them *feel*. So I zero in deeper on their emotions:

Did you feel dread anyplace? Horror?

Did you get grossed out by anything? Was it a good gross-out or a bad gross-out?

Did you feel stirred romantically? Whether yes or no, tell me more.

Did you stay up reading later than you intended?

Did you learn anything new?

Was it ever a slog?

Did the characters come alive? Which one seemed most alive? Which least? Do you feel you can clearly see them?

And then: What is X character like? I have found this simple question to be especially rewarding. Readers have different takes on characters and I learn that my characters are coming across in ways I hadn't known, sometimes quite differently than I intended. Sometimes a reader sees depth in a character that I myself missed!

With unique feedback like that, I'm able to populate my fiction more realistically.

And remember those 'vague problems' you may have felt about a chapter or a sequence of dialogue, that passage where you knew something was wrong but you couldn't put your finger on it? If you're still baffled, take the chance of pointing those out, and your beta reader might again pick up on something that would have never entered your mind.

## Consistency of Feedback

The responses you receive may be all over the map. You will hear variation after variation, and some of those variations may be exactly contradictory.

For example, from Reader A: "I like how your beginning gradually builds speed, but you didn't play fair with that random explosion at the end."

Reader B: "The beginning was slow, but you ended with a terrific bang!"

If you start rewriting in response to the specifics in every critique you receive, you will eventually find yourself fashioning a noose out of an extension cord, not knowing why. Be a bit cagey when taking comments.

But if you hear similar criticism from multiple sources, sit up and pay attention. If, after considering the feedback, you think it has merit, go ahead and revise your work accordingly.

Still, you must trust your own heartbrain above all.

I've kept notes from a years-ago phone conversation with a powerful figure in publishing who told me my novel was awful. I'd better stop submitting it, she said, and get some remedial training in storytelling.

I didn't listen. I knew in my heart that she was wrong, that my novel was publishable—if not the next *Light in August*—and moreover, the other feedback I'd gotten on it didn't remotely reflect what she'd said. (I soon sold the manuscript to another publisher.)

On the other hand, when my agent talks, I listen, even though she's only one person. I listen very hard. Why? Because a) she's made a career out of distinguishing great writing from mediocre, and b) she can articulate exactly why a particular plot point or passage of writing works or doesn't work for her. We don't always agree, but I give her opinions a great deal of weight.

In the end, consider what a 45-year-old Jack Kerouac told *The Paris Review*: "I spent my entire youth writing slowly with revisions and endless re-hashing speculation and deleting and got so I was writing one sentence a day and the sentence had no FEELING. Goddamn it, FEELING is what I like in art, not craftiness and the hiding of feelings."

He taught himself to write fast and free, and then he wrote *On the Road*.

Don't make too much of revising.

## ACTIONS

- Gather your touchstone material and sort through it for your best, most useful pages. Read over them before you get going on revisions.
- Make a list of people you might want to beta test your book.
- Make your book better!

CHAPTER 25

# A Short Section on a Big Subject

A separate part of your making-it-better process should be a review of the title you've chosen. By now you've lived with your title and you've either gotten happily used to it or you're still a little unsettled about it.

Choosing the right title for your book is like choosing the right name for your baby. No single perfect choice exists; several probably do, and as many as a zillion titles might be adequate.

Whether you're pleased with your title or not, be sure to ask your beta readers what they think of it. Ask for suggestions. If you get consistent feedback like "It's too long," or "I don't get it," you should reconsider. Sometimes when we live with a title for a long time we get overly possessive of it. Keep an open mind and play with a few ideas.

Sample great fiction titles:

*Rubyfruit Jungle* (Rita Mae Brown)
*Jurassic Park* (Michael Crichton)
*Jaws* (Peter Benchley)
*The Maltese Falcon* (Dashiell Hammett)

Sample great nonfiction titles:

*The Oregon Trail* (Francis Parkman)

*The Stranger Beside Me* (Ann Rule)

*Guerrilla Marketing* (Jay Conrad Levinson)

*What to Expect When You're Expecting* (Heidi Murkoff and Sharon Mazurel)

*What about subtitles?*

Good question. For fiction, you don't need a subtitle; they're rarely used, because most authors find that short and snappy for fiction works best.

For nonfiction, a subtitle can and should tell a lot about your book. It should magnify, or sharpen, your title, like these:

*The Long Walk: The True Story of a Trek to Freedom* (Slavomir Rawicz)

*Learning From Las Vegas: The Forgotten Symbolism of Architectural Form* (Robert Venturi, Denise Scott Brown, Steven Izenour)

*Nectarine Bounty: The Easy Way to Grow Stone Fruits* (Harriet Truxton)

*You've Got a Book in You: A Stress-Free Guide to Writing the Book of Your Dreams*

## ACTIONS

- If you're still working on your title, make a list of words and ideas that relate to your book. Mess around, get goofy, see what you come up with.
- Go to the library or on line and sport around the stacks. Pay special attention to titles. Which ones catch your eye, which ones sound boring? How come?
- Keep making your book better.

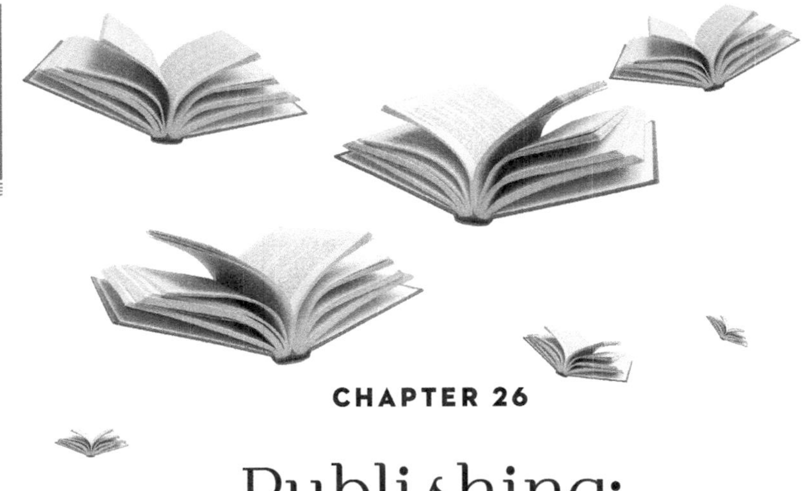

## CHAPTER 26

# Publishing:

## What It Is and How It Works

To publish a book is to make it public, to *public-ize* it. Until recently this meant printing multiple copies of it and selling them in stores or elsewhere.

Anybody who fronts the money for 1) production (which includes editing, book design, typesetting, printing, binding, and, increasingly, e-book setup), 2) distribution (shipping the books to stores and customers), 3) publicity and marketing (spreading the word via advertising or other means), 4) accounting for the book's income and sending a previously agreed-upon share to the author (royalties) is known as a publisher.

It's a big job!

Sometimes publishers even give authors advances against royalties. When you read that a certain publisher bought somebody's manuscript for X dollars, it means they agreed to advance the author that money against the future royalties.

How it works: Say you get a $10,000 advance. Usually that money is split, with half going to you upon signing the contract and the other half due after the book has been edited. (If you are a known author and you've sold a terrific *idea* for a book to a publisher, you might get half on signing and the other half when the finished manuscript is accepted: that is, before the production process, which for traditional publishers takes months.)

Then when the book comes out and starts to sell (we all hope), you get nothing more until the publisher has sold enough copies to make up that advance money via the percentage per copy you agreed to receive.

It makes sense, it really does.

This is the traditional model and it still exists.

Increasingly, however, it seems that this model exists in the same way that a street punk who has just stolen 20 kilos of heroin from an established Afghani wholesaler exists: precariously and temporarily. Even established, traditionally published authors are self-publishing these days.

As I write this, e-books are fast gaining ground on print books. And self-published books are more easily created and sold by authors than ever before, thanks to the pioneer people at Amazon and their innovative Kindle device, and those that followed. Other readers emerged before Kindle but they didn't spread like fire the way Kindle has.

But who knows? Many readers—and writers—prefer books made of paper and ink, free of any electrical umbilicus.

What routes are realistic for a first-time author? Knowing our terms will help.

**TRADITIONAL PUBLISHING.** Described above.

**SUBSIDY PUBLISHER.** This is any publishing house that charges you money to print your book. These are also called 'vanity' presses. Some of these presses typically do nothing to distribute or promote your book, but their workmanship is often quite good. You send in your money and your manuscript, and cartons of nicely bound copies of your book come back. Many subsidy publishers have promotional programs as well, usually via their Web site.

**PRINT-ON-DEMAND.** A POD publisher will not do a typical print run of your book; that is, a run of five hundred to five thousand copies for distribution in stores. Thanks to digital technology that has driven down costs and made it not ridiculously expensive to print single copies of books, these publishers will print individual copies of your book when someone places an order, either via mail-order or on line, or even if stores order copies. Some POD publishers are basically vanity presses, but some are legit small publishers with standards and editing staffs.

**PRINT YOUR OWN.** You can take your manuscript to just about any printer and pay them to format it for print, help you design a cover, and run as many copies as you want. You can also find online printers who will do this for you.

**SELF-PUBLISHING.** Doing it yourself via self-serve distribution platforms is an extremely popular choice these days. Amazon and Barnes & Noble offer these services with no upfront charges. So do companies like Smashwords, which will put up your book on multiple e-book formats and keep a share of the proceeds.

**E-BOOK.** A digital version of your book: that is, a version viewable only on an electronic device such as a computer or proprietary e-book reader. E-books are extremely cost-effective. Most publishers who offer e-book versions of books still offer print versions, but some have switched entirely to e-books. Once an e-book is up on Amazon or other e-book seller, or even your own website, you can reap profits forever. I am doing so.

## Making Sense of It All

People who work in traditional publishing tend to speak of print books as 'real' and e-books as not. Unsurprisingly, e-book publishers and authors do not make any such distinction. Some refer to print-based publishers as 'legacy' publishers, to connote backwardness.

For many writers, getting published in print is the most satisfying way to go. Fortunately, you can self-publish both ways.

Myth: You have to know somebody to get published.

Reality: The key to getting published is to write a publishable manuscript, the definition of which changes from publisher to publisher!

A great many aspiring authors yearn desperately for an agent, then a multibook contract with a major New York publishing house, then fame and fortune as a hotshot author.

Take it from me, scoring an agent who secures a multibook contract with a major New York publisher is great. You get to go to New York and have lunch. You meet the team. Your books come out in hardcover and you see them on shelves in your local library and bookstores. The fame and fortune are not automatic.

There's tons of good, detailed advice on how to get published traditionally and how to self-publish. The business keeps changing, with new players and ideas coming and going, so much so that online is really the way to learn about it. Google 'self-publishing' and other pertinent terms, and you'll learn a lot quickly.

Another good place to start is *Writer's Market*. It's where I started. *Writer's Market* is a book updated annually (I still buy one every year) that guides you in your publishing pursuits. There also is an online version.

*Writer's Digest* magazine also publishes huge amounts of useful material by battle-tested experts. Much of it is free online, with no strings attached (writersdigest.com).

## How to Figure Out What Route Is Best for You and Your Book

First of all, there's no rule that says you must publish your book.

You can keep it entirely to yourself, if you like, or share it with just a few people.

You can run copies on your home printer, you can send the digital file to friends and family, you can post it on your own Web site. No one even needs to know you wrote a book! (I've written fiction that will never see the light of day because I want it that way.)

Most writers, though, want to get their work out in the world one way or another.

If your book is nonfiction and would have a very narrow audience, and I mean like a few hundred people or less, self-publishing is the way to go. Say you've written a family history that you want to hand out to everybody at the reunion next year. That's an easy call: self-publish with a printer or subsidy publisher. Run the number of copies you want, plus a few more for good measure, and you're golden.

Other examples of nonfiction that's good for self-publishing:

- A history of your small town, school, organization, or business. I wrote a history of my local nonprofit symphony (the Port Angeles Symphony Orchestra) when I was living in the woods in Washington, and it was printed privately and sold as a fundraiser.
- A how-to with a highly specialized audience to whom you could distribute through a trade journal, like concrete wholesalers or pet shop owners.
- The memoir of your childhood that wasn't especially unusual, but worthwhile for its historical details and accounts of local color. (Your descendants will bless you.)

Nonfiction books for larger audiences might be right for either self-publishing or traditional publishing. Examples:

- A memoir or biography of a person whose life had regional or national impact. (Or would, if the story got out there.)
- A how-to for something of wider interest, such as movie making, bowling, or playing a musical instrument.
- A book about a topic of wide relevance, such as home organization, dogs, or coin collecting.

Novels and short story collections are always candidates for either self- or traditional publishing. In this case, the quality of the writing has much bearing on whether a traditional publisher will be interested.

Lots of writing gurus point out how few authors make it through the process of finding representation with an agent and getting a publishing contract versus how many authors want to get published.

I say this: If you'd like a publishing contract with a major house, don't let the numbers dissuade you. Give it a shot and accept the outcome. You can always self-publish later. Otherwise you'll always wonder.

When you send your book to any agent or publisher for consideration, it's called a submission. Most major publishers will only consider agented submissions, meaning they'll look only at material submitted to them by a literary agent. No slush pile = less work for them!

*What's a slush pile?*

Slush pile refers to manuscripts that come in over the transom.

*What's a transom?*

The little window over an old-style office door.

*Did writers actually drop their manuscripts into publishing offices that way?*

Yes, they did. Today, the transom = the e-mail in-box.

*What is an agent and how do I get one?*

A literary agent is a person who represents authors. They have contacts in the business. They pitch manuscripts to publishers, they negotiate contracts for their authors, and they generally act as a go-between. Some agents get heavily involved in their authors' writing process; others are more hands-off.

To get an agent, first write a great book, then study up on agents and pick some to approach.

Again, *Writer's Digest* can help you identify suitable agents, or you can browse online, in bookstores, or your local library for guides to literary agents. Get in touch with agents by writing what is known as a query. Almost everybody prefers e-mail these days.

In the query you:

- introduce yourself
- tell why you're approaching that particular agent
- describe your book in attractive yet honest terms
- offer to send all or part of your manuscript for consideration.

If the agent likes your material and thinks she can sell it to a publisher, she will offer to represent you.

Whole books and workshops are devoted to developing the perfect query. My feeling is, don't obsess on it, learn a little, then go forward and be natural in all of your correspondence.

*How much do I pay my agent?*

You don't pay your agent; your agent pays you. As your representative, your agent acts on your behalf and receives all monies due you from any deal the agent has made for you. The agent then turns over 85 percent of that money to you, keeping 15 percent for his or her work. (Fifteen is the typical percentage, but it can vary a little, depending on the kind of deal.)

You can also query publishers directly. That's how I sold my first novel, *Holy Hell*, after I became fed up querying agents who did not immediately grasp my brilliance.

Between getting that magic phone call that said, "We'd like to offer you a contract," and receiving the contract in the mail, I hurried out and bought books on negotiating book deals. Their advice helped me get more of what I wanted. I recommend *Negotiating a Book Contract* by Mark L. Levine.

As I said before, if your heart is set on getting an agent and a traditional publishing contract, go for it.

And if the complete control of self-publishing (including income, which is not a trivial matter) attracts you, go for it.

I've done both, and both have their pros and cons, including intangibles.

There's the prestige of a traditional publisher. When you say "I have a book out," people wonder if it's self-published. The unspoken idea being that if it's self-published it might not be any good.

On the other hand, if you self-publish, there's the incomparable feeling of running your own show, of not being dependent on anybody for your success or failure.

Increasingly, the Web and social media are making it possible to jump over the gatekeepers, build an online presence and market your own material.

Most traditional publishers are also doing simultaneous e-book releases. That would seem like the best of all worlds, and it is, in a way. You get the maximum exposure. However, with a traditional publisher your royalty rate is a much lower share of the sale price per copy than it would be if you self-published.

Companies like Amazon do not charge anything up front to publish your book in e-book form and print-on-demand. This is significant.

There are tons of companies online that will work with you to format your book for all the different e-book markets, as well as print-on-demand and audio.

Most offer either of two deals:

- You pay nothing up front, but the company keeps a percentage of your proceeds forever.
- You pay a one-time fee for the company to set things up for you, and any income you get is yours to keep.

Skim around and you'll find a lot of information, as well as opinions by users of every service out there.

If you have a modicum of computer skills, you can do a lot yourself.

## ACTIONS

- When the time comes, give some thought as to whether you'd like to publish your book. What sort of publishing might work for you? Mull it over.
- Browse the available information on publishing and read about other authors' experiences. You'll learn a heck of a lot, and what you learn might help you decide what to do.
- Keep writing.

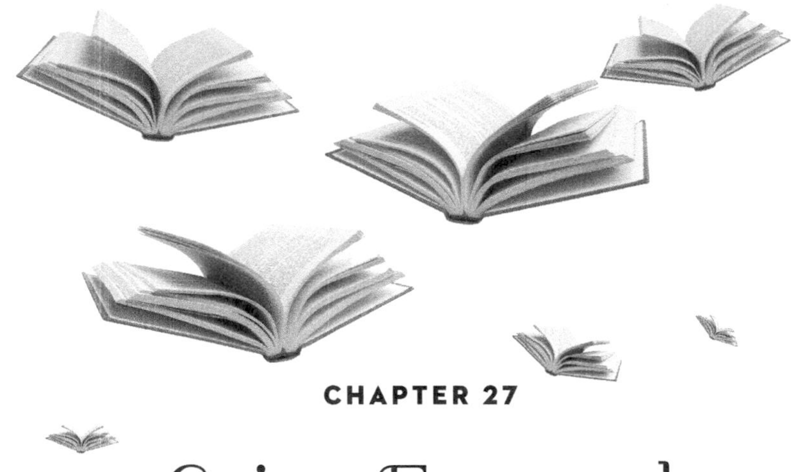

CHAPTER 27

# Going Forward

Everybody needs friends. Writers need friends. Sometimes it's nice to get together with other writers. If you think you might like that, sport around the bulletin boards at your local library, church, cafés, and online for writing groups in your area.

Or start your own. Spread the word and see what happens.

To start a writing group, all you need is a space, which can be your living room, a corner of your library (ask first), or a table in a café (where you will be sure to order refreshments and tip nicely).

Meet once a week. Let each person read some of their work aloud for five or ten minutes. Talk about it. Share stuff you've learned. Hang out. Play. Start a collective short story with everybody writing one sentence. Keep passing the paper around. For sure you'll have a good laugh and you might learn something new. Be supportive of all your writing friends. If somebody wants constructive criticism, give it in a nice way. Constructive criticism is the act of pointing out what isn't too great about a piece and then offering an idea for how it could be improved.

(You're not going to tell somebody their piece of writing is fantastic if it isn't, unless you want to ask them out, but you can find *something* nice to say about it.)

You can also take a writing class through your local community college, or online (search on keywords 'writing classes,' 'writing courses'). You can go to a writing conference, which can be a lot of fun. If one comes to your area, consider registering. You won't be out airfare or hotel money if you decide you don't like it. But you probably will like it, because writing mojo abounds at conferences.

For anything: Group, class, or conference, you'll get out of it what you put into it. Be open, receptive, and giving. Smile!

Most writers hit bumps in the road sooner or later. Remember that you have a friend in this book. Turn back to it, reread, and refresh your core. I'll always be right here.

## More Help

I mentioned *Writer's Digest* magazine earlier. When I was an aspiring novelist I subscribed and learned a lot from its pages. When the short story contest came around, I entered and came in twelfth place out of about two thousand entries. That was a shot in the arm! I kept writing fiction and started to get published. I remember thinking, boy, I sure would like to get good enough to write for *Writer's Digest* some day. I did and I do. I have a ball writing articles and reading what other writers are up to. I've been writing for them since 2006.

I also bought books from Writer's Digest Books (writersdigestshop.com), the publishing arm of the company, which publishes top-quality books on writing and publishing.

Today, besides the magazine and books, WD's website offers all kinds of writing help, discussion opportunities, and newsletters for free, plus online classes, downloads, contests, and more.

## Keep It Simple and Thrive

To end up with a worthwhile book that you and others will enjoy for years to come, keep it simple:

1. Stormwrite.
2. Write With the Masters.
3. Welcome fear and doubt, and watch them disappear.
4. Keep at it.
5. Celebrate as you go.

## Your Life Is Changing Already

It's not just when you're done writing that your book will change your life. The writing process itself will change you on a deep level. I'll wager you've seen that already.

In several different ways, writing integrates you. And by that, I mean it makes you whole. It engages your best mind versus just talking, where you can be in a conversation and trail off, figuring that people know what you mean, even if you don't quite know yourself!

Writing drives you to seek depths within yourself and others.

Writing does not take from you, it gives to you.

It's easy, in these hurry-go-faster times, for your mind and heart to get fragmented.

One way to get reintegrated is to get into nature for a while. Take a camping trip or retreat to a rustic cabin with no amenities, a place where there's no chatter, nothing much between you and your environment.

When you step off the pavement, the bullshit of life fades. The unmitigated shriek of the Web and television and radio and advertisements—all that goes away. At first you miss all that, because it's become so familiar. So normal. Yet you set off and you get into the rhythm of walking in the quiet, living in the quiet, and you begin to feel connected with something more than yourself, and you get—slowly, maybe even imperceptibly—integrated. You find yourself becoming whole.

Writing is like that, too. Writing makes the extraneous drop away. It's just you and your pen or keyboard.

### BUILD...THEN MOVE FORWARD

If one thing drives us all, it's desire, and if there's one common sin, it's self-deception. Focus on those two human factors and let idea build on idea.

Going forward, read the most powerful stories you can, whether books, plays, or screenplays. Read stuff that makes people fall down dead.

Then go your own way.

Writing fosters your creativity at the same time that it's an outlet for it. You're producing something *new to the world.* This is inherently satisfying to humans. It's making art. We've done it since some naked person with a bad haircut picked up a stick and drew a squiggle in the mud.

Tune into your desire to write. It comes from the innermost core of you. Tune into it while you write. Just feel it. Feel what the desire to write changes to as you write. Watch your deep self-focus and get excited or calmly thrilled or silently peaceful. You'll feel a balanced aliveness. Fearlessness. An acceptance of whatever comes, a feeling of smooth power.

You know this intuitively; you are pursuing writing because you already know this.

Before you write, you're a guest on the planet.

When you write, you own it.

Now go write something amazing.

- THE END -

# Index